HIKING WITH KIDS
NEW ENGLAND

HELP US KEEP THIS GUIDE UP TO DATE

Every effort has been made by the author and editors to make this guide as accurate and useful as possible. However, many things can change after a guide is published—trails are rerouted, regulations change, facilities come under new management, and so forth.

We would love to hear from you concerning your experiences with this guide and how you feel it could be improved and kept up to date. While we may not be able to respond to all comments and suggestions, we'll take them to heart, and we'll also make certain to share them with the author. Please send your comments and suggestions to the following email address: editorial@GlobePequot.com.

Thanks for your input, and happy trails!

Tulip trees flank either side of the trail and are beautiful when in bloom.

HIKING WITH KIDS
NEW ENGLAND

50 GREAT HIKES FOR FAMILIES

Sarah Lamagna

FALCONGUIDES

ESSEX, CONNECTICUT

For Everett, always—who allowed me the honor of showing him the wonders and magic of the same trails I fell in love with as a child.

And for my own mother—who instilled in me a lifelong love of the outdoors and always helped me find my place in the world through the soles of my feet.

FALCONGUIDES®

An imprint of Globe Pequot, the trade division of
The Rowman & Littlefield Publishing Group, Inc.
4501 Forbes Blvd., Ste. 200
Lanham, MD 20706
www.rowman.com

Falcon and FalconGuides are registered trademarks and Make Adventure Your Story is a trademark of The Rowman & Littlefield Publishing Group, Inc.

Distributed by NATIONAL BOOK NETWORK

Photos by Sarah Lamagna unless otherwise noted
Maps by The Rowman & Littlefield Publishing Group, Inc.

British Library Cataloguing in Publication Information available

Library of Congress Cataloging-in-Publication Data

Names: Lamagna, Sarah, author.
Title: Hiking with kids New England : 50 great hikes for families / Sarah Lamagna.
Description: Essex, Connecticut : FalconGuides, [2023] | Summary: "A guide to fifty hiking adventures for parents and their elementary school-age kids alike, featuring color photos and maps throughout"— Provided by publisher.
Identifiers: LCCN 2022043722 (print) | LCCN 2022043723 (ebook) | ISBN 9781493069774 (paperback) | ISBN 9781493069781 (epub)
Subjects: LCSH: Hiking—New England—Guidebooks. | Hiking for children—New England—Guidebooks. | Trails—New England—Guidebooks. | Family recreation—New England—Guidebooks. | New England—Guidebooks.
Classification: LCC GV199.42.N38 L36 2023 (print) | LCC GV199.42.N38 (ebook) | DDC 796.510974—dc23/eng/20220930
LC record available at https://lccn.loc.gov/2022043722
LC ebook record available at https://lccn.loc.gov/2022043723

∞™ The paper used in this publication meets the minimum requirements of American National Standard for Information Sciences—Permanence of Paper for Printed Library Materials, ANSI/NISO Z39.48-1992.

The author and The Rowman & Littlefield Publishing Group, Inc., assume no liability for accidents happening to, or injuries sustained by, readers who engage in the activities described in this book.

CONTENTS

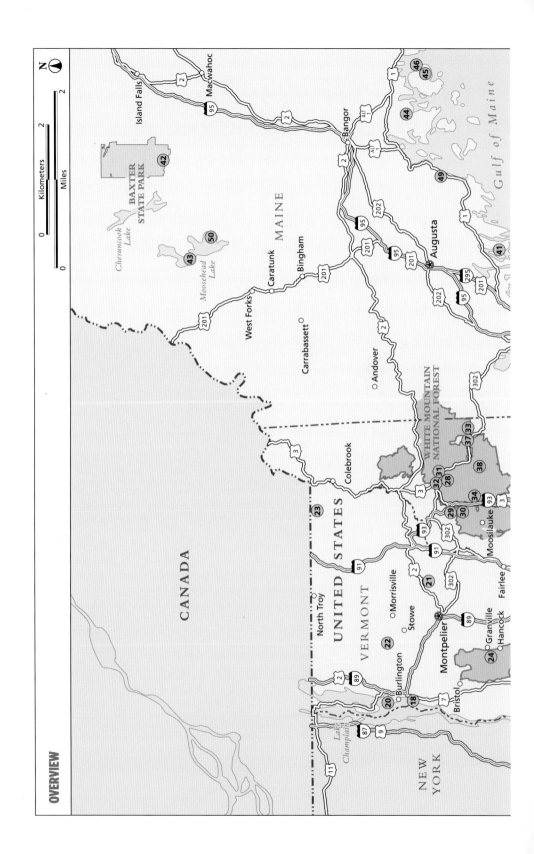

OVERVIEW

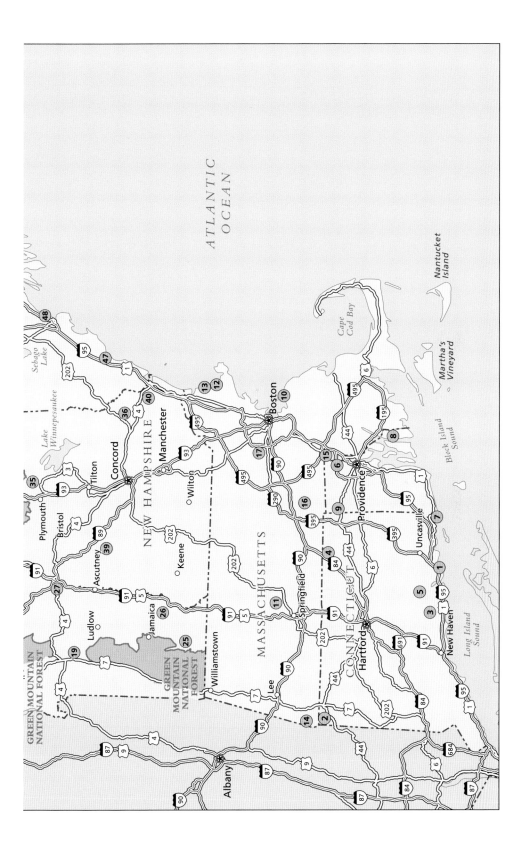

ACKNOWLEDGMENTS

First and foremost, I would not have written this book without my son, Everett, who made me a mom in 2017. Being able to walk the same trails with him as I did as a child with my own mother brought up more memories than I had anticipated. I hope you remember these days on the trail as fondly as I most certainly will.

Thank you to my family, who has always supported my weird dreams, including switching careers in my mid-thirties. Thank you to my dad for taking me fishing all those years ago, where I had my first glimpses into how wonderful nature can be. Thank you to my brother Adam, who never left my side when I wanted to find just one more salamander in the swamp next to our house. Thank you to my sister Nikki, for teaching me about the power and magic of writing—without her, I don't think I ever would've become a writer.

Last, a huge thanks goes out to my mother. She is the sole reason I started down the career path I have now. She had me out on the trail before I could even walk, and I am forever grateful she brought me outside all those years ago. My love for the outdoors blossomed because of the seed that took root from her. She taught me how to be an outdoorsy mom, and I am only just beginning to understand how truly incredible that is.

Hanging out under the suspension bridge watching anglers and other folks play in the water

Also thanks to my friend Heather, who took me under her wing as a budding freelance writer and taught me how to find a niche within the writing world. I am forever grateful for the knowledge she has given me so freely and the opportunities that have come my way because of her.

And a huge thank you to my writing partners, Meri and Leah, who I randomly met on social media and quickly became two of my most favorite people in the entire world. The way these two have stuck with me in my frustrations and celebrations is unprecedented. I love them more than they know.

To all the folks who hiked with me, allowed me to take photos of them randomly at the top of a summit, or scouted hikes for me—this book would not be what it is without them. So thank you to Audrey, Reed, and Mike Spinney for guiding me throughout the beauty of Rhode Island. To Kelli, Andrew, and Kinsley Millick for not getting too weirded out when I asked to take their photo at Owl's Head (see—I really did write a book!). To Rebecca McCormick—even though our kids went at a snail's pace up to Sterling Pond, I wouldn't have traded it for the world. And thanks to Nora Belcher, Kate Murray, Sarah White, Adria Milewski, Lauren Depina, and Meghan Jacokes for all the hike suggestions when I was at a loss.

Finally, thank you to my husband, who solo-parented for days on end so that I could travel around the region from trailhead to trailhead without worrying about our kid. Thank you for not complaining when my office light clearly kept you up at night as I was finishing this book. Thank you for never questioning me as I wanted to raise a child outdoors. Words will never begin to express how grateful I am for you.

And to all the staff of the public lands I visited—thank you for answering my endless questions with ease and grace. Thank you for keeping these lands healthy and thriving; without which, there would be no book.

MEET YOUR GUIDE

Sarah Lamagna is an ecologist-turned-freelance writer who grew up on the trails of New England. The biggest mountain she climbed as a kid was just over 2,300 feet above sea level. At the time, it felt like she was on top of the world. College brought her to Upstate New York and into the heart of the Adirondacks and then to the Pacific Northwest for graduate school.

Jobs led Sarah to the Rocky Mountains of Colorado, where she adventured throughout the Southwest. Her career as an ecologist for thirteen years allowed her endless opportunities to be outside and immerse herself in nature. Becoming a mom shifted her priorities, and so began her tenure as a stay-at-home mom. The adventures she had with her newborn were epic, and she will always be forever grateful for those initial years.

But New England was always calling to her, and when the opportunity arose, she and her family moved back East to be closer to family and closer to the mountains she loved. She makes her living as a full-time freelance writer specializing in parenting in the outdoors, sustainability, and eco-tourism. She now lives in southern New Hampshire, where hikers see her regularly on the trails in her favorite mountain range, the White Mountains, with her kiddo in tow.

The author and her son taking a break before heading back up to Mount Sunapee

Some of the Crane Beach Loop trail meanders along pine forests before heading back into sand dune ecosystems.

INTRODUCTION

Getting outside with kids is not always easy. I remember as a child the number of times I would complain to my mother about the steepness of the trail or the hardness of the ground beneath my feet. She would always tell me that it only made me stronger, and that someday I'd look back fondly on these days. I can now admit that she was 100 percent right.

Now, as I bring my own kid on the trail, I hear the same complaints and see the same frustrations I had when I was on the trail thirty years ago. But I also know that he'll look back on these days the same way I recall my hiking adventures with my mother. So, it's true: Hiking with kids can be frustrating, and you might ask yourself why you are putting yourself through this torture. But it *is* worth it, I swear.

This guide is meant to help introduce your kids to the outdoors or enhance their skills and abilities. Most of the "hiking with kids" guidebooks that I have read and seen only reference very easy, short hikes. These are great as introductory trails (I have some like this in this guide), but kids can do hard things. They are capable of so much more than a half-mile hike along a beach. They can climb 4,000-footers (albeit, with some experience) and can walk 6.0 miles without breaking a sweat. They just need to start somewhere and make their way up.

You also don't need the fanciest gear or even the priciest. The only things you truly need to get outdoors with your kids are some sturdy shoes (for safety reasons), a bag to fit things in, and a good attitude. It will not matter if your rain jacket is from Patagonia or Wal-Mart. Sure, there are reasons to buy a more expensive item every now and then, such as sustainability and longevity of a piece of gear, but you don't have to head out to Eastern Mountain Sports or L.L.Bean and buy all the things right this minute. I have built my own gear closet over decades, many items being hand-me-downs from my mother.

When it comes to getting gear for your kids, you also have to think about how quickly they might grow out of something. Buying a $200 jacket for a child who will use it for only one season might not make sense. However, if you want to camp season after season, getting a decent sleeping bag for your kid might be worth the effort and the money, because kids can grow into a sleeping bag. Thrift shops often have good clothing, and outdoor gear shops like REI have "Garage Sales" where you can find used gear at severely discounted prices. Even buying gear off-season can help your budget.

The point of this guide isn't to give you gear recommendations but rather to show you that you can build your gear closet throughout the years you adventure with your kids. The point is to show you that you don't need everything right now to start hiking. You just have to get out there and try!

HOW TO USE THIS GUIDE

Hiking with children is no easy feat, and writing a guide on the best hikes to do with children only proves this point. This guide is meant to provide you with a range of hikes for the inherent range of skill that accompanies children of all ages. Not every child will be able, nor want, to do every single hike in this guide. As a parent, you are the sole decision maker on whether your kids will be able to do a hike listed in this guide.

This guide is split among the six states that make up New England: Connecticut, Rhode Island, Massachusetts, Vermont, New Hampshire, and Maine. I tried my best to ensure an even spread of hikes to cover all the corners of the region, but New England covers a large amount of land, obviously, so many areas are not covered.

Each trail was chosen with children in mind. There are hundreds of thousands of trails across New England, but not all of them are well-suited or very fun for children. I also did not want to assume that kids can do only easy, half-mile jaunts around some lake, so there are several harder hikes in this guide for more advanced hikers.

In addition to the trail beta (i.e., all the basic information for a trail) at the beginning of each hike, driving directions are also provided from the major cities that surround the hike. You will also find step-by-step directions of the trail itself and what you'll encounter along the way.

THE BASICS

There are a few basic pieces of information at the beginning of each hike to ensure a safe and fun adventure for you and your kiddos.

Start: The trailhead you start from.

Elevation gain: How many feet of elevation gain you'll encounter. This is a huge deciding factor on how difficult a trail is, so keep this number in mind when deciding if a trail is right for you and your kids.

Distance: Round-trip distance of the trail in miles. This is another factor in deciding the plausibility of a hike for you and your kids.

Seasons/Schedule: When you can hike the trail and if access is ever restricted. Sometimes access is restricted due to hazards (e.g., rockfall, landslide, avalanche, and the like) and sometimes for other reasons, like nesting peregrine falcons.

Trail contact: The phone number and address of the management agency.

Dog-friendly: Whether or not dogs are allowed on the trail.

Trail surface: The type of surface (e.g., gravel, dirt, boardwalk) you'll encounter.

Land status: Who owns the land the trail resides on.

Nearest town: The name of the town closest to the trail.

Other trail users: Other trail users allowed on the trail (e.g., horses, bikers, snowmobiles, and so on).

Water availability: If and where you can find water near the trail.

Maps: Maps that can be downloaded or printed prior to your adventure.

Toilets: If and where toilets are available nearby.

Stroller/Wheelchair compatibility: Whether or not strollers or wheelchairs can be used on any portion of the trail.

Resting benches: Whether or not there are places for children and adults (e.g., nursing mamas) to rest or feed a hungry baby.

Difficulty: This is one of the most subjective pieces of information I provide in this guide. There are several factors that go into how strenuous a trail might be, including the ending elevation above sea level, the change in elevation throughout the trail, the length of the trail, and what hazards might be encountered along the way. I tried my best to standardize these difficulty ratings in the following categories:

Easy trails are those suitable for any hiker and any skill level. Distances for these trails are typically capped at 2.0 miles, with minimal elevation gain (less than 300 feet). These trails usually include those that are stroller- and wheelchair-friendly and will never require any rock scrambling or encounter many hazards.

Moderate trails are suitable for those with a bit more experience in the outdoors and who are comfortable hiking longer distances and more elevation gain. These trails will range from 1.0 to 4.0 miles with no more than 1,000 feet of elevation gain. Some areas along these trails may require more assistance from the adults.

Strenuous trails are suitable only for those with more advanced experience on the trail. Usually this means older kiddos, younger ones with more trail experience, or, at the very least, adults carrying their kids on their backs (in some cases, this is not suitable though). These trails are longer than 4.0 miles, usually have more than 1,000 feet of elevation gain, and, almost always, have some sort of hazard along the trail not safe for younger children.

Hiking time: This is a subjective piece of information that I provided. Hiking time varies with the skill level and age of the child, as well as with the difficulty of the hike. For most adults, the average hiking time is usually 2.0 to 3.0 miles per hour, but with smaller kids (and, subsequently, smaller legs), hiking times can double or triple your usual pace. As such, I conservatively estimate that most kids can do a mile in an hour, and the hiking times provided reflect that number.

Fees and permits: Depending on the management agency, fees and permits may be required for entrance onto their land. Most state and national parks require a fee, and some of the more popular trails even require a timed permit to enter. Many times the America the Beautiful National Parks Pass covers more than just getting into national parks—it also covers parking in wilderness areas and on land owned by the Forest Service. In Connecticut, if you are a resident, all state parks are free when you drive your CT-licensed vehicle into the park.

I have tried my best to accurately depict any fees required to park and recreate on the land a trail is on, but this can change quickly depending on the trail usage or political climate. Always call the local land management agency prior to your adventure to ensure you have what you need to get access.

Please adhere to permitting and fee regulations to keep trails open. The money collected goes directly back to managing the land, whether it be hiring more staff, maintaining trails and removing hazards, or simply buying trash cans to place at the trailheads. These management agencies are usually severely understaffed and could use all the help they can get from our recreational use.

Age range: It is hard to assess what ages are best suited for each trail, because a kid's skill is based not only on age but also experience. A 10-year-old who has never hiked before might find a 2-mile loop difficult, where a 3-year-old with ample experience might think nothing of it. The most difficult ages to assess are those toddler years, when kids don't really want to be in a carrier anymore but can't quite make it very far on their own.

Despite whatever I have written as guidance for this section, as the parent you are the only one who can decide whether a hike is suitable for your child. Use this section as it is meant to be—as a guide, not a rule.

Potential child hazards: Hiking with kids means you have to worry more about what you might encounter on the trail. A quick rock scramble to the top of a summit might be a breeze for you, but kids with little legs will have more difficulty. I try to point out every possible hazard that can be found on each trail, but be advised that trail conditions might have changed since the publication of this guide.

Gear suggestions: I could list everything but the kitchen sink for the gear I suggest for each hike. However, the things I list in this section are what I would find most useful for each hike on top of the Ten Essentials you should always carry when going out on an adventure. If you need guidance on what the Ten Essentials are, keep reading the next section.

BEFORE YOU HIT THE TRAIL

There is a lot of preparation for a day full of adventure, and that prep time only increases when children are involved. This section will give you a leg up (metaphorically speaking) on preparing for your hike with your little ones to ensure a safe and fun trip for everyone. It will also help you understand the importance of preserving these areas for your kids and the generations to come.

TRAIL ETIQUETTE

There are some basic codes of conduct along the trail. Some of these are not hard-and-fast rules but more of a courtesy and always good to know prior to any hike.

Right of Way

On most trails in the United States, the uphill hiker has the right of way. If you are like me, though, sometimes I need a break going uphill to catch my breath. The point is that the uphill hiker gets to decide whether they want to keep their pace.

Some novice hikers have a hard time wrapping their heads around this one, but there are distinct reasons why uphill hikers have the right of way.

1. Uphill hikers have a narrower field of vision and might not see folks coming down as quickly as those descending a trail can.

2. Uphill hikers have a harder time picking up their momentum again. Yes, downhill hikers might be going faster and have a harder time stopping, but the point is that it would be easy for them to get going again after stopping. Uphill hikers have to put in a lot more effort to get going again if they are abruptly stopped.

All this changes, though, when other trail users come into play. The general rule of thumb is that bikers yield to everyone and everyone yields to horses. If, however, bikers are huffing it up the trail and come up behind you, it's just polite for hikers to step aside and let them pass.

Also, if you are a solo hiker and you come across a group of folks, it's generally good etiquette to let the group go no matter if they are going up or down. Making an entire group step aside can do a lot more damage to the edges of a trail than a single hiker.

Dog Etiquette

This seems like a no-brainer, but please adhere to all leash laws. I cannot tell you the number of times someone has had their dog off-leash and simply stated, "Don't worry! My dog is friendly." At the crux of it, it doesn't matter whether your dog is friendly or not. There is a reason leash laws are put into effect for particular trails, and it is on the trail user to know ahead of time what those laws are.

Also, please pick up all feces from your pets while on the trail. This means not only picking up the poop and placing it in a doggie bag but also picking up the bag and throwing it out in a trash receptacle. Many trails on this list do not have garbage cans at the trailheads, so you need to pack out what you pack in. Do not leave bags on the trail for someone else to pick up.

Don't Forget to Knock Off the Dirt

This is one of those things that people often forget, or, perhaps, were never taught. Before you leave any trailhead after you have hiked the trail, check your gear for any mud, plants, or insects that might have caught a ride down the mountain.

One of the easiest ways to spread nonnative or invasive plant and animal species is through the soles of your hiking boots, the gear you carry, the clothing you wear, and the treads of your tires. So just do a quick check to make sure you aren't inadvertently giving anything or anyone a ride.

Stay on the Trail

Again, this seems like a given, but please stay on the official trails. Trail erosion is a real threat to many of the trails in New England due to the sheer volume of people recreating on them. If trail users start making their own trails (called social trails), more erosion can take place. This is especially important for those of us with kids since children love to wander. Make sure they understand that they need to stay on the trail for both their safety and the health of the ecosystem.

Understanding Trail Blazes

If you are new to New England, you may never have heard of a "trail blaze." Trail blazes are painted symbols (usually just a rectangle) on trees or rocks that show you the direction of the trail. Trail blazes are very common in New England and are how most trails are marked.

The general rule of thumb is that if you stand at one trail blaze, you should be able to see the next one up the trail, but that is not always the case. Also, if there are two blazes next to each other but slightly offset, that means there is a turn in the trail. If the blaze on the right is higher on the tree than the left one, it means the trail goes right. If the blaze on the left is higher on the tree than the right one, it means the trail goes left.

Blazes also can be placed on solid rock when you are above the tree line (i.e., the point on a mountain where trees can no longer grow). This happens on many of the trails in New Hampshire, which tends to have a lot of solid granite trails. Rock cairns do not work as well in this state, because winds and precipitation tend to knock them over.

LEAVE NO TRACE

There are seven basic principles to Leave No Trace—an organization dedicated to keeping the environment safe and healthy while also keeping trail users safe. For more in-depth information, head to its website: https://lnt.org. Here are the Seven Principles:

1. **Plan Ahead and Prepare:** Basically, know what you are getting yourself and your kids into. This hiking guide can assist in some of the logistics of planning

ahead, but you also need to think of other things. Know the skills and abilities of all the people in your party, check weather, and have a backup plan.

2. **Travel and Camp on Durable Surfaces:** Stay on the trail. This is what is meant by "travel on durable surfaces." But also, when you find a trail that opens up onto rock, stay as close to the blazes as possible and do not walk on the plant life that grows between rocks.

3. **Dispose of Waste Properly:** This one is fairly straightforward. Don't litter, and pack out what you pack in. This helps keep an area clean but also helps prevent wildlife from becoming nuisances on the trail.

4. **Leave What You Find:** This is the hardest one for those of us with kids. Children want to pick all the wildflowers and pinecones and rocks. Mistakes happen, of course, but there are ways to help prevent kids from picking up all the things. I tend to bring a toy (like a plastic car) for my kid to hold, or he uses one of my trekking poles to play "trail swords." Also, bubbles are a huge distraction in a pickle.

5. **Minimize Campfire Impacts:** If you don't need to build a fire, then don't. And if you do build one, make sure it's completely out before you move on. There is no need to start a wildfire because you didn't know how to properly douse your fire.

6. **Respect Wildlife:** This means do not pick up, aggravate, or try to pet any wildlife. Whether the wildlife be venomous snakes or harmless salamanders, please do not touch any wildlife for both your and their safety.

7. **Be Considerate of Others:** This is something you should think about in your life and not just on the trail. Common decency can go a long way on the trail, so just try to be a good person and a good trail user.

THE TEN ESSENTIALS OF HIKING

There are so many different types of gear that you could buy to get you and your kids outside, but I will not list all of them here. Instead, there are ten essential items that you should always carry with you no matter the size of your adventure.

1. **First-aid kit:** Any first-aid kit will do as long it fits the needs of your adventure. A longer adventure will need a more extensive first-aid kit. The only three things I ever added to a first-aid kit for my child is children's Tylenol, the NoseFrida (if you know, you know), and some child-friendly adhesive bandages.

2. **Navigation:** Either a GPS unit or map/compass will do. Your phone can technically be used at the very least, but you never know what service will be like in places.

3. **Knife/Multitool:** You can find great lightweight knives that easily fit in a small pack.

4. **Safety items:** A light, such as a headlamp, and fire-making tool (matches will suffice)

5. **Sun protection:** Bring both sunscreen and a hat.

6. **Water:** This seems obvious, but it needs to be stated. For an added kick, bring powdered electrolytes to add to your water bottle when you start to feel lethargic.

7. **Food:** Not just any food, but *enough* food for everyone. Also make sure that the food you bring is nourishing enough to fuel you and your companions for the entirety of the hike. Foods that can provide ample energy include nutrition/protein bars, energy chews, fresh veggies and fruit, trail mix, and tuna/salmon packets.

8. **Layers:** No matter the season, always come prepared with a base layer, a midlayer (like a sweatshirt), and an outer layer (like a raincoat).

9. **Appropriate footwear:** Footwear with proper protection, traction, and support should be taken under consideration.

10. **Shelter:** It doesn't have to be a three-person tent, but, at the very least, carry an emergency bivvy at all times.

HIKING SAFETY
Weather and Seasons

Anyone who has lived in New England knows how the weather and seasons change throughout the year. Winter can be brutally cold, summer is full of biting insects, and fall can have endless rain. Just because you are headed out on a hike doesn't mean Mother Nature will keep the skies blue and the rain at bay. Always check the weather prior to any adventure, especially for those hikes above the tree line. Storms can come in fast in places like the White Mountains. Always be prepared to turn around if weather comes in quickly.

Wildlife Encounters

On any given trail and at any given time, you can encounter wildlife. It might be only a caterpillar or a toad rather than a bear or a moose, but whatever it is, it should be taken seriously nonetheless. At the start of every trail, I always discuss with my kid the potential wildlife we might see on the trail and what to do if we encounter them.

When I ask him what animals he thinks we'll see, he almost always says, "Dinosaurs." (Spoiler: We have yet to see a dinosaur on the trail.) But then he gives me real answers such as "bunny rabbits" and "moooooooooose," emphasis on the "ooo." And now, at almost 5 years old, he also knows the answers when I ask him what he should do in case we encounter {insert any animal here}. Because the answer is always the same—"Walk to mama slowly."

There are, of course, nuances to wildlife encounters and the type of wildlife you see (i.e., what you do when you encounter a bear is different from what to do if you encounter a snake or a salamander). But ultimately, teach your kids to walk to you slowly no matter what the wildlife they encounter, and then assess the situation from there.

Ticks and Brown-tail Moths

Unfortunately, ticks and brown-tail moths are a regular part of outdoor life here in New England. They are pesky little buggers that are the bane of most parents' existence. The best advice I can give you is to spray your gear with permethrin at the beginning of the season (always check the label though) and use picaridin on your clothes and skin (I have never been a fan of DEET, so I try to stay away from it). Also, simply wearing long sleeves and tucking your pants into your socks works like a charm.

Poisonous Plants

There are several poisonous plants in New England, but the most common one found on the trail is poison ivy. In the Bash Bish Falls hike (hike 14), I describe how to identify poison ivy. There are a few trails in this guide where poison ivy is plentiful, so make sure to keep an eye on the trails when you hike. Again, wearing long sleeves and tucking your pants into your socks helps keep the dangerous oils off the skin and prevents irritation.

HIKING TIPS AND SUGGESTIONS

There are so many things I could put in this section, but the top tips that have proven to be useful and make for a happier kiddo on the trail include the following:

1. **Bring all the snacks**. I bring options for my kid as well as things he doesn't usually get at home but would consider a treat on the trail. I never know what mood my kid will be in, so having options is always a good thing.

2. **Always carry mini M&Ms**. I tried using gummy bears to entice my kid to get moving on the trail; however, the few times I did it, he didn't poop for three days! So, instead, I use mini M&Ms. They are not only great for bowels, they are also small enough to put in a fanny pack or your day backpack without taking up too much space.

3. **Buy good outerwear**. Remember where I said you didn't have to buy the most expensive or fancy gear? The one thing I never cheap out on is winter outerwear. I knew I wanted to bring my kid outdoors no matter the weather, which meant a lot of hiking in rain and snow, as New England experiences all the seasons. I noticed that the cheaper raincoats and snowsuits I bought him would get his base layers wet easily and he'd become cranky on the trail (who wouldn't?). I buy better outwear now and just size up so he can use it for multiple seasons.

4. **Bring guidebooks or educational apps**. I am not against screens in the outdoors. My son and I use the Seek app by iNaturalist every time we get out on a trail. It's a great resource to learn about new plants and animals, plus it works without service.

5. **Bring bubbles**. Seriously, bubbles can lift anyone out of a bad mood, adults included. I carry a small bottle of bubbles everywhere we go.

6. **Plan a fun treat for after the hike**. This might be something big (like heading up a tramway to summit a 4,000-footer) or something small (like grabbing a lollipop at the gas station on the way home). Sometimes kids need incentives, and that's OK.

MAP LEGEND

(91)	Interstate Highway	Bench	
(301)	US Highway	Boardwalk	
(41)	State Highway	Bridge	
	Local Road	Building/Point of Interest	
	Railroad	Campground	
	Featured Trail	City/Town	
	Trail	Cliffs	
	Paved Trail	Gate	
	State Border	Mountain/Peak	
	Small River/Creek	Parking	
	Body of Water	Picnic Area	
	Swamp/Marsh	Scenic View/Viewpoint	
	National Park/Forest	Tower	
	Wilderness Area	Trailhead	
	State/County Park	Tunnel	
	Refuge/Sanctuary/Reservation/Natural Area	Visitor Center	
		Waterfall	

CONNECTICUT HIKES

Gillette Castle nestled among the greenery

1 ROCKY NECK STATE PARK LOOP

Connecticut might be the third-smallest state, but it has more than 100 state parks and forests across its entirety. Rocky Neck State Park is one of the more popular state parks due to its expansive, stone-free beach and family-friendly activities. Besides hiking, you can crab or fish from one of the many piers or bridges across the park. There is a plethora of wildlife that call Rocky Neck State Park home including many species of birds, fish, and mammals. On most days throughout the spring and summer, you can catch ospreys flying from their nests in the salt marsh to catch dinner for their young ones.

Start: From the southern end of the Red Blaze Trail
Elevation gain: 140 feet
Distance: 2.2 miles
Difficulty: Easy
Hiking time: 2 hours but add more if you're headed to the beach afterward
Seasons/Schedule: Year-round
Fees and permits: Fee required, free for CT residents
Trail contact: Rocky Neck State Park, P.O. Box 676, Niantic, CT; (860) 424-3200; portal.ct.gov/DEEP/State-Parks/Parks/Rocky-Neck-State-Park
Dog-friendly: Allowed on leash on trails, not on the beach
Trail surface: Dirt, sand, and boardwalk

Land status: State of Connecticut, Department of Energy and Environmental Protection
Nearest town: Niantic, CT
Other trail users: None
Water availability: Concession stand and water fountains near toilets
Maps: Rocky Neck State Park map
Age range: All ages
Toilets: Yes, at the trailhead
Stroller/Wheelchair compatibility: Only on boardwalk at the beach
Resting benches: Picnic tables at the trailhead
Potential child hazards: Poison ivy
Gear suggestions: Sun hat, insect repellent, binoculars, swimsuit, and plenty of beach toys for after the hike

FINDING THE TRAILHEAD

From Hartford, take I-91 South for 10 miles. Use the left two lanes to take exit 22 South to merge onto Route 9 South toward Middletown/Old Saybrook. Continue on Route 9 for 29 miles and then use the left lane to merge onto I-95 North/Route 1 North toward New London/Providence. After 6 miles, take exit 72 toward Rocky Neck State Park. At the light take a left onto West Main Street and continue for 0.2 mile. The entrance to the park is on your right. Once through the gate, proceed around the roundabout and take the second exit toward the beach. Continue on the only road toward the beach for approximately 1 mile and then turn right (away from the beach side of the parking area) and park in the northwestern section at the trailhead. **GPS:** 41.302540 / -72.243776

THE HIKE

Rocky Neck State Park has been a go-to beach destination for those who reside in the Constitution State. With its campground, sandy beach, and ample hiking trails, this state park is a perfect place for a family-friendly adventure.

Rocky Neck is located on the shores of Long Island Sound and is flanked by a tidal river to the west and an extensive salt marsh to its east. The trail starts at the northwestern

Top: The view looking to the east across the salt marsh
Bottom: Mountain laurel flanks both sides of the trail and resembles a magical tunnel

corner of the large parking area. When you approach the parking area, most cars will likely be on your left and closer to the paths that grant access to the beach. You'll head to the far end of the parking lot and then turn right, away from the beach.

You'll head north on the Red Blaze Trail through a tiny grove of trees, where you will then reach a bridge that brings you across the salt marsh. Take a moment here to enjoy the sights and sounds of salt marsh life. Great blue herons and egrets will likely be stalking their prey in preternatural stillness among the reeds. Ospreys will be flying overhead, waiting to swoop down on the unsuspecting fish below.

Continue north on the trail, where you'll encounter a tunnel of mountain laurel after 0.5 mile. My own child described this tunnel as a "magical pathway," and he

The pavilion—a perfect place for a picnic

Some fun rocks to climb on the trail

continued to run through it for several minutes. Mountain laurel is Connecticut's state flower and blooms in May and June (depending on weather during the spring). The flowers are usually white and sometimes pale pink.

Mountain laurel is seen throughout the entirety of the trail as you continue north. Follow the red blazes to stay on the trail. Just under a mile from the trailhead, you'll reach the northernmost tip of the trail. When you hit the Blue Blaze Trail, continue to follow the red blazes, which will lead you back south to where you came from.

At 1.25 mile, you'll meet up with the Blue Blaze Trail again, and you'll stay on both the Red and Blue Blaze Trails to continue your jaunt south, back to your car. The Blue Blaze Trail will veer to the right after 0.15 mile, but follow the red blazes. Eventually you'll meet up with the park road, so be on the lookout for cars. As you travel down the road, look to your right and you'll see a bunch of rocks that are known as "Bakers Cave." The entrance is under an overhang and hidden a bit from the road. Supposedly it's named after a local man who avoided military service during the American Revolution by hiding there; however, even the local historical society has its doubts about this claim.

After the cave you'll be able to see the concession stand and bathrooms near the entrance to the beach. If you want, head to your car from here (which should be visible) to grab swimsuits, beach toys, and all the gear you'll need for a day in the sun. Then you can head through the tunnel that goes under the train tracks to get to the pristine beach.

Set up your beach gear wherever you'd like and enjoy looking for shells or discovering life in the tide pools near the rock groyne just below the pavilion. Or set up a picnic at the pavilion or the picnic tables below while your kids explore the surrounding area. Stay off the rocks that surround the pavilion, as they are usually covered in poison ivy!

MILES AND DIRECTIONS

0.00 Begin at the trailhead on the northwest side of the large parking area (farthest from the beach).

0.10 Cross over a boardwalk and look out across the wetland to view ospreys searching for their next meal.

0.25 Come to the intersection of the White Blaze Trail. Continue on the Red Blaze Trail.

0.50 Enter a tunnel of mountain laurel (Connecticut's state flower). Depending on weather, blooms occur in May or June.

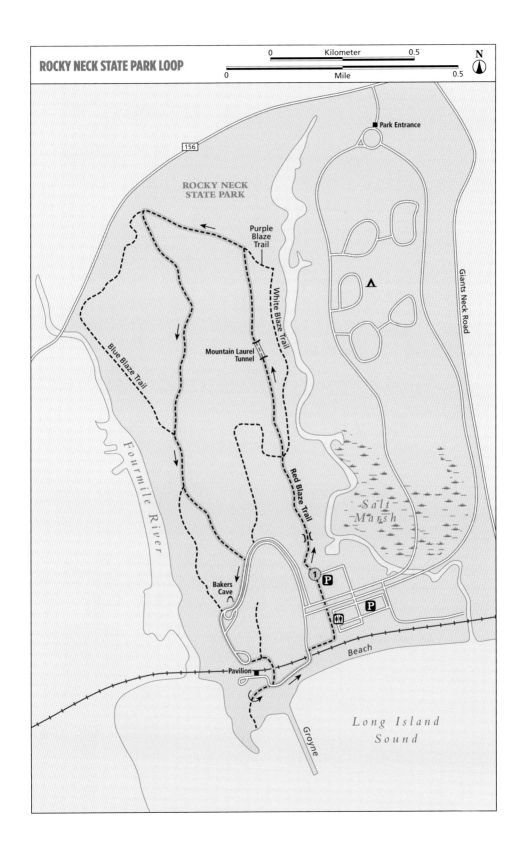

ROCKY NECK STATE PARK LOOP

Kilometer
0   0.5

Mile
0   0.5

N

156

ROCKY NECK
STATE PARK

Purple
Blaze
Trail

White Blaze Trail

Blue Blaze Trail

Mountain Laurel
Tunnel

Fourmile River

Red Blaze Trail

Park Entrance

Giants Neck Road

Salt
Marsh

1

P

P

Bakers
Cave

Beach

Pavilion

Groyne

Long Island
Sound

A stone-free beach for playing and boulders for tide-pooling

0.70   Veer slightly left to continue on the Red Blaze Trail. Do not take the right onto the Purple Blaze Trail.

0.90   This is where you'll first encounter the Blue Blaze Trail, but continue on the Red Blaze Trail. It will seem as if you're heading back south in the direction you came from (and you'd be correct).

1.25   Here you will join the Blue Blaze Trail.

1.40   At the fork in the trail, stay left to leave the Blue Blaze Trail and continue on the Red Blaze Trail.

1.60   Here you will meet up with a road, so be on the lookout for cars. Take a right along the road.

1.65   Here you'll see Bakers Cave. Once you've checked out the cave, head toward the concession stand and the tunnel under the train tracks to get to the beach.

1.90   Reach the tunnel underneath the train tracks. Take a right toward the pavilion.

2.00   Have a snack here at the pavilion or check out the views to Long Island Sound.

2.10   Head back through the tunnel underneath the train tracks.

2.20   Arrive back at the parking lot where your car is located. Grab your swim trunks and beach toys to head back to the beach for a day in the sun.

THAT'S SO GNEISS (I MEAN, NICE)!

Take a longer look around the pavilion to observe the large metamorphic rock that it sits on. These outcrops are made of granitic gneiss (yes, pronounced as "nice"), which was subjected to intense pressure and heat as it formed hundreds of thousands of years ago. Gneiss is one of the easiest rock formations to observe, because it has very distinct layers (or "bands" as geologists like to say). Its layers usually vary between light and dark stone due to the separation of different types of minerals during its alteration process.

2 APPALACHIAN TRAIL TO LION'S HEAD

The Appalachian Trail runs 2,194 miles from Georgia to Maine with only about 50 miles within the Constitution State's borders. About 3,000 people attempt the entire trail every year, while close to 3 million people visit it annually. Surprisingly this trail is much less crowded than others along the long-distance trek. The views are glorious at the top, so make sure to have plenty of battery life left on your phone to snap those photos.

Start: Appalachian trailhead off Route 41
Elevation gain: 1,170 feet
Distance: 4.4 miles
Difficulty: Strenuous
Hiking time: 4 hours
Seasons/Schedule: Year-round
Fees and permits: None
Trail contact: Appalachian Mountain Club—CT Chapter, P.O. Box 371, Marlborough, CT; (800) 372-1758; https://ct-amc.org
Dog-friendly: Allowed on leash on trails
Trail surface: Dirt and rock

Land status: Appalachian Trail Conservancy
Nearest town: Salisbury, CT
Other trail users: None
Water availability: None
Maps: Appalachian Trail map
Age range: Kids in carriers and those with extensive trail experience
Toilets: Yes, just past the trailhead
Stroller/Wheelchair compatibility: No
Resting benches: None
Potential child hazards: Poison ivy
Gear suggestions: Insect repellent and trekking poles

FINDING THE TRAILHEAD

From Hartford, take Route 44 West for 46.5 miles. Take a right onto Cobble Road, continue for 0.4 mile, and turn right onto Route 41 North. After just 0.25 mile, the small parking lot will be on your left. Only about ten cars can fit in the parking lot—do not park on the side of the road. **GPS:** 41.993970 / -73.426512

THE HIKE

The northwestern part of the state is a popular place to visit, because the tallest point, Bear Mountain, is located here along with other prominent mountains. Lion's Head lies just south of Bear Mountain and tends to be a bit quieter than its northern mountain neighbor but has just as good of views.

You start right on the Appalachian Trail (white blazes) and head north through a forested path. Within a tenth of a mile, there is a pit toilet just off-trail to your right. If you or your kids need a washroom, now is the time, because there aren't any other facilities in the area. It's not the cleanest of toilets, but it suffices for what needs to be done. There's even a fun graphic that greets you, describing "privy basics" while you sit and do your business.

After you've taken care of emptying your tanks, continue on the trail toward the summit. Make sure to stop every now and then to enjoy the beauty of nature, which includes many species of birds, deer, tons of wildflowers, and an a.rray of fungi. But also

Top: The sun peeks through the canopy on your way up the trail.
Bottom: View from Lion's Head summit looking north

be adamant with your children to stay on the trail. This path is riddled with poison ivy throughout its entirety, which can easily irritate your skin.

You'll encounter several perennial (aka springfed) streams throughout the trail. Depending on the time of year and whether or not it has rained recently, the streams could either be nonexistent or a bit hazardous. Always wear proper, waterproof footwear and be prepared to assist your kids across the small streams. The first stream crossing is about a half-mile in while the fourth one isn't until 1.3 miles.

At the 1.6-mile mark, the trail will start to ascend quickly. Up until this point, the trail was relatively flat with a few small sections of incline. But here, the trail climbs almost 600 feet in under 0.5 mile with switchbacks throughout. Eventually, at 2.0 miles you'll reach

View from Lion's Head summit looking south

the junction of the trail that leads south to Bunker Hill. If you aren't up for the big ascent from the Appalachian trailhead, you can park near the Bunker Hill summit just off Bunker Hill Road, which cuts your hike by more than half.

Keep right at the junction and climb the few tenths of a mile to the summit of Lion's Head. You can take a left when you reach a second fork before the summit to take the long way around and take in the views from the loop. Or you can just go right at the junction for the best views of them all at the rocky outcrop. At the summit enjoy sweeping views of Connecticut and New York off to your right. The huge swaths of forest make this a great place to view the leaves in autumn.

Turn around and go back the way you came. If you see folks with large back-packs along the trail, they're likely thru- or section-hikers. Thru-hikers are doing the entire Appalachian Trail in one go, while those who are section-hiking only do sections of the hike (hence the name) over the course of several years. Be nice and say hello to them, or, better yet, offer them a treat that they likely would love (like a Snickers bar or something). They will be forever grateful!

At the junction for the last push up to the summit

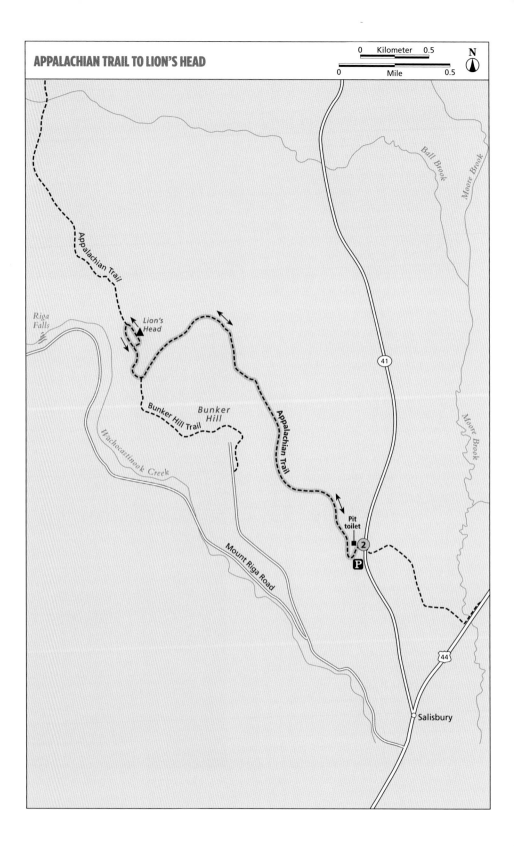

Kilometer

Mile

N

Appalachian Trail

Riga
Falls

Lion's
Head

Bunker Hill Trail

Bunker
Hill

Appalachian Trail

Hrachocastinook Creek

Mount Riga Road

Ball Brook

Moore Brook

41

Moore Brook

Pit
toilet

2

P

44

Salisbury

MILES AND DIRECTIONS

0.00 Begin at the trailhead just off Route 41.

0.10 Pass by the pit toilet on your right—this is the only facility along the trail.

0.55 First stream crossing.

1.10 Second stream crossing.

1.20 Third stream crossing.

1.30 Fourth stream crossing.

1.60 Here is where the big ascent begins.

2.00 Meet up with the junction to Bunker Hill—stay right to go up to the summit of Lion's Head.

2.20 Arrive at the summit! Take in the views and have a snack before descending back the way you came.

2.40 Reach the junction of Bunker Hill Trail. Take a left to stay on the Appalachian Trail.

2.80 The steep descent tapers off here, and it's a smooth hike back to your car.

3.10 Cross back over the fourth stream crossing.

3.20 Cross back over the third stream crossing.

3.30 Cross back over the second stream crossing.

3.85 Cross back over the first (and now your last) stream crossing.

4.30 Pass by the pit toilet, now on your left—if you need to go before getting back in your car, do it now.

4.40 Arrive back at the trailhead.

MILLIPEDES DON'T HAVE A THOUSAND LEGS

You'd think with a name like "millipede" that this creature would have a thousand legs. However, the most pairs ever found in nature in the eastern United States is 375. That number, though, is uncommon. Most millipedes have only around 50 to 75 pairs of legs. That is still an amazing feat (no pun intended!), and those legs easily transport these little arthropods (millipedes are, in fact, not insects) to where they need to go. Despite their creepy appearance, millipedes are an important part of the ecosystem. They help with the decomposition process and even provide sanitary services for certain species of ants!

A giant millipede found on the trail up to Lion's Head

3 INDIAN CAVES AT CHATFIELD HOLLOW

There aren't many places where you can swim in a lake, sunbathe on a beach, walk through a covered bridge, and explore caves all in one day, let alone on the same trail. But that's exactly what you get when you visit Chatfield Hollow State Park. The park is filled with unique geological features and loads of fun activities, including a nature center. No matter what your kids enjoy, there is bound to be something for them here at Chatfield Hollow.

Start: Red Blaze/Ridge trailhead
Elevation gain: 280 feet
Distance: 3.1 miles
Difficulty: Moderate
Hiking time: 3 hours
Seasons/Schedule: Year-round
Fees and permits: Fee required during the summer, free for CT residents
Trail contact: Chatfield Hollow State Park, 381 CT-80, Killingworth, CT; (860) 663-2030; https://portal .ct.gov/DEEP/State-Parks/Parks/ Chatfield-Hollow-State-Park
Dog-friendly: Allowed on leash on trails; not allowed in the water or at the beach
Trail surface: Dirt, rock, and pavement

Land status: State of Connecticut, Department of Energy and Environmental Protection
Nearest town: Killingworth, CT
Other trail users: None
Water availability: At picnic areas and restroom facilities at the beach
Maps: Chatfield Hollow State Park map
Age range: All ages
Toilets: Yes
Stroller/Wheelchair compatibility: No
Resting benches: Yes, picnic tables throughout the park
Potential child hazards: Walking on a road
Gear suggestions: Insect repellent, sun hat, beach accessories, and clothing you don't mind getting dirty in the caves

FINDING THE TRAILHEAD

From Hartford, Connecticut, take I-91 for 10 miles to exit 22S to merge onto Route 9 toward Middletown/Old Saybrook. Continue on Route 9 for 14 miles. Take exit 9 toward Killingworth/Clinton. Take a right onto Route 81 South and continue for 8 miles until you hit a traffic circle. Take the first exit in the traffic circle onto Route 80 West. After 1 mile, turn right into the Chatfield Hollow State Park entrance. Park near the beach; the trail starts just before the restroom facilities at the beach. This place is crowded on the weekends during the summer.

From New Haven, Connecticut, take Route 80 east for 14 miles. At the traffic circle, take the second exit to stay on Route 80. After 3 miles, turn left into the park entrance and proceed to the swim beach area. **GPS:** 41.369290 / -72.588472

THE HIKE

Chatfield Hollow State Park has something for even the pickiest of kids. It's got caves, a swim beach, fishing, a nature center, and a genuine covered bridge. After you park, find the trailhead for the Red Blaze/Ridge Trail just south of the restroom facilities in the beach area (it's across the road from where you park).

The large rock face that houses the caves on the other side

Follow the red blazes for about the first mile. Most of this section is forested with no real significant views—but it's beautiful nonetheless. You know you've reached the end of the red blazes when you make it to a junction for the Purple Blaze/Covered Bridge Trail. If you don't want to see the covered bridge, take a left here to walk parallel to the stream back toward the swim beach area. If you do want to see the covered bridge (and I suggest you do), take the quick walk a few hundred feet straight to the bridge.

Top: A quaint covered bridge along the path
Bottom: Looking across the pond to the beach and picnic area

After you've gotten your fill of the covered bridge, make your way back onto the Purple Blaze Trail and head south (right). You'll meander along this trail next to the stream, which can be pleasant most months of the year, except when mosquitos come out in late spring and early summer. The Purple Blaze Trail is only about 0.5 mile long and will end when you reach the Park Road. Be careful as you walk alongside the road, as most visitors don't travel at the required 10 mph speed limit.

You'll likely walk past your car, so if you need to stock up on any items or need to use the restrooms, feel free to do so at the swim beach area. After that, continue south on the Park Road, again taking heed of the cars. After 0.5 mile, you'll see the Green Blaze/Chimney Trail on your left. Take this left to wander through some wetlands before coming across the caves.

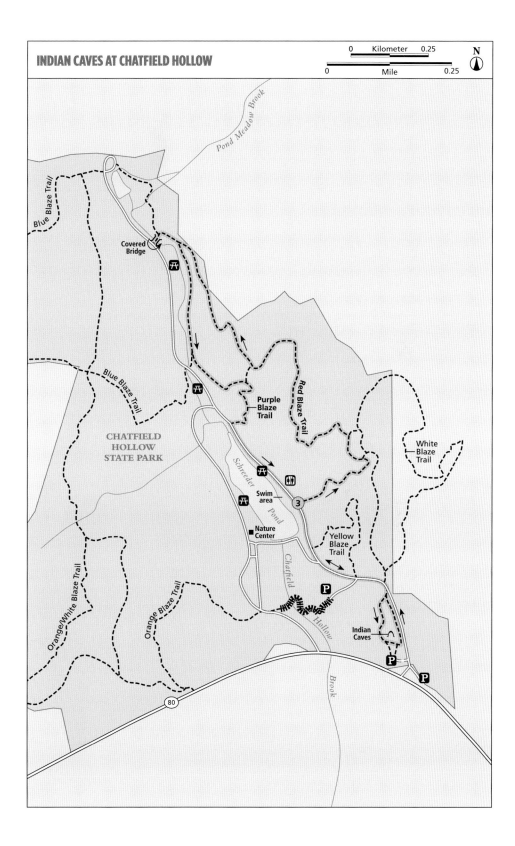

INDIAN CAVES AT CHATFIELD HOLLOW

Pond Meadow Brook

Blue Blaze Trail

Blue Blaze Trail

Covered Bridge

Purple Blaze Trail

Red Blaze Trail

CHATFIELD HOLLOW STATE PARK

White Blaze Trail

Schreeder Pond

Swim area

3

Nature Center

Yellow Blaze Trail

Orange/White Blaze Trail

Orange Blaze Trail

Chatfield Hollow Brook

Indian Caves

P

P

P

80

0   Kilometer   0.25

0   Mile   0.25

N

The caves aren't large or deep, but they are great to hang out in during a hot summer day. The minute you round the corner to the cave, nature's air-conditioning greets you with a smile and you're instantly cooled off. After you and the kids are done romping around the caves and cliff faces, head back on the trail and back to the road.

Head north on the Park Road until you get back to your car at the swim beach area. Grab all your beach goodies and head down to the small sand beach on Schreeder Pond. Kids can make sandcastles or swim in the water to get more energy out, even after 3.0 miles of walking. Ensure you've got a good book stashed in your car to relax while your kids make more memories.

MILES AND DIRECTIONS

0.00 Begin at the trailhead just across the road from the parking area and south of the restrooms.

1.20 Hit the junction of the Purple Blaze/Covered Bridge Trail. Take a left to continue on the Purple Blaze Trail, or take a quick jaunt straight to the covered bridge and then find your way back to this spot.

1.80 Make it to the Park Road. Follow it south back toward the swim beach area.

2.00 Arrive at the swim beach area. You can stop the hike here if you or your kiddos are getting tired (or cranky). Or you can grab some provisions and keep going to check out the caves.

2.30 Leave the road and connect with the Green Blaze/Chimney Trail.

2.40 Arrive at the caves!

2.50 Leave the trail to head back onto the road and hike north back toward your car and the swim beach area.

3.10 Arrive back at your car. Get ready for the beach and enjoy the sunshine!

WHY ARE CAVES SO COLD?

Caves don't change dramatically when it comes to their core temperature. It's probably one of the few things about caves that doesn't ever really change, considering stalactites and stalagmites are added to (albeit slowly) every year. The temperature stays relatively the same mostly because rock is very slow to transmit heat, which means it stays "ground temperature" for the majority of the year. By the time the scorching heat of summer and the frigid air of winter reach the cave, the temperature has effectively balanced out. This is why people have used basements to store vegetables and other perishable items since the dawn of time. It's nature's refrigerator!

Looking into the caves. Bundle up—it's cold in here!

4 BREAKNECK POND LOOP

Breakneck Pond lies within Bigelow Hollow State Park, a quaint swath of land in northeastern Connecticut. Local tradition claims that the man who owned land near the pond fell after trying to traverse the steep sections surrounding it and was badly hurt. The name "Breakneck" was quickly attached to the mile-long pond soon after. Although the hike is one of the longer ones on the list, the elevation gain makes this a leisurely stroll through the woods and around a pond fluttering with beaver activity.

Start: White Blaze/East Ridge trailhead
Elevation gain: 215 feet
Distance: 6.0 miles
Difficulty: Moderate
Hiking time: 4 hours
Seasons/Schedule: Year-round
Fees and permits: Fee required, free for Connecticut residents
Trail contact: Bigelow Hollow State Park, 298 Bigelow Hollow Rd., Union, CT; (860) 684-3430; https://portal.ct.gov/DEEP/State-Parks/Parks/Bigelow-Hollow-State-Park-Nipmuck-State-Forest
Dog-friendly: Allowed on leash on trails
Trail surface: Dirt and rock
Land status: State of Connecticut, Department of Energy and Environmental Protection

Nearest town: Union, CT
Other trail users: Yes, except only foot traffic on the Blue Blaze/Nipmuck Trail
Water availability: None
Maps: Bigelow Hollow State Park map
Age range: All ages; toddlers may have difficulty if not being carried
Toilets: Yes, at the trailhead
Stroller/Wheelchair compatibility: No
Resting benches: Yes, picnic tables throughout the park
Potential child hazards: Trail is close to water's edge
Gear suggestions: Insect repellent and binoculars (to view the beaver activity)

FINDING THE TRAILHEAD

From Hartford, Connecticut, take I-84 East for 30 miles. Take exit 73 toward Union and turn right onto Route 190 East for 2 miles. Turn right onto Route 171 East for 1.4 miles, until you see the entrance for the park on your left. Drive on Park Road until you reach the East Ridge trailhead parking lot on the northern tip of Bigelow Pond.

From Norwich, Connecticut, take Route 32 north for 9 miles, then turn right onto Route 203 north. Continue on Route 203 north for 5.3 miles, then turn right onto Route 6 east for 2 miles. Turn left onto Route 198 north for 12 miles and then turn left onto Route 171 west for 5.4 miles. The entrance to the park is on your left. Drive on Park Road until you reach the East Ridge trailhead parking lot on the northern tip of Bigelow Pond. **GPS:** 41.99862 / -72.126274

THE HIKE

I remember going to Bigelow Hollow State Park with my own mother dozens of times as a kid. We would always walk the loop around Breakneck Pond, opting for the longer hike instead of the shorter one around Bigelow Pond. We'd always cap off our day at the

Top: You traverse an old forest road to get to Breakneck Pond.
Bottom: The trail heading back to the parking area

Vanilla Bean in Pomfret on our way home and order one of the decadent sandwiches or a huge chunk of chocolate cake. Bringing my kiddo here brought back a lot of memories, and I love that I can share this hike with you.

The trail starts at the White Blaze/East Ridge trailhead, but you are only on this trail for a short while. At the first junction, go right on the No Blaze/Forest Road Trail and then stay left at the next junction. Once you hit the Blue Blaze Trail (which is the junction after that), go left to head north to Breakneck Pond.

This trail is rather wide and flat and brings you to the southern tip of Breakneck Pond after 0.75 mile. Just off the trail is one of two lean-tos around the pond that you can reserve for an overnight stay. Go right toward the eastern side of the pond and head north to continue on the Blue Blaze/Nipmuck Trail.

A view from the southern edge of Breakneck Pond

INTRODUCE BACKPACKING TO YOUR KIDS

Breakneck Pond has one of the best places to introduce your kids to backpacking. The South Shelter lean-to is only a mile from the trailhead and has little-to-no elevation gain. It's a great place to introduce backcountry camping to your kids without having to slog through miles of trail or worry that something might go wrong. Because even if something did go wrong, or you or your kids weren't having a great time, you're a hop, skip, and a jump from your car and an easy drive home. Plus, the sounds you get to hear when the sun dips past the horizon and the loons and owls come out to play will lull any kiddo to sleep in just a few minutes. Or perhaps they'll be too excited to sleep at all. Let's hope, for your sake, it's the former.

One of the shelters on Breakneck Pond—a great place for a picnic or to stay the night!

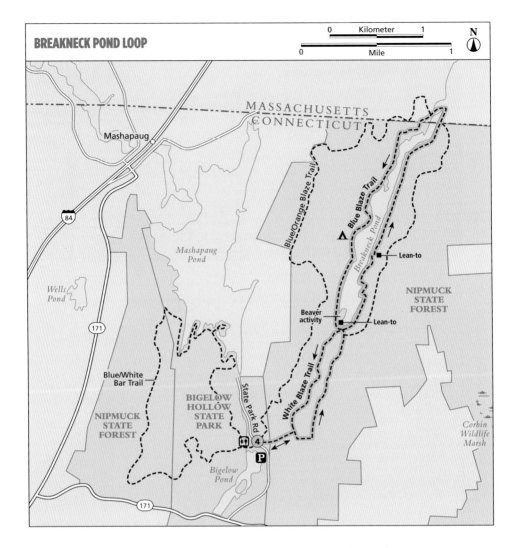

Kilometer

Mile

N

MASSACHUSETTS
CONNECTICUT

Mashapaug

84

Blue/Orange Blaze Trail

Blue Blaze Trail

Breakneck Pond

Mashapaug
Pond

Wells
Pond

171

Lean-to

NIPMUCK
STATE
FOREST

Beaver
activity

Lean-to

Blue/White
Bar Trail

White Blaze Trail

State Park Rd

BIGELOW
HOLLOW
STATE
PARK

NIPMUCK
STATE
FOREST

Corbin
Wildlife
Marsh

4

P

Bigelow
Pond

171

Eventually you'll reach the second shelter (called the East Shelter), where you can sit and relax and enjoy the view if no one is staying there at the moment. Then continue following the blue blazes until you reach a three-way junction at the northern tip of the pond. Stay all the way to the left and follow the blue blazes with the white dots in the middle all along the western edge of the pond. You'll get some great views of beaver activity along this route.

Before you know it, you'll be back at the South Shelter and ready to make the last push back to your car. Crossing the wetland area at the southern end of the pond can be tricky, especially if beavers have clogged up the culvert that runs underneath the trail. If so, tread carefully, and be on the lookout for tiger swallowtail butterflies that can often be seen sunning themselves on the rocks.

Instead of taking the same trail back, take the first junction on your right to head down the White Blaze/Park Road Trail. It's still relatively the same as the Blue Blaze Trail you took up, but it's also different. It's a wide trail with plenty of room to. get out any last-minute energy before getting back into your car.

End the hike by taking a right onto the White Blaze/East Ridge Trail, where you'll meet back up at the northern tip of Bigelow Pond. If you still feel like walking even after a 6-mile hike, you can walk the 1.3 miles around Bigelow Pond or head up the Park Road to Mashapaug Pond. Or you can do what my mom and I always did and head down to Pomfret to grab a sweet treat at the Vanilla Bean, which has been a Connecticut staple since 1989.

A tiger swallowtail butterfly suns itself on the edge of the pond.

MILES AND DIRECTIONS

0.00 Begin at the White Blaze/East Ridge trailhead at the northern tip of Bigelow Pond.

0.25 Turn right onto the No Blaze/Forest Road Trail and then almost immediately stay left on the No Blaze/Forest Road Trail.

0.35 Turn left onto the Blue Blaze/Nipmuck Trail.

1.10 Arrive at the southern tip of Breakneck Pond and the South Shelter. Stay right at the junction to follow the eastern side of the pond.

1.65 Arrive at the East Shelter but continue on the Blue Blaze Trail.

2.75 Meet up with the Blue-White Dot/Breakneck Pond View Trail. At this point, other trail users such as horse riders and mountain bikers can use the trail along with hikers.

2.95 Stay left at the three-way junction to continue on the Blue-White Dot/Breakneck Pond View Trail.

4.10 Arrive at the established backcountry campsite right at the water's edge.

4.85 Arrive again at the South Shelter and the southern tip of Breakneck Pond. Take the first right after rounding the tip of the pond and take the White Blaze/Park Road Trail back toward your car.

5.70 Turn right off the Park Road and continue on the White Blaze/East Ridge Trail.

6.00 Arrive back at the trailhead.

5 GILLETTE CASTLE RAILROAD LOOP

Whether your kid loves trains or Sherlock Holmes or being a princess in a Disney movie, you should not miss the Train Trail at Gillette Castle State Park. As if plucked from medieval times, the looming presence of Gillette Castle towers over the Connecticut River and is quite the sight! The castle is named for famous actor, director, and playwright William Hooker Gillette, who built this home and surrounding estate. He was best known for his portrayal of Sherlock Holmes, and the castle reflects the mystery of the noted fictional character.

Start: Purple Blaze/Train trailhead
Elevation gain: 115 feet
Distance: 2.0 miles
Difficulty: Easy
Hiking time: 2 hours (longer if touring the castle)
Seasons/Schedule: Year-round
Fees and permits: None to visit the park grounds, but fees are required for entrance to the castle.
Trail contact: Gillette Castle State Park, 67 River Rd., East Haddam, CT; (860) 526-2336; https://portal .ct.gov/DEEP/State-Parks/Parks/ Gillette-Castle-State-Park
Dog-friendly: Allowed on leash on trails but not inside any buildings, including the castle
Trail surface: Dirt, rock, and pavement

Land status: State of Connecticut, Department of Energy and Environmental Protection
Nearest town: East Haddam, CT
Other trail users: None
Water availability: Yes, at the visitor center
Maps: Gillette Castle State Park map
Age range: All ages
Toilets: Yes, at the visitor center
Stroller/Wheelchair compatibility: No
Resting benches: Yes, along the trail and around the castle
Potential child hazards: Jagged steps around the castle, raised sections on the trail
Gear suggestions: Camera, because this place is very photogenic

FINDING THE TRAILHEAD

From Hartford, Connecticut, take CT 2 East for 20 miles. Take exit 16 toward Westchester/Moodus. Turn right onto Route 149 South for 6 miles and then turn left onto Falls Bashan Road. After 1 mile, turn right onto East Haddam/ Colchester Turnpike. Follow the turnpike for 2 miles and then turn left onto Route 151 South for 1.2 miles, where it turns into Route 82 South. Continue on Route 82 for another 1.3 miles and then turn right onto CT 431. After 1.5 miles, turn right into the park entrance and park at the main parking area outside the visitor center. **GPS:** 41.423671 / -72.426853

THE HIKE

When I was a kid, I dreamed of living in Gillette Castle. Its mysterious crevices and creepy exterior reminded me of the fantastical stories I'd read before bed. I loved finding new places and corners to discover throughout the grounds of the estate.

My most favorite of the trails was the Purple Blaze/Train Trail, which runs along the same tracks that William Gillette constructed around his estate. He used to tour guests

Top: The model train that once traversed the property
Bottom: The well-established trail along the Railroad Loop

around the grounds by using an electric and steam engine. The Sherlock Holmes actor was passionate about trains and has famously said, "Some folks were born with a silver spoon in their mouths; me, a locomotive." Extensive restoration has been done on the trails to follow the same train stations, trestles, and tunnels that Gillette used during his lifetime.

One of Gillette's original trains, the electric one, finally made its way back home to the castle in 2007 and now resides for the public to view in the visitor center. To take the path that these trains traveled, park in the main parking area outside the visitor center and take the White Blaze Trail located in the northeast corner. You'll pass a pond on your left—look o.ut for pileated woodpeckers, turtles, and ducks!

Top: William Gillette was an actor who oftened played Sherlock Holmes.
Bottom: Gillette Castle in the distance

When you reach a T-intersection of the White Blaze Trail, go straight a few dozen feet to get on the Purple Blaze/Train Trail and go right. After a tenth of a mile, you'll head through some small tunnels and then make your way onto a few footbridges. The trail makes a small loop at the end, and you'll return back the way you came over the footbridges and through the tunnels.

Instead of going back on the White Blaze Trail, take a right to stay on the Purple Blaze/Train Trail toward the smaller pond. Picnic tables are dotted around the pond to take in the wildlife and beautiful gardens. Go over the stream on a small footbridge to head toward the road. When you reach the road, make sure to hold your kids' hands as you cross and hop on the Purple Blaze/Train Trail once again and head right. You'll follow the road for short time and then veer west (left) toward the forest.

Stay on the Purple Blaze/Train Trail and have some fun with your kids by asking them if they think they can walk as fast as a train—trust me, it'll be a good motivator. You'll

You can walk through the castle when it's opened for the season.

eventually pass the 125th Street Station, where you can sit and relax before continuing your hike. When you reach the Yellow Blaze Trail, turn right to head toward the castle. When you hit the road, Gillette Castle should be in full view.

If you've purchased tour tickets (which I highly suggest you do), wait for your tour group to enter the castle. Tours are offered every 15 minutes and keep groups to only twelve visitors at a time. There's a great viewpoint at the southern part of the castle that overlooks the Connecticut River. You might be lucky and see the Chester/Hadlyme Ferry making its way across the river.

When you've finished taking a gazillion photos and doing your tour, follow the signs back to the visitor center to grab a snack and a souvenir before heading back to your car in the parking lot. Don't forget to take one last look back through the trees to see the glory of Gillette Castle.

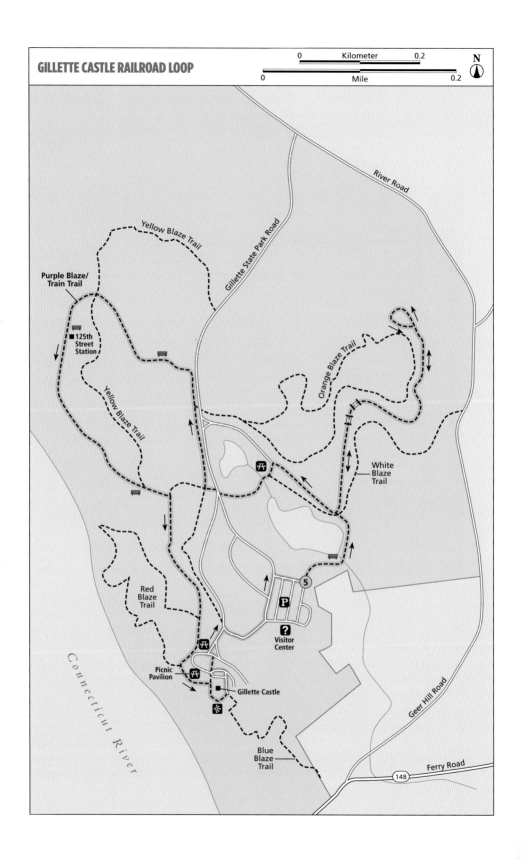

GILLETTE CASTLE RAILROAD LOOP

0 Kilometer 0.2

0 Mile 0.2

N

River Road

Yellow Blaze Trail

Gillette State Park Road

Purple Blaze/
Train Trail

■ 125th
Street
Station

Yellow Blaze Trail

Orange Blaze Trail

White
Blaze
Trail

Red
Blaze
Trail

5

P

? Visitor
Center

Picnic
Pavilion

■ Gillette Castle

Connecticut River

Blue
Blaze
Trail

Geer Hill Road

148 Ferry Road

MILES AND DIRECTIONS

0.00 Begin in the northeast part of the parking area on the White Blaze Trail.

0.10 Hit the T-junction of the White Blaze Trail and go straight and then immediately right onto the Purple Blaze/Train Trail—do not go left or right to stay on the White Blaze Trail.

0.20 Go through two tunnels.

0.40 Round the small loop and head back the way you came.

0.60 Go back through the tunnels.

0.70 Take a right to stay on the Purple Blaze/Train Trail and head toward the small pond.

0.80 Take a left back onto the White Blaze Trail and head toward the road.

0.90 Cross the road and then head right onto the Purple Blaze/Train Trail.

1.20 Arrive at the 125th Street Station.

1.40 Take a right onto the Yellow Blaze Trail to head toward Gillette Castle.

1.60 Eventually you'll hit a road, although there is no public access by car here, so you shouldn't have to worry about any vehicles other than the state park employees. At this point, Gillette Castle will be in full view.

1.65 Stay right on the road, tour through Grand Central Station, and sit at one of the many picnic tables to grab a snack.

1.70 Walk around the castle grounds and take in the views of the Connecticut River at the overlook. Head back to the road.

1.80 Follow signs for the visitor center by heading northeast on the roads.

1.90 Stop by the visitor center for snacks and some souvenirs.

2.00 Arrive back at the trailhead.

SEE ONE OF TWO UNDERWATER PRESERVES IN THE STATE

Gillette Castle was completed in 1919 atop the southernmost summit of a chain of hills called The Seven Sisters. In fact, before the castle was named Gillette Castle, William Hooker Gillette called his home "The Seventh Sister" after the mountain it sat on. He originally thought to build his retirement home on Long Island, but when he saw the cliffs along the Connecticut River, he knew what he wanted to do.

The twenty-four-room mansion is filled with hidden mirrors and secret nooks and crannies, and no two doors are alike in the entirety of the castle. Your kids will walk around enchanted by the mystery of the castle, which has been lovingly restored and maintained to keep the look of medieval times with a dash of European flare.

But the castle isn't the only cool thing to see here. If you time your visit correctly, during low tide, you might get a glimpse of one of the two underwater preserves in the state. While Gillette Castle was being built, William Gillette lived on his houseboat called the *Aunt Polly*. He had it docked at his home when he finally moved into the castle and used the boat as a greenhouse. Unfortunately, the boat burned in 1932 and was a total loss. You can still see 100 feet of the boat's hull when low tide arrives along the Connecticut River.

RHODE ISLAND HIKES

Walking along
Napatree
Conservation Area
Trail at sunrise

6 CUMBERLAND MONASTERY LOOP

Have your kids take a vow of silence as you traverse the trails located at the Cumberland Monastery. Although monks no longer use the buildings, they now house the Cumberland Public Library and a senior center. This loop brings you on the same trails the monks used to tend their fields and quarry granite for the buildings on the property. You'll see beautiful wetlands, white pine groves, several ponds, and gorgeous fields along both wide and narrow paths. If your kids aren't keeping their voices down, no need to worry; these trails (although popular) are vast, so you likely won't see too many people the farther you get from the parking area.

Start: The kiosk behind the Cumberland Public Library
Elevation gain: 210 feet
Distance: 2.7 miles
Difficulty: Easy
Hiking time: 2.5 hours
Seasons/Schedule: Sunrise to sunset, year-round
Fees and permits: None
Trail contact: The Rhode Island Land Trust, PO Box 633, Saunderstown, RI 02874; (401) 212-0832; www.rilandtrusts.org. Town of Cumberland, 45 Broad St., Cumberland, RI 02864; (401) 728-2400; www.cumberlandri.org
Dog-friendly: Allowed on leash
Trail surface: Dirt and gravel

Land status: Rhode Island Land Trust Council and the Cumberland Conservation Commission
Nearest town: Cumberland, RI
Other trail users: Mountain bikers
Water availability: Yes, at the library
Maps: Cumberland Monastery trail map
Age range: All ages
Toilets: Yes; restrooms are available in the adjacent town library when the library is open.
Stroller/Wheelchair compatibility: The trails nearest the town buildings are nearly level and wheelchair accessible. However, these trails may not meet ADA standards.
Resting benches: None
Potential child hazards: Poison ivy
Gear suggestions: Insect repellent

FINDING THE TRAILHEAD

From Providence, Rhode Island, take I-95 North to exit 23 for Route 146 toward Woonsocket. Continue onto Route 146 North for approximately 7.6 miles, following signs for Lincoln/Woonsocket. Take the I-295 North/Rhode Island 99 North exit toward Boston/Warwick. Keep right at the fork to continue on exit 8A, follow signs for I-295 North/Boston, and merge onto I-295 North for about 3.7 miles. Take exit 22 for Route 114 toward Cumberland. At the traffic circle, take the first exit onto Route 114 South/Diamond Hill Road. Turn right onto Monastery Drive. Your destination is on your left. Park behind the Cumberland Public Library in the large parking lot. **GPS:** 41.934307 / -71.406198

THE HIKE

There's a lot of history among the trees and trails on the 305 acres of the Cumberland Monastery. Walk the same trails as the monks of the Cistercian Order of the Strict

Top: Walking along the wide path of the Cumberland Monastery
Bottom: A pond along the path—you might get lucky and see some eastern painted turtles

Observance (aka Trappists). Their strict lifestyle of isolation, dedication to prayer, and self-denial made them a near-silent community who even developed their own sign language to speak to each other. Unfortunately for those of us with kids, silence won't likely be on the trails here, and that's all right. Kids are supposed to have fun and talk about all the things that make them go, "Mom, isn't this cool?" or "Look at this neat bug!"

Start your hike on the western side of the property, behind the library. There's a large parking lot for you to use. At the kiosk, take the trail directly behind it to head down to the Beauregard Loop. You'll take a right at your first junction onto this trail but won't stay on it very long. Take the trail to your left, the Old Road Trail, which is a wide, gravelly path easily traversed by most hikers.

Top: The monks' quarry
Bottom: View of the Cumberland Monastery

You'll come to a fork in the trail. Stay left and then right to stay on the Old Road Trail. After 0.3 mile, take a right onto the Whipple Trail. There is an overlook off this trail, but it just looks over a huge gravel mine and isn't that picturesque, so I would skip it. Continue on the Whipple Trail until you see a narrower path to your right, which brings you through some beautiful white pine groves.

At the next intersection, take a left to get back on the Whipple Trail. Veer right onto the monks' Quarry Trail to head toward the named landmark. Monks who lived on the property decades ago used stone from the quarry to construct many of the buildings. You can still see all the unused stone at the quarry even now. Talk to your kids about how hard it was to bring stone from this far back on the property to where the buildings now reside.

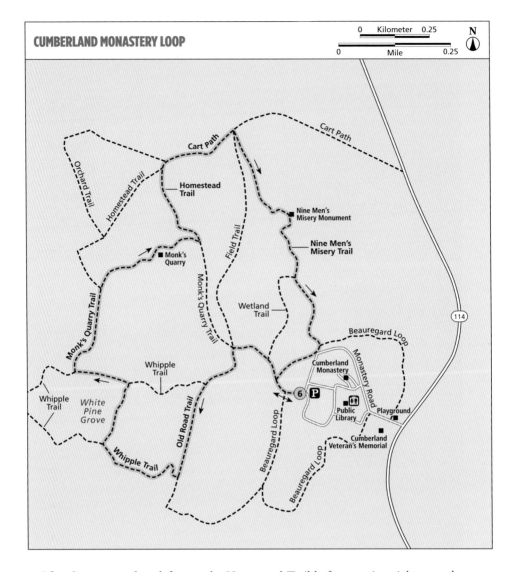

Kilometer 0.25

Mile 0.25

N

Orchard Trail

Homestead Trail

Cart Path

Cart Path

Homestead Trail

Nine Men's Misery Monument

Nine Men's Misery Trail

Field Trail

Monk's Quarry

Monk's Quarry Trail

Monk's Quarry Trail

Wetland Trail

Whipple Trail

Beauregard Loop

Cumberland Monastery

Monastery Road

114

Whipple Trail

White Pine Grove

Old Road Trail

6 P

Public Library

Playground

Beauregard Loop

Cumberland Veteran's Memorial

Whipple Trail

Beauregard Loop

After the quarry, take a left onto the Homestead Trail before turning right onto the Cart Path. You'll pass fields the monks used to tend when they were living here. Most of their food was grown right on the property. Take the next right onto Nine Men's Misery Trail, which brings you to the monument. This is the place where Native Americans killed nine soldiers back in 1876. The monument doesn't describe the horrific instances of soldiers slaughtering Native Americans, but it undoubtedly happened.

Moving on from the monument, you head back down the Nine Men's Misery Trail until you reach the end and take a left onto Beauregard Loop. You'll travel close to the road that will bring you back to your car. End the day by heading to the library for story time, getting more energy out on the playground on the property, or simply sitting and relaxing at the picnic tables before heading home.

MILES AND DIRECTIONS

0.00 Begin at the kiosk behind the monastery and at the forest's edge. Take the trail directly behind.

0.05 Stay right at the T-intersection and then left onto the Old Road Trail.

0.20 Stay on the Old Road Trail by taking a left at the junction and then stay right to stay on the Old Road Trail.

0.50 Take a right onto the Whipple Trail.

0.80 Veer right off the Whipple Trail for a narrower path.

0.85 Go through the White Pine Grove.

0.95 Take a left to get back on the Whipple Trail.

1.10 Go right for the Monk's Quarry Trail.

1.20 Stay right to keep on the Monk's Quarry Trail.

1.40 Look to your right to see the old quarry the monks used to use.

1.55 At the next junction take a left onto the Homestead Trail.

1.70 Stay right at the junction to head onto the Cart Path.

1.90 Take a right onto the Nine Men's Misery Trail.

2.20 Follow the trail off to your left to view the Nine Men's Misery Monument.

2.30 Stay straight to continue on the Nine Men's Misery Trail.

2.50 Take a right at the next junction onto the Beauregard Loop.

2.60 Take a left at the junction and then another left to head back to your car.

2.70 Arrive back at the trailhead.

A SERIES OF FIRES

The trail that you're walking on is all part of the land owned by the Monastery of Our Lady of the Valley. Back in 1892, monks of the Cistercian Order of the Strict Observance had a devastating fire rip through the Abbey of Petit Clairvaus in Nova Scotia. They relocated to Rhode Island, where they built the Cumberland Monastery over several years using the granite stone on the property to erect most of the buildings.

Despite the fact that many of the buildings were made of stone, another fire broke out in 1950 in the original building, where the interior was made solely of wood so easily flammable. In fact, the building would've been torn down and reconstructed if it hadn't burned first. The fire began in the Guest House (which was the main area at the time) and then jumped to the church. Fortunately, no monks were killed. Damage was significant, and the monastic community finally moved north to Massachusetts, to St. Joseph's Abbey, where they still reside today. Now the monastery is used as the Cumberland Public Library.

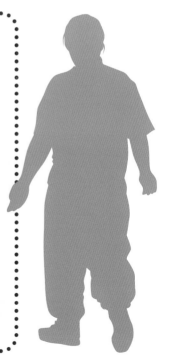

7 NAPATREE POINT CONSERVATION AREA TRAIL

Have you ever been on a hike where you could also ride a carousel? I thought not! If you do the Napatree Point Conservation Area Trail, you can cross "hike a trail with a carousel" off your bucket list. Besides the Watch Hill Carousel, Napatree Point Conservation Area is filled with incredible views of Block Island Sound and the Atlantic Ocean. Bring the sand buckets and trowels to spend hours making sandcastles or digging to China. You're forewarned, though, because this trail is very popular in the summer and parking can be an absolute nightmare. It's well worth it, though, so don't let that deter you.

Start: At the corner of Bay Street and Fort Road
Elevation gain: 26 feet
Distance: 3.2 miles
Difficulty: Easy
Hiking time: 3 hours
Seasons/Schedule: Open 24 hours a day year-round
Fees and permits: None
Trail contact: The Watch Hill Conservancy, One Bay St., Watch Hill, RI; (401) 315-5399; thewatchhillconservancy.org
Dog-friendly: Allowed on leash anytime from the day after Labor Day through May 1 and then prohibited from 8:00 a.m. to 6:00 p.m., from May 2 through Labor Day.

Trail surface: Sand, pavement, and some rock scrambles
Nearest town: Westerly, RI
Land status: Watch Hill Conservancy
Other trail users: None
Water availability: None
Maps: None
Age range: All ages
Toilets: Yes
Stroller/Wheelchair compatibility: No
Resting benches: No
Potential child hazards: Ocean currents and tides
Gear suggestions: Lots of sunscreen, sun hat, bathing suit, and beach accessories

FINDING THE TRAILHEAD

From Westerly, Rhode Island on Route 1, turn onto Route 1A/Shore Road toward the Weekapaug Golf Club. Follow Shore Road for about 5 miles and then turn left onto Watch Hill Road. Continue for about 2 miles onto Wauwinnet Avenue and Bay Street. Turn right onto Fort Road. Napatree Point Conservation Area does not have its own designated parking facilities.

Parking in Watch Hill in the summer is, unfortunately, very difficult to find. What's even harder is finding free parking. There are several private parking lots that charge anywhere from $20 to $40 a day, which may or may not be in your budget. If you want free parking, I suggest going early (think 7:00 a.m.) and parking along the street, where you can park for free for 2 hours. **GPS:** 41.310502 / -71.861057

THE HIKE

If you're lucky enough to have snagged a good parking spot, you can start the hike at the corner of Fort Road and Bay Street. Here you'll walk the pavement behind the Watch Hill beach cottages and the Misquamicut Club. You'll pass by the Watch Hill Yacht Club on your right.

Top: A perfect place to watch the sunrise over the town of Watch Hill
Bottom: Pondering about life as the sunrise casts hues of pinks and purples

From the kiosk, walk along the northern edge of the beach to take in the views. Often you'll see dogs in the early morning hours—they are allowed prior to 8:00 a.m. and after 6:00 p.m. from May 2 until Labor Day. As you walk along the beach, take a look at the seaweed in the water or what shells might've washed up onshore. Personally, my kiddo and I create background stories for the shells and who might have inhabited them at one time or another.

Impress your kids by saying you're about to walk on a spit. Hopefully they'll refrain from actually spitting, because it's not that type of spit. Instead, coastal geologists have named Napatree Point a "barrier spit." These are considered landforms that protect the shoreline of the mainland from waves—in this case, Napatree Point protects Watch Hill,

Looking back toward town

Westerly, Pawcatuck, and Stonington. Because Napatree Point protects the rest of the mainland from waves and wind, the landscape changes frequently around the point. Since 1939, the point itself has moved almost a full width north!

When you reach the end of Napatree Point, there's a bit of a scramble to get around it, so it's good to have solid shoes (not to have bare feet). You'll see a large structure, which are the remnants of Fort Mansfield. The remains are from three concrete gun emplacements left after the fort was demolished in 1928. You can't access the remains, as fencing borders its entirety, but you can see what it looks like inside. There's a lot of graffiti from visitors who illegally jump the fence.

Continue on the south side of the point, where there is a long stretch of sandy beach in front of you for you and your kids to frolic on. Feel free to hang out as long as you'd like (unless you've parked in the 2-hour parking spot) and enjoy a dip in the ocean. There are no lifeguards on the beach, so be careful with your kids and always keep an eye on them. The current can be quite strong in the area.

FIND A PREHISTORIC CREATURE RIGHT ON THE BEACH!

There aren't any dinosaur bones on the beach around Napatree Point, but there *are* horseshoe crabs! These ancient-looking creatures haven't changed much since they first popped up 445 million years ago. Surprisingly, they are not crabs, they're more closely related to arachnids (like spiders and scorpions). Is your mind blown yet?

Horseshoe crabs have an armored shell that has proven to be the best defense for almost 450 million years. Their sharp tail isn't used as a weapon, instead it's used to flip themselves over when they undoubtedly land on their back when a wave crashes into them. They are clumsy creatures.

But if prehistoric creatures aren't your thing, you can find plenty of other species including more than 300 bird species! Napatree Point Conservation Area has been designated a Globally Important Bird Area by the National Audubon Society. The most common birds found in the area are nesting piping plovers (please adhere to all signage when the birds are nesting), American oystercatchers, and ospreys.

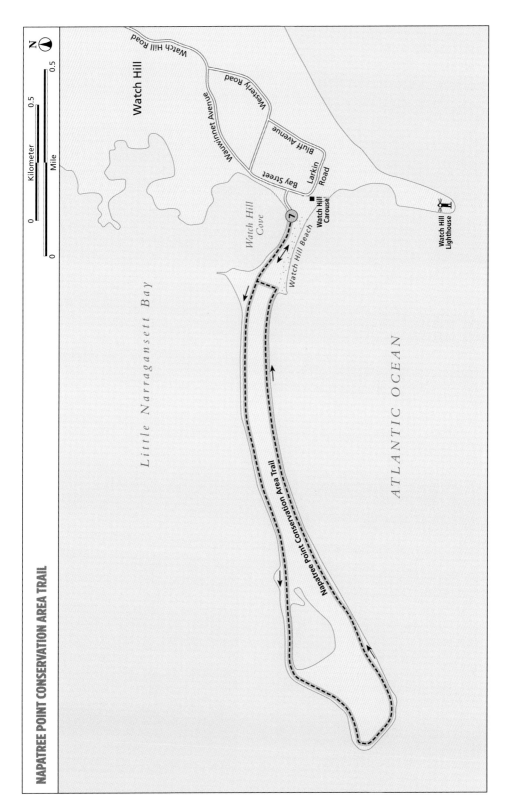

NAPATREE POINT CONSERVATION AREA TRAIL

Watch Hill

Little Narragansett Bay

Watch Hill Cove

Waluwinnet Avenue

Watch Hill Road

Westerly Road

Bluff Avenue

Bay Street

Larkin Road

Watch Hill Beach

Watch Hill Carousel

Napatree Point Conservation Area Trail

ATLANTIC OCEAN

Watch Hill Lighthouse

N

Kilometer

0   0.5

Mile

0   0.5

Looking out toward Napatree Point

After you've had your fill of sand and ocean, feel free to continue to walk along the beach until you reach a large path through the dunes to head back to the kiosk on the other side. Then follow the road back to wherever you've parked.

Don't forget to take a ride on the Watch Hill Carousel if you've got time. Honestly, make the time! Tickets are fairly cheap if you want to ride on one of the inside horses of the carousel ($1 at time of publication). The carousel was constructed in the late 1800s and is still going strong. I suggest riding one of the outside horses, though, so you can have a chance to catch the brass ring on the outside. There's an arm with a brass loop that protrudes out into the carousel where folks riding on the outside can try to grab it. If you are lucky enough to grab one of the rings, you'll earn a free ride the next time!

MILES AND DIRECTIONS

- 0.00 Start at the corner of Fort Road and Bay Street.
- 0.20 Read the information on the kiosk—sometimes there will be information on nesting plovers.
- 1.50 Round the tip of Napatree Point.
- 1.70 There's a trail to your left that heads up to the remnants of Fort Mansfield.
- 2.80 Head left on the trail that goes up and over the dunes.
- 3.00 Hit Fort Road again and make your way back to Bay Street (stop and do some shopping if you'd like).
- 3.20 Arrive back at the trailhead.

Searching for seashells and other beach treasures

8 WEETAMOO WOODS LOOP

Weetamoo Woods is named after the last sachem of the Pocasset—a female whose name meant "speak to them." The trees and wildlife that surround you as you walk along Weetamoo Woods will speak to you through the wind and whistles of birds. You'll travel through historical features including an Early American slab bridge and the foundation of an 1800s sawmill, as well as natural features like a holly-oak forest, wetlands, and a large rock outcrop called High Rock.

Start: At the end of Lafayette Road at the Red Blaze trailhead
Elevation gain: 170 feet
Distance: 3.1 miles
Difficulty: Easy
Hiking time: 3 hours
Seasons/Schedule: Sunrise to sunset, year-round
Fees and permits: None
Trail contact: Town of Tiverton Open Space Commission, Town Hall, 343 Highland Rd., Tiverton, RI; (401) 625-6710; www.tiverton.ri.gov
Dog-friendly: Allowed on leash or under voice control. If not leashed, a leash must be carried by the person controlling the dog to be used when encountering other hikers with dogs.

Trail surface: Dirt and rock
Land status: Town of Tiverton
Nearest town: Tiverton, RI
Other trail users: Mountain bikers, snowshoers, cross-country skiers, and horseback riders (parking lot cannot accommodate trailers)
Water availability: None
Maps: Weetamoo Woods and Pardon Gray Preserve trail map
Age range: All ages; toddlers may have difficulty if not carried
Toilets: None
Stroller/Wheelchair compatibility: No
Resting benches: No
Potential child hazards: Poison ivy
Gear suggestions: Insect repellent

FINDING THE TRAILHEAD

From Providence, Rhode Island, take I-195 East entering into Massachusetts. Stay on I-195 for about 16.5 miles to exit 14A. Take exit 14A for Route 24 South toward Tiverton/Newport. Continue onto Route 24, entering back into Rhode Island. Take exit 5 toward Fish Road. Keep left at the fork and follow signs for Fish Road. Turn left onto Fish Road and travel 1.4 miles. Turn right onto Route 177 West for 1 mile. Turn left onto Lafayette Road, and the trailhead parking lot will be on your right when the road ends. **GPS:** 41.595480 / -71.188488

THE HIKE

Most first-time visitors use the trailhead just off East Road, which is only a quarter mile east of Tiverton Four Corners. This trailhead at the end of Lafayette Road is less trafficked and just as beautiful. Don't forget the insect repellent on this hike though—mosquitos run rampant from spring until late summer.

Start off on the Red Blaze Trail, where you'll immediately meander through Weetamoo Woods's famed holly-oak forest. These types of forests in New England are dominated by oak, maple, and tupelo trees, while American holly blankets the understory. Holly-oak forests are great for wildlife, and you might see several types on your hike, including white-tailed deer, gray squirrels, red squirrels, chipmunks, wood frogs, dozens of bird species, and more.

Top: A family walking along the trail in Weetamoo Woods
Bottom: Heading up High Rock with little legs

After 0.5 mile, you'll reach the Yellow Blaze Trail. As you meander along the trail, you'll eventually see a trail with green blazes on your left about a mile in. Keep going straight here, because you'll come back that way. At the next intersection, you'll take a left onto the Blue Blaze Trail. Walk just over a quarter mile and take the narrow path up a large rock. Those with shorter legs might need some help. When you get to the top, you'll be standing on High Rock, which is one of the best views in Rhode Island!

Climb back down the rock and back onto the Blue Blaze Trail, where you'll come across the ruins of an old (think 1800s) sawmill. You can see where the general layout was, and there's even an arched bridge still standing over the small creek that runs through it. You might notice the strange color of the water—see the "Fun Factor" sidebar to learn more about why this may be.

Top: The view from the summit of High Rock—it's beautiful in the autumn!
Bottom: The ruins of the old mill

After you and your kids have had fun romping around the old ruins (although be extra careful here), head back on the Blue Blaze Trail. You'll reach the next junction in just under a tenth of a mile, where you'll meet up with the Red Blaze Trail. Go left (or north) here for another tenth of a mile until you reach the junction of the Green Blaze Trail.

The Green Blaze Trail brings you up and over several wetter areas in Weetamoo Woods. The trail skirts the southern side of the Cedar Swamp, and you'll most likely hear the calls of the wood frogs that call this area home. The Green Blaze Trail will come to an end at a T-intersection. Turn right to get back onto the Yellow Blaze Trail and then head the mile back to your car.

If you're still up for some adventure, you can head to Tiverton Four Corners and grab some ice cream or lunch at Gray's Ice Cream or Groundswell Café. Then head down

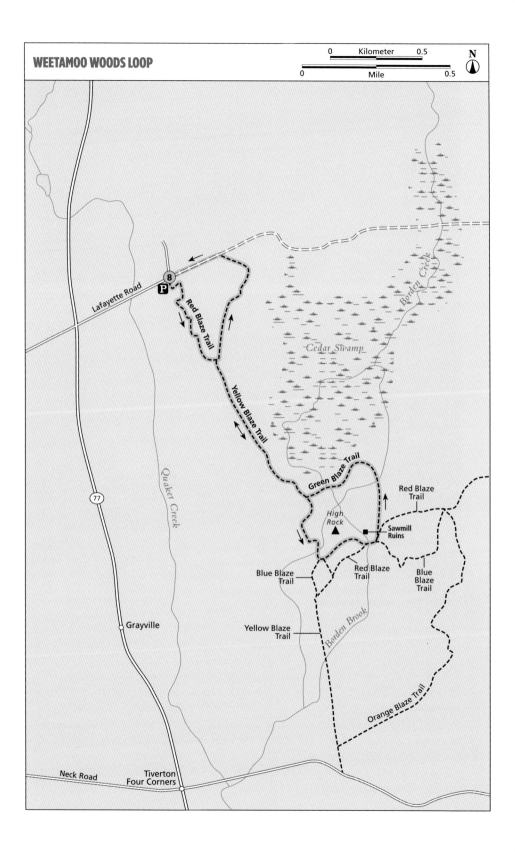

0 Kilometer 0.5

0 Mile 0.5

N

Lafayette Road

Red Blaze Trail

Yellow Blaze Trail

Green Blaze Trail

Borden Creek

Cedar Swamp

High Rock

Sawmill Ruins

Red Blaze Trail

Red Blaze Trail

Blue Blaze Trail

Blue Blaze Trail

Yellow Blaze Trail

Borden Brook

Quaker Creek

Grayville

77

Orange Blaze Trail

Neck Road

Tiverton Four Corners

8

Main Road/Route 77 until you hit Pond Bridge Road. Take a right and then take a left onto Fogland Road toward Fogland Beach. Kids will love this area, so be sure to conserve some energy after your hike.

MILES AND DIRECTIONS

0.00 Start at the parking lot off Lafayette Road on the Red Blaze Trail.

0.50 Reach the junction of the Yellow and Red Blaze Trails. Veer right to go on the Yellow Blaze Trail.

1.00 Reach the junction of the Yellow and Green Blaze Trails. Stay straight to continue on the Yellow Blaze Trail.

1.25 Turn left onto the Blue Blaze Trail.

1.30 Head left up the narrow path and the large boulder. Make your way to the top of High Rock to see sweeping views of the surrounding landscape.

1.40 Reach the remnants of an 1800s sawmill.

1.45 Take a left onto the Red Blaze Trail.

1.60 Veer left at the fork to head on the Green Blaze Trail through the southern section of Cedar Swamp.

2.00 Turn right onto the Yellow Blaze Trail to head back to your car.

2.90 Veer right onto an unmarked trail to get back to Lafayette Road.

3.00 Take a left onto the wide road.

3.10 Arrive back at the trailhead.

WHY IS THE WATER RED?

You might notice that the water near the remnants of the 1800s sawmill is a certain, and perhaps alarming, shade of red. But it likely doesn't warrant a call to a land management agency. There are many reasons that waters turn color, and not all are that bad.

First, it could be a sign of an algal bloom. "Red tide" is a phenomenon that happens when there is an overgrowth of algae caused by slow water buildup, sunlight, or nutrient disruption (depleting or augmenting).

Second, there could be runoff from the surrounding soil. This usually happens after large weather events such as floods, large storms, or significant amounts of erosion that occur in a short time.

Last, there are certain minerals that occur naturally in the sediment surrounding an area. Limestone, which is highly abundant in New England, naturally carries manganese and iron,

The water along the trail looks red due to the iron in the soil.

which can cause a red or orange hue to the waters that run through an area. This is likely the case here in Weetamoo Woods and isn't cause for alarm. With that being said, don't drink this water.

9 CASIMIR PULASKI PARK LOOP

There is a lot to discover on this 100-acre park, despite it being one of the smaller parks in this. guide. The loop around Casimir Pulaski Memorial State Park has a combination of recreational opportunities, including trout fishing, swimming in the pond, wildlife viewing, and hiking. But the real way to visit this park is in winter, when you can traverse the many miles of groomed cross-country ski trails. No skis? No worries! You can also snowshoe or hike. Don't forget to bring the hot cocoa and marshmallows, though!

Start: At the Blue Dot trailhead
Elevation gain: 200 feet
Distance: 3.2 miles
Difficulty: Easy
Hiking time: 3.5 hours
Seasons/Schedule: Sunrise to sunset, year-round
Fees and permits: None
Trail contact: Casimir Pulaski Memorial State Park and Recreational Area, 151 Pulaski Rd., Chepachet, RI; (401) 723-7892; www.riparks.com/Locations/LocationPulaski.html
Dog-friendly: Allowed on leash on trails but not on the beach area
Trail surface: Dirt and rock
Land status: George Washington Management Area

Nearest town: Putnam, CT
Other trail users: Snowshoers and cross-country skiers in winter
Water availability: Yes, at the changing rooms
Maps: Pulaski State Park trail map
Age range: All ages
Toilets: Yes
Stroller/Wheelchair compatibility: No
Resting benches: Yes, picnic tables at the pavilion
Potential child hazards: Angry Canada geese
Gear suggestions: Sun hat, insect repellent, beach accessories, swimsuit, and a hard-backed cooler (because geese frequent the area)

FINDING THE TRAILHEAD

From Providence, Rhode Island, take Route 6 west toward Woonsocket/Hartford, Connecticut, for almost 12 miles. Continue straight onto Route 101 West (do not veer left to stay on Route 6). Stay on Route 101 for 8 miles. Turn right onto Route 94 North for 5.6 miles and then turn left onto Route 44 West. After 1 mile, turn right onto Pulaski Road and into the state park. Find your way to the main parking area for beach access. **GPS:** 41.931816 / -71.797199

THE HIKE

The loop around Casimir Pulaski Memorial State Park is a still-undiscovered gem in northern Rhode Island. It sits right at the border of Connecticut but is still within an hour's drive of Providence. While many other outdoor enthusiasts might be headed toward the shores of Rhode Island, there's a reason not to miss out on this less-trafficked park.

Start the hike to the east of the parking lot. In summertime the parking lot can fill up on hot weekends, as most visitors will likely be headed to the beach to cool down. Even if the beach is busy, you likely won't see many on the trail even on crowded weekends. The trail starts along the Blue Dot Trail, which is easily identified by a white blaze with a blue dot in the middle of it.

Top: The Blue Dot trail is easy to follow with blazes on the trees.
Bottom: Beaver activity along the pond at Casimir Pulaski Memorial State Park

You'll pass the White Blaze Trail on your right, but continue straight and then immediately take the right fork to get off the Blue Dot Trail. You'll be veering away from Peck Pond at this point. Unfortunately the trails don't have that many blazes here, so it might be a bit confusing, as the next few forks occur one on top of the other. In the course of 0.2 mile, you'll stay right at a fork and then left until you finally hit a T-intersection.

If you go right at the T, the trail will bring you back to the Park Road, so take a left to head northeast along the Center Trail. There are various trails on your left and right, but continue straight until you reach a gate. Go through it if it's open or around it if it's not. Take the trail all the way to your left (there are three trails) and head toward the covered bridge.

Lots of old pine needles blanket the trail, making for slippery conditions.

Take a left to go through the covered bridge or hang out and relax with your kiddos. The covered bridge is fun! As you walk along the Covered Bridge Trail (green blazes), you'll walk through wetlands and swamps, so the trail may be wet or muddy in some places. Remember to walk right through the mud to minimize trail erosion.

When you reach another T-intersection, take a left onto the George Washington Trail, indicated by orange blazes. The wetlands and swamps will be to your left as you walk southwest to get back to the trailhead. Hemlocks line this trail, meaning there will be plenty of pinecones on the ground. As enticing as they might be for your kids to collect, make sure they stay on the trail per Leave No Trace guidelines. If your kid is having difficulty refraining from collecting them, tell them they can choose one to hold during the hike but must discard it before getting back to the car. You can always distract them with bubbles too!

THE FAIRY TALE OF HOW TREES RECEIVED THEIR PINECONES

During my college years I had a great dendrology (study of trees) professor who told us about the pinecone fairy. You see, way back when the world was created, there was a pinecone fairy. All the pines, hemlocks, cedars, larches, and more lined up to see the pinecone fairy to receive their unique pinecone size and characteristics. The sugar pine was first in line and was given the largest pinecone on the planet. Their pinecones can grow up to 2 feet long! The sugar pine was so proud, they stand tall (and is the tallest pine in the world) to this day.

As the pinecone fairy went through the line, they gave out all the pinecones they had in their arsenal. Some tree species, like jack pine, annoyed the pinecone fairy and were given cones that would only release their seeds with high heat (scientists call these cones "serotinous"). The Douglas firs were a bit scared of the pinecone fairy, so they were given unique cones that looked like a mouse was hiding under each of the scales of the cone.

But the poor eastern hemlock was last in line. As the pinecone fairy dug through what they had left, there was only one cone. It was the smallest of the cones and given to the eastern hemlock. The eastern hemlock felt ashamed by how tiny their cones were compared to the others. And to this day, the eastern hemlock hangs its head in shame. You can always tell an eastern hemlock from far away if the top of the tree hangs limply to one side.

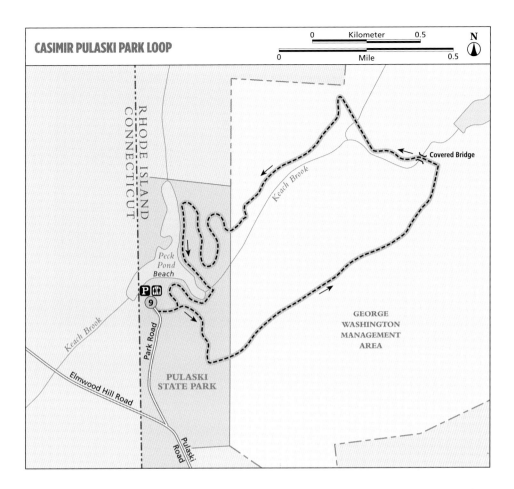

CASIMIR PULASKI PARK LOOP

0   Kilometer   0.5

0   Mile   0.5

N

Covered Bridge

RHODE ISLAND
CONNECTICUT

Keach Brook

Peck
Pond
Beach

P ♿

9

Keach Brook

Park Road

GEORGE
WASHINGTON
MANAGEMENT
AREA

Elmwood Hill Road

PULASKI
STATE PARK

Pulaski
Road

Eventually, after about 0.5 mile, the trail will veer left and then you'll take the trail on your right to get back on the Blue Dot Trail. This trail is filled with lots of roots and wet spots the closer you get to Peck Pond. Be on the lookout for beavers as you get closer. You'll likely see a lot of beaver evidence among the trees that line the pond. The Blue Dot Trail will bring you all the way back to your car, where you can then grab your beach accessories and head to the pond to cool off and wash the sweat away.

If you've brought food, keep it put away when you're not eating it, because this area is frequented by Canada geese. These migrating birds are known for their aggressive habits in getting food, especially if they've gotten used to people feeding them. Remember the sixth Leave No Trace principle and respect wildlife, which means refraining from feeding them. The geese are already a nuisance, so there is no need to further encourage that.

MILES AND DIRECTIONS

0.00 Start on the east side of the parking lot at the Blue Dot trailhead.

0.02 The White Blaze Trail veers to the right, but stay straight.

0.04 At the fork in the trail, take the right fork to get off the Blue Dot Trail.

The beach at Casimir Pulaski Memorial State Park

0.10 Stay right at the fork.

0.20 Stay left at the next fork.

0.30 At the T-intersection take a left onto the Center Trail.

1.20 Take a left onto the Covered Bridge Trail, which follows green blazes.

1.30 Go through the covered bridge.

1.60 Take a left onto the George Washington Trail, which follows orange blazes.

2.10 Take a right back onto the Blue Dot Trail.

2.90 Take a right to stay on the Blue Dot Trail.

3.20 End back at the trailhead.

MASSACHUSETTS HIKES

Among the reeds along the Hellcat Interpretative Trail in Parker River Wildlife Refuge

10 WORLD'S END TRAIL

The trail might be called World's End, but the adventure is only just beginning when you head out to this unique spot just south of Boston. You can make this trail as long or as short as you like, with views of the ocean in almost every direction. The paths were designed by Frederick Law Olmsted (a famous landscape architect) so that people of all shapes, sizes, and abilities could enjoy this area. Thankfully, prior plans to turn this area into the United Nations headquarters and a nuclear power plant never progressed further than the development phase. Instead, it's now a 450-acre preserve offering sweeping views of the Boston skyline.

Start: At the parking area
Elevation gain: 250 feet
Distance: 3.1 miles
Difficulty: Easy to moderate
Hiking time: 3 hours
Seasons/Schedule: 8:00 a.m. to sunset, year-round
Fees and permits: Fee required
Trail contact: Managed by the Trustees of Reservations, 200 High St., Boston, MA; (617) 542-7696; https://thetrustees.org/place/worlds -end-hingham
Dog-friendly: Allowed on leash
Trail surface: Gravel

Land status: Boston Harbor Island National Park Service
Nearest town: Hingham, MA
Other trail users: Mountain bikers
Water availability: None
Maps: World's End trail map
Age range: All ages
Toilets: Yes, at the trailhead
Stroller/Wheelchair compatibility: Yes
Resting benches: Yes, throughout the trail
Potential child hazards: Some large drop-offs
Gear suggestions: Binoculars to view the wildlife and the Boston skyline

FINDING THE TRAILHEAD

From Boston, take I-93 South to Quincy Shore Drive, about 7 miles. Follow Quincy Shore Drive to Southern Artery, about 4 miles. Take MA 3A South to Summer Street in Hingham, about 6.6 miles. At the traffic circle, take the third exit onto Summer Street, and then turn left onto Martins Lane. Follow Martins Lane for 0.7 mile to the entrance and parking (seventy cars) at the end. Roadside parking is not permitted. **GPS:** 42.258891 / -70.872673

THE HIKE

You would think for an urban hike, there wouldn't be so much greenery. You'd be wrong to think that you have to drive 50 miles west of Boston to get into a little bit of wilderness. Instead, head south a few miles to the coastal drumlins of World's End.

Once you park, head back to where you turned into the parking lot and go right to enter the park. There's a kiosk (and usually an attendant) here if you have questions about anything. Cross the bridge that goes between the Damde Meadows Tidal Marsh on the right and Hingham Bay on the left. You'll veer right to stay along the bank of the tidal marsh.

The peninsula that makes up World's End was acquired by John Brewer—a wealthy farmer in the area. He built a mansion for his estate and slowly purchased the land around

Top: Walking along the trail at World's End
Bottom: There are several spots to stop and take a break to breathe in the fresh air outside the city.

it. At one point, Brewer hired Frederick Law Olmsted to design a residential subdivision, because Brewer knew he'd be able to monetize the peninsula. The landscape architect constructed paths for carts to drive on, which were flanked by beautifully large trees. Fortunately the subdivision never came to fruition and the cart paths remain!

The path is wide and open with plenty of beautiful trees, wildflowers, and sweeping vistas of the surrounding waters. You'll see lots of birds catching breakfast (or lunch or dinner, depending on the time you go), so don't forget those binoculars so you can see the action up close. Eventually you'll reach The Bar, which is a causeway that connects the southern section with the northern section of World's End.

Cross over The Bar and veer right to go in a counterclockwise direction. You'll reach a junction about 0.4 mile from The Bar. Taking a left will send you on a shortcut to the western side of the island. Taking a right will bring you around the northern tip of the island. It's up to you which way you'd like to go. Either way will bring you back to the same spot on the western side.

The overlook on the northwest side of the island has unparalleled views of the Boston skyline and Hingham Bay. Continue down the trail to head back over The Bar and onto the southern section of the park.

Go straight up the wide, grassy path when you reach the other side of The Bar. This leads you to Planters Hill, where you can get views from a higher elevation. There's a bench at the top for you to catch your breath and relax. If you visit during wildflower season, you might see the bees and butterflies jumping from flower to flower sucking up all the delicious nectar in the surrounding fields.

Head to the right to get back on Brewers Road. This road brings you back onto the main path back to your car. You'll notice signs on several trees that describe each species. A common tree found on the property is the tulip tree, which has, as you might suspect, flowers that look like tulips! Help your kids identify the different trees and what makes each species special. Ask them to describe the shape of their leaves and what the bark looks like.

WHAT'S THE DIFFERENCE BETWEEN HARDWOOD AND SOFTWOOD TREES?

Most people look at a tree and can tell if it has pine needles or leaves or something in between. But there are scientific terms for these things too. Hardwood trees, also known as angiosperms, have seeds that have a protective covering and commonly have leafy leaves (rather than needle-like). The seeds come in forms of acorns, nuts, samaras (the helicopter-like seeds on maples), and pods. Hardwood trees include maple, oak, ash, elm, and more. Most hardwood trees go dormant in winter, meaning they drop their leaves. They are also known as deciduous trees.

Softwood trees, also known as gymnosperms, do not have seeds but rather pinecones and usually possess needle-like "leaves." Typically, softwood trees are the pine, cedar, hemlock, and spruce varieties. These are trees that don't usually go dormant in winter and retain their needles all year—they are also known as nondeciduous. But deciduous does not always equal hardwood and nondeciduous does not always equal softwood.

Generally speaking, hardwood trees are actually harder (hence the name) than softwoods, but not always. The strongest wood in the world is Australian buloke, which is a hardwood. The other top-four strongest woods also happen to be hardwood. However, the softest wood in the world is actually balsa wood, which is also a hardwood, as are the next two softest woods. So, hardwood doesn't necessarily mean "harder" and vice versa. Practically speaking, the harder and denser a wood, the more difficult it is to put a nail through it without splitting the wood—whereas softwood wouldn't split as easily. That's why many pines are more commonly used in construction than maples or oaks.

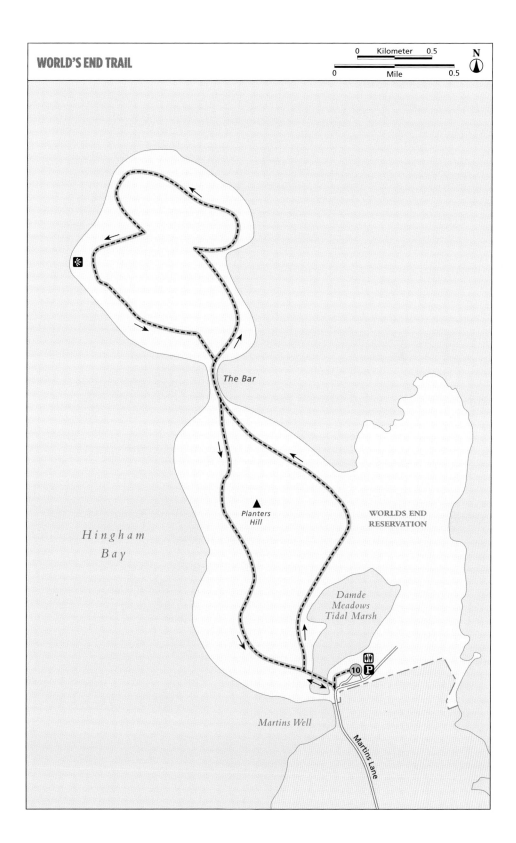

0   Kilometer   0.5

0   Mile   0.5

N

The Bar

Planters Hill

WORLDS END RESERVATION

H i n g h a m B a y

Damde Meadows Tidal Marsh

10

Martins Well

Martins Lane

Looking out across the bay with the Boston skyline in the distance

If you want more to your hike, check out the events on The Trustees website. They've got everything from full moon hikes to sunset walks and family-focused hikes to bird- and geology-focused walks. They also offer kayaking tours and even a yearly campout! This place is a great spot for kids and adults of all skill levels to picnic and go for a stroll along the water.

MILES AND DIRECTIONS

0.00 Start at the parking lot and head down the road back to the entrance.

0.10 Take a right onto Brewers Road to head over the bridge.

0.20 Veer right at the fork to walk along Barnes Road.

0.80 Head over The Bar. There are a few trails to your left but stay straight.

1.20 At the fork, take the trail to the right to traverse the northern tip of the island. You can also take a left here for a shortcut to the other side—this will shorten your hike by 0.4 mile.

1.70 Stay to the right if you've taken the longer route, turn left if you've taken the shortcut.

1.80 You can take the trail to your right here to take in the views at the overlook.

2.20 Go back over The Bar.

2.30 Stay straight once you are back on the southern section of the park to head up to Planters Hill.

2.40 Take a breather on the bench at the top of Plant- ers Hill.

2.50 Meet up with Brewers Road and head south/ straight to go back to your car.

Clover flowers are on full display!

2.90 Go back over the bridge.

3.00 Take a left to head back up the road toward your car.

3.10 Arrive back at the trailhead.

11 MOUNT NORWOTTUCK

Traverse the tallest mountain within the Holyoke Mountain Range and be rewarded with sweeping views of Amherst and surrounding towns. It is a steady climb up Mount Norwottuck, but it's well worth the effort. You'll even be greeted with "caves" (more like large over-hanging ledges) as you descend the mountain. If you want incredible views, no matter the season, look no further than this central Massachusetts gem.

Start: Behind the Notch Visitor Center located off Route 116
Elevation gain: 750 feet
Distance: 3.3 miles
Difficulty: Moderate
Hiking time: 3.5 to 4 hours
Seasons/Schedule: Year round
Fees and permits: None
Trail contact: Mount Holyoke Range State Park, 1500 West St., Amherst, MA; (413) 253-2883; www.mass.gov/locations/mount-holyoke-range-state-park
Dog-friendly: Allowed on leash
Trail surface: Dirt
Land status: Mount Holyoke Range State Park

Nearest town: Amherst, MA
Other trail users: Mountain bikers and horseback riders
Water availability: Yes, at the visitor center
Maps: Mount Holyoke Range State Park trail map
Age range: Kids in carriers and those with extensive trail experience
Toilets: Yes, at the visitor center
Stroller/Wheelchair compatibility: No
Resting benches: None
Potential child hazards: Poison ivy
Gear suggestions: Trekking poles and insect repellent

FINDING THE TRAILHEAD

From Springfield, Massachusetts, take I-91 North to I-395 North. Take exit 5 onto Main Street, turn right onto Main Street, then take a slight right onto North Canal Street. Turn left onto MA 116 North/County Bridge. Continue for 8.2 miles, then turn right at the park entrance. Park at the main parking area outside the visitor center. **GPS:** 42.305007 / -72.527833

THE HIKE

The town of Amherst is noted for its artistic and eccentric residents, including a significant number of poets. Former resident poets include Emily Dickinson, Robert Frost, and Eugene Field, while former resident authors include Helen Geisel (children's author and first wife of Dr. Seuss), Norton Juster (author of *The Phantom Tollbooth*), and even Noah Webster, who literally wrote the dictionary.

Maybe you'll find some inspiration for your own stories on the trails within Mount Holyoke Range State Park. To climb Mount Norwottuck, start behind the Notch Visitor Center. If you need to use the restroom, do so here, as there are no other facilities on the trail. Start off on the Laurel Loop, Metacomet–Monadnock, and Robert Frost Trails (there will be three blazes to follow).

After just 0.2 mile, you'll stay straight to continue on the Metacomet–Monadnock Trail with the white blazes. After just under 0.5 mile, the trail forks again, but this time

Top: The path up Mount Norwottuck starts on the New England/Robert Frost Trails (white and orange blazes).
Bottom: The path is well marked. You can take the orange-blazed trail up and the white-blazed trail down (or vice versa).

stay right to continue following the white blazes. The Robert Frost Trail has orange blazes—you'll take this trail coming back down the mountain.

At just over 0.5 mile, you'll turn left to start your steady climb up Mount Norwottuck. Pace yourself here, because it's about 600 feet of elevation gain in just under 0.7 mile. Kids might need more breaks or more motivation during this section. Luckily for you, Mount Holyoke Range State Park is filled with wildlife sounds throughout all parts of the day.

One of the most noticeable songbirds in New England is the veery. These birds blend in nicely with the typical beech, birch, and maple forests of the Northeast, but their call

Top: You'll be just over 1,100 feet above sea level at the summit.
Bottom: The views are endless.

is very unique. It has a spiraling sound, where it starts off high and circles down to lower notes. Another songbird is the eastern wood peewee. This is, quite frankly, my favorite songbird, because its call sounds like it's saying "peeeeeeee-weeeeeee." Kids love it!

After you've got your fill of songbirds, keep heading up the mountain. At just over a mile, you'll reach the summit of Mount Norwottuck and see views for what seems like days. Be careful here at the top, because some visitors have left broken glass that might be tempting to pick up for little hands. Continue down the White Blaze Trail. A little under 0.5 mile from the summit, you'll reach the Horse Caves. (See more about their history in the sidebar on the page 71.) They're not really caves but more like large overhanging ledges.

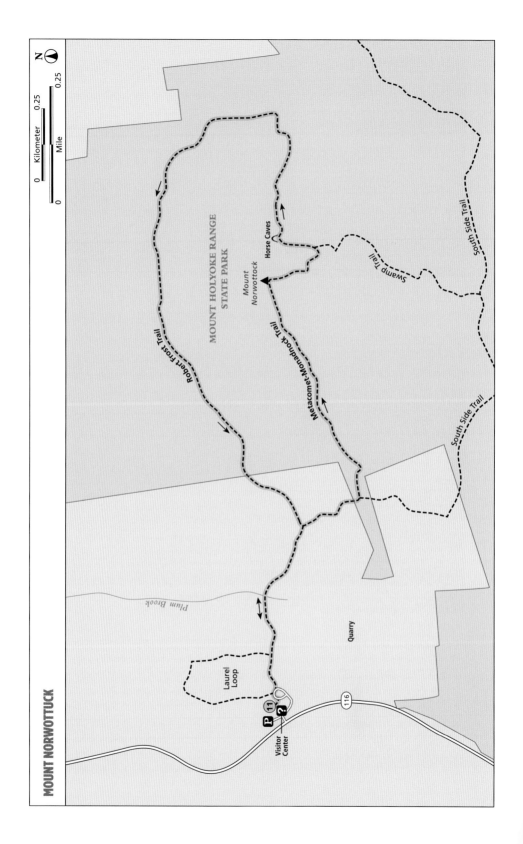

MOUNT NORWOTTUCK

MOUNT HOLYOKE RANGE
STATE PARK

Robert Frost Trail

Mount
Norwottock

Horse Caves

Metacomet-Monadnock Trail

Swamp Trail

South Side Trail

South Side Trail

Plum Brook

Laurel
Loop

Quarry

116

P 11

Visitor
Center

N

0   Kilometer   0.25

0   0.25
Mile

Once you and your kids are done horsing (no pun intended) around, get back on the trail and take a left onto the Robert Frost Trail, indicated by orange blazes. It's a nice gradual descent down the northern face of the mountain. Stay on the Robert Frost Trail until you meet up with the Metacomet-Monadnock and Laural Loop Trails once again.

MILES AND DIRECTIONS

0.00   Start at the Laurel Loop trailhead behind the Notch Visitor Center.

0.20   Stay straight to follow the white blazes and get on the Metacomet-Monadnock Trail.

0.40   At the fork, stay right to follow the white blazes—do not follow the orange blazes to the left.

0.60   Take a left at the fork to continue your steep ascent up Mount Norwottuck—it's about 600 feet of elevation gain in 0.7 mile.

1.10   Reach the summit of Mount Norwottuck.

1.20   Keep on the Metacomet-Monadnock Trail by continuing to follow the white blazes.

1.40   Reach the Horse Caves.

1.70   Take a left to get on the Robert Frost Trail, indicated by orange blazes. Follow this gradual descent down the mountain.

1.80   Take a left at this fork to stay on the Robert Frost Trail.

2.70   Keep straight to follow the orange blazes. Do not turn right on the trail.

2.90   Meet back up with the Metacomet-Monadnock Trail once again.

3.10   Stay straight to get back on the Laurel Loop.

3.30   Arrive back at the trailhead.

THE HISTORY OF THE HORSE CAVES

The Horse Caves on Mount Norwottuck are of historical significance dating all the way back to Shays' Rebellion. This rebellion was an uprising against the rigorous economic conditions and high taxes that took place in Massachusetts during the late 1700s (remember the Boston Tea Party, folks?).

Daniel Shays led the Shays' Rebellion in September 1786, during which he and his followers forced the Supreme Court in Springfield to adjourn. Then in January the following year, Shays led 1,200 men to attack the federal arsenal in Springfield, but they were defeated. Early in February, Shays, along with many of his followers, were chased by militia and forced to hide or be arrested. Some of the men ended up in the hills of Mount Holyoke Range State Park and camped out in the Horse Caves until the coast was clear. Unfortunately, Shays fled to Vermont and gave up his cause. However, after all these events, the legislature of Massachusetts created laws that loosened the strict conditions of debtors to ease those who might've gone through foreclosure.

12 CRANE BEACH LOOP

Named for Richard T. Crane, who was the original owner of the property on and around Castle Hill, Crane Beach now entertains 350,000 people annually over its 1,200 acres. Despite the popularity of the beach and surrounding estate, park management has been able to successfully maintain one of the most important nesting sites for piping plovers. You'll be able to view these nesting piping plovers, along with several other types of bird species, while traversing the dunes across the area.

Start: At the Green Trail trailhead
Elevation gain: 115 feet
Distance: 3.2 miles
Difficulty: Easy to moderate
Hiking time: 3 hours
Seasons/Schedule: 8:00 a.m. to sunset, year-round
Fees and permits: Yes, and advance passes are usually required on weekends during peak season
Trail contact: The Trustees of Reservations, 200 High St., Boston, MA; (617) 542-7696; https://thetrustees.org/place/crane-beach-on-the-crane-estate
Dog-friendly: Not allowed on trail
Trail surface: Sand and dirt
Land status: The Trustees of Reservations

Nearest town: Ipswich, MA
Other trail users: Horseback riders (permitted from October 1 to March 31)
Water availability: Yes, at the concession stand
Maps: The Crane Estate trail map
Age range: All ages
Toilets: Yes, at the concession stand
Stroller/Wheelchair compatibility: No
Resting benches: None
Potential child hazards: Ocean/water
Gear suggestions: Sun hat, insect repellent, beach accessories, and swimsuit

FINDING THE TRAILHEAD

From Boston, follow US 1 North and continue to Newburyport Turnpike, approximately 14 miles. Keep left to continue on US 1 North/Newbury Street/Newburyport Turnpike for about 4 miles. Keep right at the fork, follow signs for US 1 North/Topsfield, and continue on this route—US 1 North/Newbury Street/Newburyport Turnpike—for about 4 miles. Take a right onto Ipswich Road and follow for just under 2 miles. The road then turns into Topsfield Road for 3.6 miles and then Market Street for 0.2 mile. Turn right onto MA 133 East/MA 1A South for 0.3 mile. Turn left onto Argilla Road and stay on this road for about 4.4 miles. The entrance for Crane Beach is on your right. Park in the southeastern corner of the parking lot, away from the beach side. **GPS:** 42.683319 / -70.765600

THE HIKE

If you're heading out to Crane Beach on a holiday weekend, be prepared to share the trails and beach with other visitors. This northeastern Massachusetts beach has long stretches of sand that make this area ideal for families and out-of-town visitors to get a lot of bang for their buck.

However, despite the crowded beaches, the trails tend to have far fewer folks walking on them. Park at the southeastern side of the large parking lot to reach the trailhead for

Top: The loop around Crane Beach is mostly sand and a perfect place for kiddos to play.
Bottom: There are multiple wildlife trails that are restricted.

the Green Trail. The trail starts out on some dirt and then a short boardwalk but quickly turns to sand as you cross over the bridge. On hot summer days the sand can be scorching, so I don't suggest ever hiking in bare feet.

Take a right when you get to a T-intersection, which will bring you away from the beach—the beach will be toward the end of the hike. Make sure to keep an eye on your kids, as it's easy to veer off the trail. The ecosystem surrounding the trails is extremely sensitive; walking on the ground around here can cause irreparable harm. Sand dunes are incredibly important to many species and should not be trampled on.

You will see a trail on your left about 0.75 mile in. This is a shortcut to the beach if you or your kids aren't feeling a longer hike. However, if you are up for more hiking, keep

The grasses next to the beach are ideal habitats for nesting piping plovers.

straight to go on the Red Trail and head up to the highest section of the hike: Wigwam Hill. Descend the "hill" (because, let's face it, it's not much of a hill) until you reach the next fork.

Keep left at the fork to head toward the beach side of the park and then left again when you reach another fork. You'll walk along the sand dunes on both sides of the trail; you might get a first glimpse of some nesting piping plovers here if you come at the right time of year. When you see the trail that goes off to the right, take it—this leads you down to the beach!

If you want to avoid crowds and brought your beach accessories with you (which I highly recommend), then set up camp here. Almost all the visitors to Crane Beach don't take the trails, and, instead, use the easy access of the boardwalks on the other side of the beach to set up their spot for the day. You will be joined by far fewer people and will have way more room for your kids to romp around the beach if you prepare your beach day to coincide with your hike.

You don't have to hang on the beach for long either. You can simply dip your toes in and say hi to the piping plovers, all of whom will be out and about trying to catch some food for their nestlings. When you see a boardwalk to your left, take it to get back to the parking lot where you parked your car.

MILES AND DIRECTIONS

0.00 Start at the parking lot and head down the road back to the entrance.

0.10 Take a right at the T-intersection.

0.70 Keep straight to go on the Red Trail. If your kids are getting antsy, take a left to head toward the beach.

0.90 Arrive at Wigwam Hill, the high point of the hike.

1.30 At the fork, take the trail to the left.

1.60 Stay straight to continue on the Red Trail; do not take the Blue Trail to the right.

CRANE BEACH LOOP

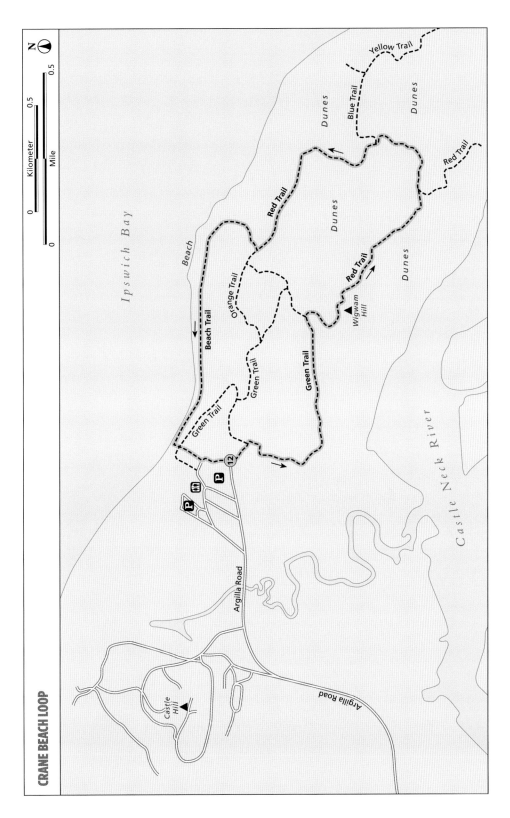

N

Kilometer
0   0.5   0.5

0   0.5   0.5
Mile

Ipswich Bay

Beach

Beach Trail

Green Trail

Orange Trail

Green Trail

Green Trail

Green Trail

Red Trail

Red Trail

Red Trail

Wigwam Hill

Blue Trail

Yellow Trail

Dunes

Dunes

Dunes

Dunes

12

P

P

Argilla Road

Argilla Road

Castle Hill

Castle Neck River

No need to bring shovels; clam shells can be used to dig through the sand.

2.20 Take the trail to the right to head down to the beach. If you've brought your beach accessories with you, you'll find way fewer people on this side of the beach. Otherwise, continue walking along the beach.

2.90 Take a left over the boardwalk bridge to get back to the parking lot.

3.20 Arrive back at the trailhead.

THE CUTEST SHOREBIRDS YOU'VE EVER SEEN

If you've seen the Disney short film called *Piper*, you have already had a glimpse into the piping plover world. They are just as cute in real life as they are in cartoon form. They resemble a wind-up toy when they scurry about on the beach trying to get their food. And don't get me started on the babies! They are so adorable; they'll break your heart. But where exactly did their name come from?

The sand-colored, black-eyed birds have what most scientists describe as a "plaintive" call. Their mournful cries echo along the beach and are easily heard before the birds are ever seen. Their cry is why these birds are called piping plovers.

If there aren't too many visitors on the beach with you, see if you and your kids can mimic their calls. Of course, keep your distance and do not disturb any piping plovers. That means refrain from chasing the birds. I know it's tempting for kids to chase the birds on the beach, but piping plovers are a threatened species in the Northeast (they're endangered in the Great Lakes region) and are federally protected.

If there were ever a trail made for every single person on this earth—no matter age, size, shape, or ability—Hellcat Interpretive Trail would be it! Not only is this trail completely stroller- and wheelchair-accessible, it's also got stunning views and offers true immersion into nature without having to break a sweat. More than 4,500 acres of upland and wetland habitat cover Parker River National Wildlife Refuge, which is home to more than 300 species of both resident and migratory birds. If you've got a bird "life list," this is the place to find them!

Start: At the Hellcat Interpretive trailhead

Elevation gain: 40 feet

Distance: 1.5 miles

Difficulty: Easy

Hiking time: 1 hour

Seasons/Schedule: Sunrise to sunset, year-round

Fees and permits: Fee required

Trail contact: Parker River National Wildlife Refuge, 6 Plum Island Turnpike, Newburyport, MA; (978) 465-5753; www.fws.gov/refuge/parker-river

Dog-friendly: Dogs not allowed, except seeing eye dogs and others that assist people with physical impairments

Trail surface: Some gravel but mostly boardwalk

Land status: US Fish and Wildlife Service

Nearest town: Newburyport, MA

Other trail users: None

Water availability: None

Maps: Parker River Wildlife Refuge trail map

Age range: All ages

Toilets: Yes

Stroller/Wheelchair compatibility: Yes

Resting benches: Yes, several along the trail

Potential child hazards: Raised boardwalks and crossing roads

Gear suggestions: Binoculars to view the many bird species that utilize this area

FINDING THE TRAILHEAD

The refuge is located 35 miles north of Boston near the City of Newburyport. From Route 95 take exit 57 and travel east on Route 113, then continue straight onto Route 1A South to the intersection with Rolfe's Lane, for a total of 3.5 miles. Turn left onto Rolfe's Lane and travel 0.5 mile to its end. Turn right onto the Plum Island Turnpike and travel 2 miles, crossing the Sgt. Donald Wilkinson Bridge to Plum Island. Take your first right onto Sunset Drive and travel 0.5 mile to the refuge entrance. The trail is located 3.5 miles south of the refuge entrance station. Parking will be on your right and can only fit about twenty cars. **GPS:** 42.741419 / -70.795469

THE HIKE

Getting to the trailhead for the Hellcat Interpretive Trail brings you through most of the Parker River National Wildlife Refuge. As you cross over onto Plum Island where the wildlife refuge resides, you're greeted with a multitude of seafood restaurants, friendly locals, and idyllic beaches.

Before even getting into the wildlife refuge, pop by the Parker River National Wildlife Refuge Visitor Center to chat with the staff. Hellcat Interpretive Trail is always open, but

Top: The raised boardwalks traverse the entirety of the loop, so it's great for strollers and wheelchairs.
Bottom: The view from the ocean overlook

if you want to visit any of the other attractions within the wildlife refuge, make sure the trails are open. As is the case with multiple beaches in New England, some close during nesting season to protect shoreline bird species.

Make sure to take it slow as you drive down the Refuge Road, as there are many pull-outs and tourists not paying attention to the cars driving by. Some trails, like the Hellcat Interpretive Trail, cross the road too. To get the full wildlife refuge experience, pull off into some of the overlooks and viewing areas to see the abundance of species that call this place home.

When you get to the trailhead, park wherever you can find a spot—there's room for a few dozen vehicles. It'll likely be busy on weekends, so prepare for that. The trailhead

Top: Running through the reeds at the marsh overlook
Bottom: The viewing tower is a great place to sit and watch the birds over the marshes.

starts at the western edge of the parking lot. If you or your kids need to use the toilet, head left to the pit toilets adjacent to the parking lot. Otherwise, go straight on the trail and then veer right at the fork.

Most of the trail is raised boardwalks and, in many cases, without a fence. Even if your child did fall, however, it usually isn't a far drop and they should be all right. Just make sure they're being mindful of how close they're getting to the edge when the fences aren't up. After 0.2 mile, you'll reach your first road crossing. Drivers should be driving slow, but always use caution when crossing.

After the road crossing, go straight at the next intersection toward the Ocean Overlook.

Once at the overlook, take in the views of the Atlantic Ocean and the ever-changing sand dunes at the shore. If you want to walk along the shore, you'll have to drive back down the road to one of the beach access points.

There are many birds that call this area home or use it as a stopover for their migration.

Head back the way you came and then take a right to continue your path. Again, you'll cross the road and then reach another junction. Take the trail to the right to check out the Marsh Overlook, then head back the way you came. Keeping to the loop, you'll head right at the junction to take a final branch to another overlook among the cattails of the North Pool.

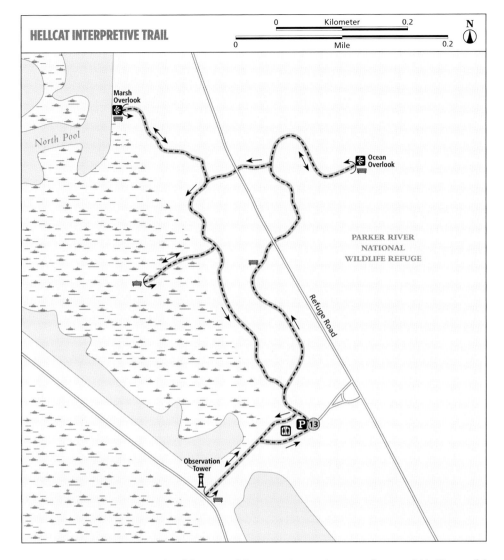

0   Kilometer   0.2

N

0   Mile   0.2

Marsh
Overlook

North Pool

Ocean
Overlook

PARKER RIVER
NATIONAL
WILDLIFE REFUGE

Refuge Road

P 13

Observation
Tower

This is a neat site and will be one of the more interesting spots for your kids. Be careful here, though, as there are areas where there is no fence, and the drop here will put them in standing water a few feet deep.

Once you're done at the last overlook, go back the way you came to once again take a right to finish off the loop. Finally, one last trail to the right will bring you to the Observation Tower.

Feel free to climb the tower, but keep an eye on the little ones heading up—the stairs are a little steep. When you're done observing the wildlife from above, climb back down and head back the way you came. This time, veer to the right and drop down back toward the toilets and the parking area.

MILES AND DIRECTIONS

0.00 Start at the Hellcat Interpretive trailhead.

0.10 Veer right at the fork.

0.30 Cross the Refuge Road, taking heed when crossing.

0.40 Take the trail in front of you to check out the Ocean Overlook.

0.50 Arrive at the Ocean Overlook. There's a bench here to relax until you're ready to head back the way you came.

0.60 Take a right onto the trail to cross the road again back to the other side.

0.70 You can take the trail to your right here to take in the views at the Marsh Overlook.

0.80 Arrive at the Marsh Overlook. When you're finished taking in the view, go back the way you came.

0.90 Go right to continue on the trail.

1.00 Take the trail to the right to head to another overlook and then return the way you came.

1.10 Take a right to continue on the trail.

1.20 Meet up with the other fork you took at the beginning of the trail. At the next fork, go right to head toward the Observation Tower.

1.40 Reach the Observation Tower. Head back the way you came, but take the trail to the right toward the toilets.

1.50 Arrive back at the trailhead.

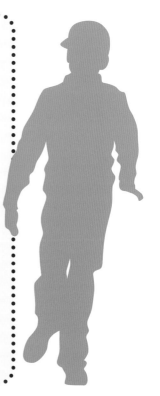

WHY OSPREYS ARE SO UNIQUE

Ospreys are one of the many bird species you can find at Parker River National Wildlife Refuge. Affectionately known as the "sea hawk" due to its proclivity for hunting fish, ospreys are truly unique birds of prey. They are found on every continent except Antarctica, making them the second-most widespread raptor species—second to the peregrine falcon.

Ospreys have a unique way of hunting, catching, and keeping hold of the prey they catch. As fairly successful hunters (most ospreys catch something at least 25 percent of the time, but some are successful upward of 75 percent), ospreys hover above the water awaiting a fish to get close to the surface. When they've zeroed in on their prey, they swoop down, feet first, and snatch it up. Sometimes they become fully submerged in the water to get what they've worked so hard for.

Once they've snatched their prey, the birds' powerful talons keep hold of it as they fly back to the nest. Ospreys' outer toes are reversible, meaning they can hold on to slippery and squirmy fish quite easily without dropping them. They bring the food back to their nest—a nest they'll usually come back to year after year. Ospreys tend to have one partner and mate for life. Aww.

14 BASH BISH FALLS TRAIL

Check out Massachusetts's tallest waterfall—Bash Bish Falls. This relatively easy stroll along a wide dirt path greets you with a massive waterfall and stunning scenery only 0.75 mile in. Immerse yourselves in the strength and beauty of crashing cascades. If you head out during spring snowmelt or after a big rainstorm, the power of the falls will be even greater!

Start: Taconic State Park at the Bash Bish Falls lower lot
Elevation gain: 239 feet
Distance: 1.5 miles
Difficulty: Easy
Hiking time: 1.5 hours
Seasons/Schedule: Sunrise to sunset, year-round
Fees and permits: None
Trail contact: Bash Bish Falls State Park, 4G85+29, Mt. Washington, MA; (413) 528-0330; www.mass.gov/locations/bash-bish-falls-state-park. Taconic State Park, 253 Route 344, Copake Falls, NY; (518) 329-3993; parks.ny.gov/parks/taconiccopake
Dog-friendly: Allowed on leash
Trail surface: Dirt
Land status: Massachusetts Department of Conservation and Recreation and New York Department of Parks, Recreation, and Historic Preservation
Nearest town: Copake, NY
Other trail users: None
Water availability: None
Maps: Bash Bish Falls State Park trail map
Age range: All ages
Toilets: Yes, at the trailhead and the waterfalls
Stroller/Wheelchair compatibility: No
Resting benches: Yes, several along the trail
Potential child hazards: Rocks around waterfalls can be slippery and poison ivy
Gear suggestions: Insect repellent

FINDING THE TRAILHEAD

From Springfield, take Route 90 west toward Albany for about 47 miles. Take exit B3 toward Austerlitz/New Lebanon. Turn left onto MA 22/NY 22 and continue for about 20 miles. Turn left onto NY 344 and then take an immediate left to continue on NY 344. After 0.75 mile, the Bash Bish Falls lower lot will be on your right. If you make it back to Massachusetts, you've gone too far. **GPS:** 42.116943 / -73.507462

THE HIKE

There are two ways to view Bash Bish Falls, but this trail is the more gradual, albeit longer, hike. You could park in the Bash Bish upper lot and hike down the very steep (but short) trail. It's only about 0.3 mile but has more than 500 feet of elevation gain/loss. If you have little kiddos with you or you've got bad knees, I don't suggest going this way.

Instead, cross over into New York and park at the Bash Bish lower lot. You will start your hike in Taconic State Park and then cross over into Bash Bish Falls State Park in Massachusetts, where the falls reside. The trail starts and continues on a very wide path with minimal elevation gain. Most of the elevation gain/loss you see in the blue overview section of this chapter is at the very end, to descend toward the rocks at the base of the pool at the falls.

Top: A wide, gravelly path leads you to the Falls.
Bottom: A quiet place to take a break along the river.

You'll walk parallel to Bash Bish Brook, which has strict signage stating no one is to enter the water or go near the water's edge. This can be difficult for little kids, so keep a close eye on them. I know they'll likely be tempted to throw rocks in the brook or dip their feet in, but make sure they refrain from doing so. Due to the trail's popularity, management has had to close off the brook so it stays as pristine as possible. However, fishing is permitted in Bash Bish Brook; you only need a fishing permit to do so.

There are several benches along the trail for you to relax, but with such a short trail, you might not need them. The wide trail makes it easy for kids to hike (or run) at their own pace without holding up (or crashing into) other hikers. After 0.75 mile, you'll reach Bash Bish Falls.

Bash Bish Falls

Bash Bish Falls is actually a series of cascades, but only the last drop is visible to visitors of the area. More than 850 linear feet, the falls drop about 210 feet. The last of the cascades, which splits between a boulder, drops about 50 feet. This is the largest of the drops among all the cascades, with most only dropping about 15 feet. So even though you can't see the other parts of the falls, you can see the biggest and grandest of them all.

Legend has it that Bash Bish Falls was named after a Mohican woman who was accused of being unfaithful to her husband. As punishment, she was sent over the top of the falls

The trail parallels the river.

tied to a canoe. According to multiple reports by visitors of the falls, a woman can be seen looking at them behind the falls. One can only assume it's Bash Bish haunting the area where she died. As eerie as that might sound, the tale is highly unlikely due to the low probability of a canoe even making it that far down the cascades (too many boulders).

LEAVES OF THREE, LET THEM BE

You can find poison ivy across New England, and this trail is no different. For most of us who have grown up in New England, we know how to easily identify poison ivy. But for those who haven't been around this pesky plant often, there are some simple ways to remember what poison ivy looks like.

"Leave of three, let it be." Technically, the leaves being referenced here are leaflets, and there are three along a single stem—one at the top and two to the sides. If there are more leaves than three on a single stem, it isn't poison ivy.

"Longer middle stem? Stay away from them!" The middle leaflet's stem is longer than the two side leaflets. This is a key difference to the similar-looking fragrant sumac plant.

"Don't put your hand where butterflies land." Butterflies land in many places, but they can also land on poison ivy, because they are not affected by the oils from the plant.

"Berries white? Run in fright!" Sure, other plants have white berries, but if you see these in combination with any of the other indicators of poison ivy, run away!

"Hairy vine? No friend of mine" As the poison ivy plant matures, the vine-like stem has a hairy appearance.

"Red leaflets in spring? It's a dangerous thing" Not all poison ivy plants turn red in spring, but many do. In summer they turn green and then back to red as autumn arrives.

"Side leaflets like mittens will itch like the dickens." This is likely my favorite saying. The side leaflets usually have a shape just like a winter mitten you put on your kiddos. Stay away from these guys!

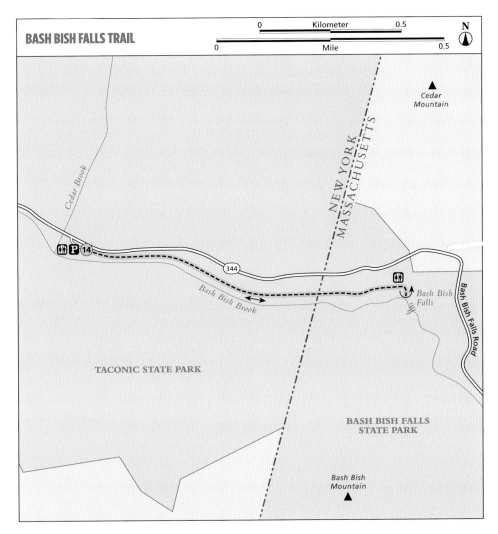

BASH BISH FALLS TRAIL

Over the decades that Bash Bish Falls has been open to the public, more than twenty-five people have died trying to do cliff jumps from the top. This area is highly dangerous, and swimming in the pool or climbing the rocks around the falls is strictly prohibited.

After you've finished watching the marvel of the falls, head back to your car the way you came.

MILES AND DIRECTIONS

0.00 Start at the lower lot of Bash Bish Falls.

0.50 Cross over into Massachusetts.

0.75 Reach Bash Bish Falls.

1.00 Head back across the border to New York, where your car is parked.

1.50 Arrive back at the trailhead.

15 WWI MEMORIAL PARK LOOP

If you need to cram a lot of activities into one day to make sure your kid gets all their energy out, look no further than WWI Memorial Park Loop. Along with the hiking trail, there is also a playground, arboretum, stunning overlook, beach area (with toys!), and zoo! What more could you ask for? How about a game of disc golf? Because this park has that too. Plus it has some neat geological features, including a balanced rock that looks like it's about to topple over. Your kids will be begging you to bring them back here once they've experienced it.

Start: From the parking area to the west of the zoo
Elevation gain: 130 feet
Distance: 1.6 miles
Difficulty: Easy
Hiking time: 2 hours
Seasons/Schedule: Year-round; opens at 7:30 a.m. on weekdays and 8:00 a.m. on weekends. From April 1 to October 31, the park closes at 8:00 p.m. From November 1 to March 31, the park closes at 4:00 p.m. Closed Thanksgiving, Christmas, and New Year's Day.
Fees and permits: None
Trail contact: World War I Memorial Park and Zoo, 365 Elmwood St., North Attleborough, MA; (508) 699-0129; https://northattleboroughma .myrec.com/info/facilities/details .aspx?FacilityID=14696
Dog-friendly: Allowed on leash

Trail surface: A paved walking path with some dirt trails
Land status: Town of North Attleborough Parks and Recreation Department
Nearest town: North Attleborough, MA
Other trail users: None
Water availability: Water fountains throughout the park
Maps: World War I Veteran's Memorial Park trail map
Age range: All ages
Toilets: Yes
Stroller/Wheelchair compatibility: Yes, for the trails along the pavement
Resting benches: Yes, picnic tables throughout the park
Potential child hazards: Crossing and walking on the road and poison ivy
Gear suggestions: Binoculars to view the birds in the arboretum

FINDING THE TRAILHEAD

From Boston, follow I-93 South and I-95 South to US 1 South in Sharon. Take exit 19 from I-95 South. Take exit 19 to merge onto US 1 South toward Foxboro/Wrentham. Continue on US 1 South to your destination in North Attleborough. About 9 miles on US 1 South look for MA 106 East. Turn left onto MA 106 East, then right onto George Street. Next turn right onto Messenger Street. Continue onto Elmwood Street; WWI Memorial Park Loop is on the left. **GPS:** 41.999161 / -71.315346

THE HIKE

The road around WWI Memorial Park is one-way, so if you miss the parking lot, you'll have to loop back around. The best parking to start this trail is the second parking lot on your right, directly west of the zoo. You'll start just behind the parking lot on an unmarked trail. The zoo will be the last thing you visit, so it'll keep your kids motivated to stay motivated.

Top: The view from the overlook
Bottom left: Signs showing how far you are to each landmark from the overlook
Bottom right: Balanced Rock is one of the many features along this loop.

One of the many playgrounds found throughout the park

About 0.1 mile in, you'll reach the junction of the West Loop Trail, indicated by yellow blazes. Here you'll take a right to traverse the entirety of the West Loop, which brings you through the Harold Burns Memorial Wildlife Arboretum. The trail winds through typical New England forests made up of beech, birch, and maple along with a multitude of wildflowers. Birds will be using their calls to alert you to their presence. If you don't want to do the entire loop, you can opt for the shortcut after you've been walking 0.4 mile on the West Loop. The trail will be to your left and will connect you with the West Loop on the other side.

If you want to walk more, keep on the West Loop Trail, which will turn back around when it hits Mount Hope Street. You'll round a corner to head back east toward the parking lot. You'll pass by Petti Field, which has two baseball diamonds used for the town's youth baseball teams.

Eventually you'll link back up with the road and combine with the South Loop Trail (indicated by white blazes). You'll head left (north) once you hit the road. At the next intersection, take a right to continue on the road until you come up on another parking lot on your right. Just south of the parking lot is another trail to your right. Take it to head to Balancing Rock—there is a wooden sign pointing the way, even though the trail is unmarked.

Make your way through the gravity-defying boulder formation until you meet up with the South Loop Trail again (white blazes). Take a left to head back to the road. Once you hit the road, you can head right (north) to check out the beach area, playground, and Sunrise Hill, which are just a few feet from here. After the kids have had their fill of playing, head down the road until you reach a fork. Take the fork to the right to head through Julia's Garden. There's a great slide in the garden that even adults won't be able to resist.

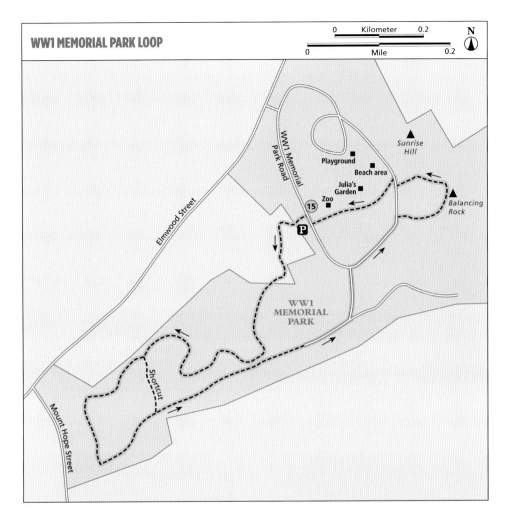

Head back out on the road to the zoo and another small playground for toddlers. The zoo is filled with goats, emus, deer, donkeys, and peacocks! There is no fee to enter the zoo, but make sure you keep fingers away from the fences and do not feed the animals with any outside food. Management provides grain machines for you to feed some of the animals, but double-check their dietary restrictions first. Once you're done at the zoo, head west back to your car.

MILES AND DIRECTIONS

0.00 Start behind the second parking lot on your right as you drive into the park.

0.05 Take a left at the fork to stay on the unmarked trail.

0.10 Veer right onto the West Loop Trail indicated by yellow blazes.

0.50 If you don't want to do the whole loop, turn left here to take the shortcut to the other side of the West Loop Trail.

0.70 Take a left to continue on the West Loop Trail and head back in the direction you came.

1.10 Reach a road and take a left.

1.20 Take a right on the road.

1.30 Take the unmarked trail to your right and follow the sign for Balancing Rock.

1.45 Balancing Rock will be on your right. Stay left after the rock to get on the South Loop Trail, indicated by white blazes.

1.50 When you reach the road again, you can go right (north) to the playground, beach, and overlook or straight to Julia's Garden and the zoo.

1.60 Arrive back at the zoo. Head across the road to get back to your car.

THE BEAUTY OF JULIA'S GARDEN

Named after a little girl who lived in North Attleborough and died of pancreatitis when she was 9, Julia's Garden is a fairy tale within a suburban oasis. Julia loved to visit the WWI Memorial Park and Zoo often, even during her concurrent medical issues of having seizures and autism. It gave her a sense of peace.

There are over forty species of trees and shrubs as well as one hundred species of perennials throughout Julia's Garden. It provides a haven for many pollinators, which have declined in recent years due to habitat destruction and urban sprawl, among other reasons. Within the garden there is also a wishing well, unicorn sculpture, and butterfly fountain—everything you need for a fantastical adventure!

The most epic of slides in Julia's Garden, which is also next to the zoo

16 PURGATORY CHASM LOOP

Don't let the name fool you. No place around here will make you suffer while you atone for your sins. Although your legs might suffer a bit trying to get up and over the boulders that make up Purgatory Chasm Loop. The trail will bring you through an immense fissure through the earth and some narrow passageways that might not be wide enough for the adults in your group. Squeeze through them if you dare and enjoy your time in Purgatory Chasm State Reservation.

Start: At the Chasm Loop trailhead
Elevation gain: 200 feet
Distance: 1.6-mile loop
Difficulty: Easy to moderate (only because of the boulders that you'll need to traverse)
Hiking time: 2 hours
Seasons/Schedule: Sunrise to sunset, closed during winter
Fees and permits: Fee required
Trail contact: Purgatory Chasm State Reservation, 198 Purgatory Rd., Sutton, MA; (508) 234-3733; www.mass.gov/locations/purgatory-chasm-state-reservation
Dog-friendly: Allowed on leash
Trail surface: Dirt, rock, and roots
Land status: Massachusetts Department of Conservation and Recreation

Nearest town: Sutton, MA
Other trail users: Cross-country skiers and rock climbers
Water availability: Yes, at the visitor center
Maps: Purgatory Chasm State Reservation trail map
Age range: All ages, although smaller kids who want to walk might need help through the chasm
Toilets: Yes, at the visitor center
Stroller/Wheelchair compatibility: No
Resting benches: No
Potential child hazards: Large boulders to traverse over and large drop-offs
Gear suggestions: Trekking poles

FINDING THE TRAILHEAD

From Worcester, follow MA 146 South for approximately 10 miles. Take exit 11 for Purgatory Road toward Northbridge. Keep right at the fork and follow signs for Purgatory Chasm and merge onto Purgatory Road. The reservation entrance and visitor center are on your right. Once you've paid the fee, park at the parking lot on your left just across from the visitor center. If there is no parking there, use the large lot outside of the visitor center. **GPS:** 42.129222 / -71.714754

THE HIKE

This is one of those hikes that provides a lot of bang for very little buck, especially if you just want to see the chasm part. From the trailhead, take the trail that points straight through the chasm. Immediately you're greeted with views of the wide fissure created thousands of years ago.

As you head deeper into the chasm, several areas of interest are scattered throughout. Lover's Leap will be the first thing you see on your right—a massive, 75-foot plummet to the ground if you were to jump from the top. Be careful traversing the boulders here; little legs might need some help climbing and descending some of the boulders. There are also several large holes that small kids could fall into—so be careful.

Top: Purgatory Chasm is filled with fallen boulders that are both fun and dangerous to climb, so tread carefully.
Bottom: A raised boardwalk keeps the sensitive natural areas pristine.

Next up you'll see Devil's Pulpit just after Lover's Leap, where a large rock juts out for, supposedly, the Devil to preach to his followers (at least that's what legend says).

Speaking of legend, Purgatory Chasm has a gruesome past. According to legend, hundreds of years ago an Algonquin woman killed a white colonial settler. She walked away hoping no one knew what she had done. But then she came across another settler. She called to the Spirit of Death, named "Hobomock," but discovered the settler she had come across had disguised himself and was really Hobomock.

According to the colonists, knowing what the woman had done, Hobomock took her to Purgatory Chasm. Legend states that the wide fissures we see today were made when

Another angle of the chasm

Hobomock threw his victim to the ground, and the deep slots scattered throughout the chasm came as a result of his swinging his tomahawk. Historians, however, have theorized that this was a way to indoctrinate the Native American population at the time to Christianity. To find out the real geological history of the chasm, read the sidebar in this chapter.

Moving through the chasm, you'll reach the end of the fissure when you've hit Devil's Coffin. Continue straight onto Charley's Loop Trail. Stay on this trail for 0.8 mile, until

Once you're done with the hike, swing by the shaded playground at the visitor center.

you reach the trailhead you started at. From here, you can end your journey and maybe go run around the playground near the visitor center. If you're still up for an adventure, head to the left to hop on the rest of the Purgatory Chasm Loop.

Points of interest on this loop include a scenic vista, Devil's Corncrib, and Fat Man's Misery, which is exactly what you think it is. This is the deepest cut in the rocks you'll find on the reservation. You can walk through (or at least attempt to walk through) the deep slot to see if you need to suck in your gut to see how far you can make it before you get stuck. Continue down the trail and take a right to go back through the chasm the other way.

After the hike, I highly recommend romping around the playground near the visitor center. The entire playground meanders through the woods and has complete shade, so it's perfect for those hotter days. Once you and your kids are all tuckered out, head back to your car.

MILES AND DIRECTIONS

0.00 Start at the Chasm Loop trailhead. Take the trail that goes straight through the chasm.

0.05 Lover's Leap and Devil's Pulpit are on your right.

0.10 Arrive at the deepest part of the chasm.

0.25 Reach Devil's Coffin.

0.30 Take a left at the three-way junction to hop on Charley's Loop Trail.

1.00 Reach the original trailhead. You can either stop here or continue to visit a few more points of interest.

1.10 Reach Devil's Corncrib.

1.15 Fat Man's Misery is on your right. Feel free to try your luck at squeezing through it.

1.35 Reach Devil's Coffin again and take a right to head back through the chasm the other way.

1.60 Arrive back at the trailhead.

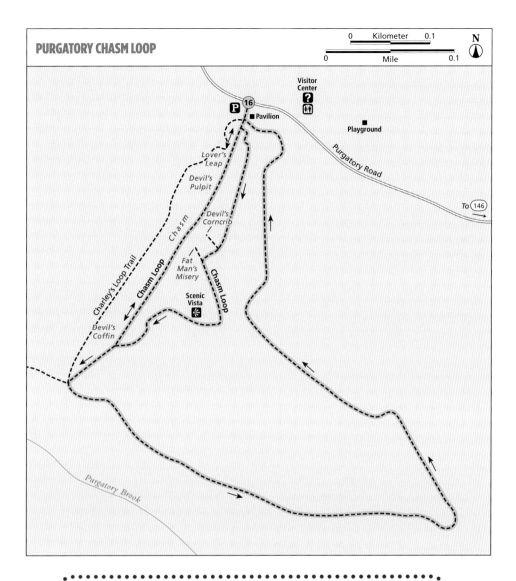

Map labels:
0 Kilometer 0.1
0 Mile 0.1
N

Visitor Center
Playground
Purgatory Road
To 146
Pavilion
Lover's Leap
Devil's Pulpit
Chasm
Devil's Corncrib
Charley's Loop Trail
Chasm Loop
Fat Man's Misery
Chasm Loop
Scenic Vista
Devil's Coffin
Purgatory Brook

THE GEOLOGIC HISTORY OF PURGATORY CHASM

Geologists have determined that Purgatory Chasm was created more than 14,000 years ago. At first look you might think the chasm was formed after a large earthquake hit the area; the large boulders look as if they tumbled down the cliff walls. And maybe they have a bit over time, but an earthquake isn't the reason behind its formation.

Instead, scientists determined that a gush of glacial water created the massive granite walls and deep fissures. After collecting for thousands of years, the glacial meltwater built up so much that it broke free and flowed down the valley in a torrent of rushing water. It was so strong that it ripped the area in two and created the deep fissures you see today.

17 DRUMLIN FARM LOOP

Drumlin Farm, managed by the Massachusetts Audubon Society, is both a working farm and wildlife sanctuary. There are several trails to explore and spots to learn about farm life. Whether you're strolling through the fields of vegetables, ascending Hathaway Hill, or absorbing all the information at the Learning Garden, there is something for everyone here.

Start: At the Ice Pond trailhead
Elevation gain: 130 feet
Distance: 1.9 miles
Difficulty: Easy
Hiking time: 2 hours
Seasons/Schedule: Tuesday through Sunday, 9:00 a.m. to 5:00 p.m.; closed Monday (except holidays)
Fees and permits: Fee required
Trail contact: Drumlin Farm, 208 S. Great Road; Lincoln, MA; (781) 259-2255; www.massaudubon.org/get-outdoors/wildlife-sanctuaries/drumlin-farm
Dog-friendly: Not allowed
Trail surface: Pavement, gravel, grass, and dirt

Land status: Massachusetts Audubon Society
Nearest town: Lincoln, MA
Other trail users: None
Water availability: None
Maps: Drumlin Farm trail map
Age range: All ages
Toilets: Yes
Stroller/Wheelchair compatibility: Some trails; the sections around Bird Hill, the Farm Life Center, and the Goat Shed are all ADA accessible.
Resting benches: Yes
Potential child hazards: Poison ivy directly on the trail up Hathaway Hill
Gear suggestions: None

FINDING THE TRAILHEAD

From Boston, take I-93 North for 4 miles. Take exit 22 to merge onto MA 16 West/Mystic Valley Parkway toward Arlington. Merge onto MA 16 West for 2 miles and then take the second exit to stay on MA 16 West for another 1.4 miles. Merge onto Route 2 West via the ramp to Concord. Stay on Route 2 for 8.5 miles. Take a slight right onto the ramp for Bedford Road and stay on this road for 1 mile, where it turns into Lincoln Road. Stay on Lincoln Road for 2 miles until you hit a T-intersection. Take a left onto MA 117 East and then an immediate right into the parking lot for Drumlin Farm. **GPS:** 42.408660 / -71.329873

THE HIKE

Drumlin Farm is a great alternative to the busier (and bigger) zoos in the Greater Boston area. As a still-working farm, visitors are able to experience what life on a farm is truly like. Before you head on your hike, make sure to pop by the Farm Stand and Visitor Center.

Once you have paid the fee, head back to the parking lot, hop on the Ice Pond Trail, skirt the southern edge of the parking lot, and then take a left to get onto the Hayfield Loop. Ignore any of the trails that go off to your left or right, just continue straight along until you reach a fork in the trail. Stay left to continue on the Hayfield Loop and make your way up to Hathaway Hill. This is the highest point on the property, and although it doesn't have too big a view, it's a nice spot to relax. There's a big boulder at the top that is perfect for little kids to climb on or for tired parents to rest.

Top: Headed up the trail to the overlook
Bottom: The boulder at the top of the overlook is perfect for climbing on.

From Hathaway Hill, turn right to head down Drumlin Loop Trail. At the first fork, stay left and right at the second fork. You'll head down a grassy meadow, so be careful of scurrying creatures and poison ivy that seems to grow right on the trail. It's a good habit to wear closed-toe shoes. When you reach a large gravel path and field in front of you, you've made it to Boyce Field. Take a left here to round the northern side of the field.

Take a left at the T-intersection to head toward the main area of Drumlin Farm and where the real fun starts. As you approach the Crossroads Barn, the trail will turn to pavement and is ADA-accessible and stroller-friendly. You can take this trail as a sole loop if you are traveling with anyone who needs a wheelchair or stroller.

Take a right to head toward the Farm Life Center and the Red Barn. You'll see Bird Hill to your left before you hit the Farm Life Center. Bird Hill is filled with native raptors of the area including vultures,

The farm has sheep, goats, horses, pigs, bunnies, chickens, and more!

owls, falcons, and hawks. There is also a fisher that has an enclosure on Bird Hill—don't worry, she's away from the birds.

Just before you make it to the Farm Life Center, the New England Wildlife Explorations building is on your right, where the farm's resident red fox lives. Continue on the path to the Goat Shed, Red Barn, Pig Barn, and Green Barn, where you can see kid goats (in spring), sheep, pigs, cows, and a pony! Make your way around the other side and see the chickens in the Poultry House (there's a bunny here too!).

The Learning Garden to your left allows you to see what types of plants are native and good for pollinators and other animals. You can participate in harvesting the crops in the fall when they're ready to be picked! There is also a small playground for kids to get more energy out. Pass by the Farm Life Center to go back toward the Farm Stand and Visitor Center. Restrooms are on your right on the way out.

MILES AND DIRECTIONS

0.00 Start at the parking lot and head up to the Farm Stand and toilets. Use the restrooms here, because other toilets won't be available until farther along on the trail.

0.10 The Farm Stand and toilets are located here. Go back the way you came after you've paid the fee. Head out on the Ice Pond Trail.

0.20 Take a left onto Hayfield Loop. Ignore any trails to your left or right, and continue straight.

0.70 Take the trail to your left to continue up Hayfield Loop.

DRUMLIN FARM LOOP

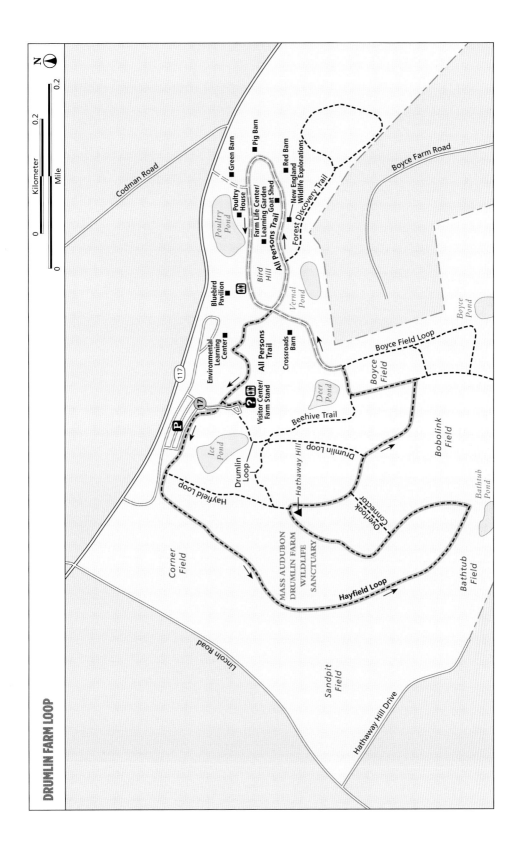

Top: The playground in the garden has a steering wheel so kiddos can pretend to ride a tractor.
Bottom: The experimental garden with the goats in the background

BOBOLINKS! BOBO-WHAT?

Massachusetts Audubon Society has worked with farmers across the state as well as Vermont and New York over countless years to adjust their haying schedule and support grassland nesting birds. Bobolinks are one such bird!

Bobolinks used to be fairly common across northeastern forests until farming practices destroyed their nesting habitat. Farmers have gradually plowed their fields earlier and more often due to economic pressures, so Massachusetts Audubon Society helps them with financial incentives to delay their plowing. Over the course of several years, the Bobolink Project has helped bobolinks come back in the area.

If you're lucky enough to see one while you're at Drumlin Farm, look for a black belly with a white and yellow back/wings. You'll likely hear their beautiful chirping in the meadows before you see them. The male calls are reminiscent of a metallic, happy chirping song and usually bring a smile across my face every time I hear them. I hope it does for you too!

0.90   Reach the highest point on the property at Hathaway Hill. Go down the Drumlin Loop Trail.

1.00   Stay left at the fork to continue on Drumlin Loop. At the next fork, stay right to go on the Overlook Connector Trail.

1.10   Take a left when you hit Boyce Field and a large gravel path. Continue around the north section of the field.

1.20   As you round the field, take a left to head toward the main area of the farm.

1.40   Take the trail to the right to head toward the Farm Life Center and the Red Barn.

1.50   Here is the Goat Shed after passing the Learning Garden and Farm Life Center on your left.

1.60   The Poultry House occurs on the northern side of this ADA-accessible trail after you've passed the Red Barn and Pig Barn. There is also a small playground in the Learning Garden to your left.

1.70   Turn right to head back to the Farm Stand and Visitor Center.

1.90   Arrive back at the trailhead.

VERMONT HIKES

Sunset along the
Colchester Causeway

18 SHELBURNE FARMS TRAIL

With sweeping views of Lake Champlain and some of the most stunning formal gardens, the trails around Shelburne Farms should not be missed. You can get a behind-the-scenes look at how artisanal cheddar is made at the on-site cheese-making room, view the many animals that call Shelburne Farms home, or take a walk to check out the maple sugaring process. There is so much going on at this working farm!

Start: At the Farm trailhead
Elevation gain: 600 feet
Distance: Up to 5.1 miles
Difficulty: Easy to strenuous, depending on the route you choose
Hiking time: 2 to 5 hours
Seasons/Schedule: Year-round, sunrise to sunset; the Welcome Center is open daily from 10:00 a.m. to 6:00 p.m.; closed Thanksgiving and Christmas
Fees and permits: Fee required
Trail contact: Shelburne Farms, 1611 Harbor Rd., Shelburne, VT; (802) 985-8686; https://shelburnefarms .org
Dog-friendly: Not allowed
Trail surface: Pavement, gravel, grass, and dirt

Land status: Shelburne Farms
Nearest town: Burlington, VT
Other trail users: None
Water availability: Yes, at the Farm Barn, Welcome Center, and near the Formal Gardens
Maps: Shelburne Farms trail map
Age range: All ages
Toilets: Yes, at the Farm Barn and Welcome Center
Stroller/Wheelchair compatibility: Yes, but only on parts of the Farm Trail and North Gate Path
Resting benches: Yes, several along the trail
Potential child hazards: Crossing some roads and potential for bees in the garden areas
Gear suggestions: Insect repellent

FINDING THE TRAILHEAD

From Burlington, head south on Route 7 for approximately 5 miles. Turn right onto Bay Road for 1.7 miles. At the stop sign, go straight to cross over Harbor Road and into the entrance to Shelburne Farms. A large parking lot is off to the right. Park anywhere. **GPS:** 44.395615 / -73.247695

THE HIKE

Shelburne Farms lies on the banks of Lake Champlain just south of Burlington. When you arrive at the parking lot, pop into the Farm Store and Welcome Center to donate what you can. Entrance to the farms is free, but they rely on donations to help keep these trails accessible to everyone.

There are two ways to start your trek around Shelburne Farms. You can walk the 0.5 mile to the Farm Barn, or you can take the tractor shuttle that leaves from the parking lot every half-hour. If you take the tractor shuttle, it'll shave off about 1.5 miles from your round-trip length.

When you arrive at the massive Farm Barn, bask in the immense beauty of this late-nineteeth–century building. It underwent a $3 million renovation back in the mid-1990s to make it what it is today. Not only is it home to the farm's animals, it is also a

Top: A happy kiddo with a lollipop and a skip in his step as he heads toward the Farm Barn
Bottom: The Farm Barn is full of cows, sheep, goats, horses, chickens, and more!

cheese-making facility, an organic bakery, an independent furniture maker, an elementary school, an education center, and the farm's administrative offices.

You might spend quite a bit of time here and throughout the buildings. There are several rooms with games and things to play. Many times there are children's programs, including wool weaving and nature walks. Ask the staff at the Welcome Center what is on the calendar for the day to make sure you don't miss out.

Once you have seen everything you want at the Farm Barn, continue on the trail. Head around the back of the Farm Barn to head up the Lone Tree Hill Trail. On the way, look to your left to see the tubes connecting the dozens of sugar maple trees that they use to make maple syrup in late winter (usually February). Make the ascent up Lone

Tree Hill, the highest point on the property. If you look out to the west, across Lake Champlain, you will see the many mountains of the High Peaks region of the Adirondacks in New York.

Take a left to head down the wide path of the Farm Trail, and then take your next left to head toward the western side of the property. The trail brings you to Sugarbush Road, which you'll walk alongside. There shouldn't be that many cars on this road, because the only people who use it are the guests at the inn and the farm staff. Still, take caution with your kids on all roads.

Eventually a small trail will veer off the road to the right. Follow this, the Garden Trail, for 0.2 mile. At that point you'll be back on the North Gate Path, which you'll follow to an unmarked trail to head toward the Formal Gardens.

Make sure your nose is booger-free so you can smell all the scents wafting in the air here. Check each flower for bees and other pollinators before putting your nose anywhere near the plants though! When you've smelled all the beautiful fragrances, head back the way you came.

Once you make it back to the the Farm Barn, check out where the cheese-

There are some great play spaces for kids where you can pull your own horse and cart.

making process is. Has the whey been drained yet? Are curds forming? Maybe they're in the process of chopping up the cheese into smaller sections, called "fingers," and about to cool them rapidly. Give one last look at all the farm animals before you head down the trail and back to the Welcome Center. You can also take the tractor shuttle the 0.5 mile back. Shuttles run daily from 10:00 a.m. until 4:00 p.m., from late spring through Labor Day. End your day at the Farm Store and Welcome Center to pick up some cheese and maple syrup to take home.

MILES AND DIRECTIONS

0.00 Start at the main parking lot next to the Farm Store and Welcome Center and take the Farm Trail.

0.50 Reach the Farm Barn, where you can view many different types of animals and the cheese-making area.

0.70 Take a left onto the Lone Tree Hill Trail.

0.80 Go left to continue on the Lone Tree Hill Trail to keep ascending.

Top: A view of the Farm Barn from the lookout in the farm's northwestern corner
Bottom: At the summit of Lone Tree Hill looking west toward the High Peaks of the Adirondack Mountains across Lake Champlain

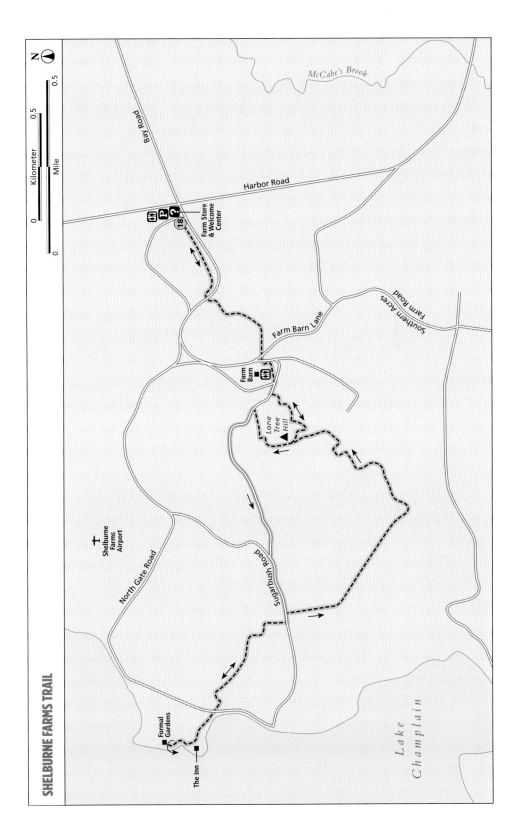

SHELBURNE FARMS TRAIL

McCabe's Brook

Bay Road

Harbor Road

N

Kilometer
0   0.5   0.5

Mile
0   0.5

Farm Store & Welcome Center

18 ⟨2⟩

Farm Barn Lane

Southern Acres Farm Road

Farm Barn

Lone Tree Hill

Shelburne Farms Airport

North Gate Road

Sugarbush Road

Formal Gardens

The Inn

Lake Champlain

0.90 Reach the highest point on the property at Lone Tree Hill. Continue north along the Farm Trail.

1.20 Take a left to get back on the wide gravel path of the Farm Trail. Ignore other trails that spur off this one and continue straight on the Farm Trail.

1.70 Here you'll hit Sugarbush Road and walk alongside it.

1.90 Veer right off Sugarbush Road to get on the Garden Trail.

2.10 Hit the North Gate Path and turn right.

2.30 Cross over the North Gate Road and continue straight on an unmarked path to the Formal Gardens.

2.50 These are the Formal Gardens in front of the inn. Turn back around when you're finished smelling all the fragrant flowers.

2.70 Reach North Gate Road again and continue straight to get on North Gate Path.

2.80 Keep straight to get back on the Garden Trail.

3.10 Turn left onto Sugarbush Road, which follows the North Gate Path, but then take an immediate right onto the Farm Trail.

3.20 At the fork, stay left.

3.30 At this fork, also stay left.

3.60 Turn left to continue on the Farm Trail and head back to the Farm Barn.

3.90 Stay right at the fork to summit Lone Tree Hill once again.

4.10 Arrive at the summit of Lone Tree Hill. Descend the hill by taking the Lone Tree Hill Trail down and back to the Farm Barn.

4.40 Reach the Farm Barn once again.

5.10 Arrive back at the trailhead and the Farm Store and Welcome Center.

CUT THE CHEESE!

Shelburne Farms is known for many things, but what sets this farm apart from other farms is the artisanal cheese they make on-site. Visitors can view the process through glass windows that look into the cheese-making room.

Every day fresh milk is brought into the cheese-making room around eight in the morning. The milk is hosed into the vat in the cheese-making room, and then slowly warmed while culture is added to the mixture. After an hour an enzyme called rennet is added to help the cheese begin to solidify. Curds start to form only after about half an hour and then separate into quarter-inch cubes. About 10 percent of the milk is made into those quarter-inch cubed curds, while the other 90 percent separates out as liquid whey, which the farm uses as fertilizer.

The liquid whey is drained, and the curds are cut into slabs and stacked to continue acidification. Once those slabs are at the desirable pH, they're cut up into curd "fingers" and cool slowly while a cheesemaker uses a pitchfork to flip them. Next, salt is added and the cheese is put into molds. Approximately 7 hours after the milk was first delivered, the cheese is ready to be formed into 40-pound blocks. Then they age for anywhere from six months to four years before they reach the shelves of the Farm Store.

19 CLARENDON GORGE VIA LONG TRAIL

The Long Trail traverses the main ridge throughout Green Mountain National Forest. As the oldest continuous footpath in the United States, the Long Trail is thru-hiked by many every year. But if you don't have time to hike all 272 miles, walk the section between Clarendon Gorge in the north and Route 140 in the south.

Start: At the Long Trail trailhead
Elevation gain: Up to 2,550 feet
Distance: Up to 10 miles
Difficulty: Moderate to strenuous depending on length
Hiking time: 2 to 8 hours
Seasons/Schedule: Year-round
Fees and permits: None
Trail contact: US Forest Service, Green Mountain and Finger Lakes National Forests, PO Box 220, Rutland, VT; (802) 747-6700; www.greenmountainclub.org/the-long-trail
Dog-friendly: Allowed on leash
Trail surface: Dirt

Land status: US Forest Service
Nearest town: Clarendon, VT
Other trail users: None
Water availability: None
Maps: Long Trail map—Upper Falls section
Age range: Kids in carriers or those with extensive trail experience if doing the full 10 miles
Toilets: None
Stroller/Wheelchair compatibility: No
Resting benches: None
Potential child hazards: Drop-offs around the suspension bridge
Gear suggestions: Trekking poles

FINDING THE TRAILHEAD

From Lebanon, take I-91 South for 18.6 miles. Take exit 8 for VT 131 toward US 5/VT 12. Turn right onto VT 131 West for 16 miles. Turn right onto VT 103 North for approximately 20 miles. Look for signs for Long Trail parking on your left and pull into the parking lot. **GPS:** 43.521232 / -72.925272

THE HIKE

Start your hike at the northern tip of this out-and-back trail. When you've parked, head over to the kiosk and look for any alerts in the area before making your way down the narrow path to the suspension bridge. Sometimes there are notices about bears or other wildlife in the area, as well as fire restrictions. If all is clear, then head out.

Within just 0.1 mile, the suspension bridge will come into view. If you've got toddlers or very small children with you, make sure to watch them as they go across the bridge. The bridge itself is completely fenced in, so there's no way for a child to accidentally fall into the boulders and rushing water below.

Cross the bridge and continue straight on the Long Trail. However, if you aren't doing the full 10.0 miles, this is a great place to stay and hang out for a few hours. If you traverse down the path to your left, you can head down to the river below. Be careful on the rocks, as they can be slippery when wet. Kids can spend hours flipping the rocks to see what creatures might be hiding underneath or skipping rocks along the water's edge.

Top: It's a short walk down the path to Clarendon Gorge.
Bottom: Only a few tenths of a mile from the trailhead, Clarendon Gorge has some dramatic views.

SECTION- VERSUS THRU-HIKING

Many outdoor enthusiasts have heard the terms *section-hiking* and *thru-hiking*. But what exactly is the difference? Thru-hiking is what you often see in movies and on the news. The film *Wild* with Reese Witherspoon depicts Cheryl Strayed's thru-hiking experience along the Pacific Crest Trail.

Thru-hiking simply means hiking a long-distance trail in one go. For instance, thousands of hikers start in April down in Georgia to try their hand (or should I say foot) at hiking the Appalachian Trail, which heads all the way up to Mount Katahdin in Maine.

However, not everyone can nor desires to hike 2,000-plus miles in one fell swoop. Instead, they do sections at a time. This is called section-hiking. Hikers can do a little bit here and there, not necessarily in geographic order, but still finish the entirety of the Appalachian Trail without having to take months off work.

Talk to your children about section- versus thru-hiking and see if they'd be interested in doing a long-distance trek. Start slowly by trying a few overnight backpacking trips along the Long Trail in Vermont to spark their interest.

The suspension bridge over Clarendon Gorge

Back over the suspension bridge
to head back to the car

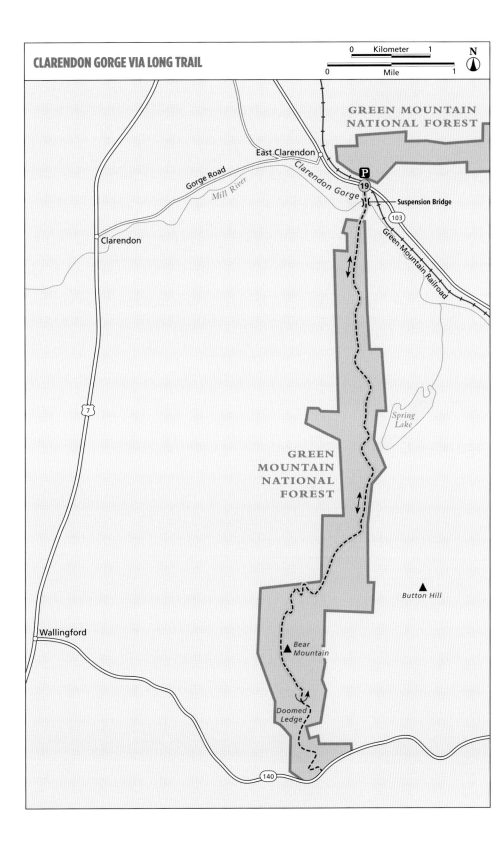

0   Kilometer   1

0   Mile   1

N

GREEN MOUNTAIN
NATIONAL FOREST

East Clarendon

Gorge Road

Clarendon Gorge

Mill River

P

19

Suspension Bridge

103

Clarendon

Green Mountain Railroad

Spring
Lake

GREEN
MOUNTAIN
NATIONAL
FOREST

7

Button Hill

Wallingford

Bear
Mountain

Doomed
Ledge

140

If you and your kids are up for a trek, then keep hiking down the Long Trail. Green Mountain National Forest is called "Green" because of the trees that blanket the entire area, including mountain summits. You'll traverse through hemlock and pine forest as well as beech, birch, and maple stands. There are not a lot of viewpoints along this trail, so it might not be as exciting for young children.

Nearly 4.5 miles from the start, you will reach the summit of Bear Mountain, which stands at 2,231 feet above sea level. Unfortunately, like many summits in Green Mountain National Forest, the view is obscured by trees. If you happen to do this trail in late fall or winter, when leaves have dropped from the trees, you'll be able to see through the trunks at the surrounding mountains around you.

Head down the trail another 0.75 mile to Doomed Ledge, a rocky outcrop with a vista looking southwest. You can keep heading south to Route 140 if you've got a car or shuttle to bring you back to the car you parked off Route 103. If not, head back the way you came.

The hike back can feel long, so if you've got smaller kids with you, make sure to take plenty of breaks to rest their little legs. This trail is meant mostly for kids who are still in carriers (usually around the age of 2 or younger) and those with much more trail experience. But what's nice about this trail is that the really exciting part is just 0.1 mile in, and you can turn around anytime you like. On your way back, again, stop at the suspension bridge to take in the views of Clarendon Gorge. Head back up to your car at the trailhead when the kids are tuckered out.

MILES AND DIRECTIONS

0.00 Start at the parking lot and head south on the Long Trail.

0.10 Head over the suspension bridge.

4.30 Reach the summit of Bear Mountain.

5.05 Reach Doomed Ledge. Turn around here, or you can continue south to Route 140 if you have a car/shuttle waiting for you.

5.80 Summit Bear Mountain again and continue north on the trail.

9.90 Head back over the suspension bridge.

10.0 Arrive back at the trailhead.

20 COLCHESTER CAUSEWAY

Sometimes you have to hang up your hiking boots for a bike helmet instead. The Colchester Causeway is the perfect "hike" to do just that. Although you can walk this trail, it's best experienced as a bike ride. I highly suggest taking this trail as either a sunrise or sunset ride, as the views over Lake Champlain are unparalleled in the early morning or late evening orange, pink, and purple glow.

Start: At the Causeway Connector Path
Elevation gain: 100 feet
Distance: 9.4 miles
Difficulty: Moderate only because of length
Hiking time: 2 to 5 hours
Seasons/Schedule: Year-round
Fees and permits: None
Trail contact: Town of Colchester, 781 Blakely Rd., Colchester, VT; (802) 264-5500; https://colchestervt.gov/facilities/facility/details/Causeway-Park-6
Dog-friendly: Allowed on leash
Trail surface: Dirt, gravel, and pavement

Land status: Town of Colchester
Nearest town: Colchester, VT
Other trail users: Mountain bikers
Water availability: None
Maps: Causeway Park trail map
Age range: All ages
Toilets: Yes, at Airport Park
Stroller/Wheelchair compatibility: Yes
Resting benches: Yes, picnic tables at the trailhead
Potential child hazards: Crossing some roads and drop-offs into Lake Champlain
Gear suggestions: Bikes (as they are the most common way to do this trail) and headlamps

FINDING THE TRAILHEAD

From Montpelier, follow I-89 North to US 2 West/US 7 North in Colchester. Take exit 16 from I-89 North to US 2/US 7 toward Winooski/Colchester, about 38 miles. At the end of the ramp, take a left onto VT 127 South. Continue straight onto West Lakeshore Drive, then onto Holy Cross Road, and then take a slight left onto Colchester Point Road. After about 0.5 mile, take a right and then turn left. Parking is available at Airport Park and at the Mills Point Road lot. **GPS:** 44.543375 / -73.279817

THE HIKE

Start the trail on the southwestern side of the parking lot at Airport Park. If you are biking, you can park even closer at the Causeway Bike Path Parking Lot off Mills Point Road. If parking here, it takes about 2.0 miles off your round-trip length, which could mean everything if you have a cranky kid by the time the hike or bike ride is over.

Head out on the Island Line Trail, which is the bike path that leads down to the causeway. Because this is a bike path, take caution with your kids and educate them about safety around bikes and on bike paths. It's polite to stay off to one side so you can allow bikes to pass you as you hike down. For 0.25 mile, the trail parallels Colchester Point Road, which can be busy at times.

Eventually the trail veers right off the road and makes a beeline for Mills Point Road and where the other parking lot is located. There's a crosswalk to cross Mills Point Road with a button that flashes warning lights to anyone on the road.

Top: The trail starts out on a tree-covered gravel path—make sure to watch out for bikes!
Bottom: Sunset is a great time to walk along this path.

After about another 0.5 mile, the path will open up to a wide sky and endless views of Lake Champlain. Make your way across the causeway. You can go as little or far as you and your kids' hearts desire. As you walk farther out onto the causeway, you will pass Law Island, Sunset Island, and Stave Island on your left. The large landmass to your right is the mainland of Vermont, while to your left is the mainland of New York. Lake Champlain is split in half north to south and creates part of the border between the two states.

About 4.0 miles into the hike/bike ride, you'll reach a gap in the causeway for boats to travel from one side to the other. If you want to continue on the trail, there is a bike/pedestrian ferry to usher you across to the other side. You can also choose to turn around here if you desire.

Top: Looking out to Lake Champlain
Bottom: The path is flanked by lots of flowers and plants, which also means there's quite a few bugs.

If you make it to the other side of the causeway, you'll be on one of the islands that are peppered throughout Lake Champlain. Turn back around to make your way back across the causeway. If you are doing this trail in the early morning or late evening for a sunrise or sunset hike/ride, have headlamps and the lights on your bike turned on to stay safe.

When you make it back to the trailhead, take a break at Airport Park. There's a nice playground for kids to play on, as well as basketball and tennis courts. In case an almost 10.0-mile hike/bike ride didn't get all their energy out, you can really drain them for a quiet car ride home.

The sun is just about to dip in the horizon over the mountains across Lake Champlain.

MILES AND DIRECTIONS

0.00 Start at the Colchester Connector Path in the southwestern part of the parking lot at Airport Park.

0.30 Veer right off the road to stay on the path.

1.00 Cross Mills Point Road to continue on the bike path.

1.40 Begin hiking or biking the causeway.

4.10 Take the bike/pedestrian ferry to the other side.

4.70 Reach the other side of Colchester Causeway and then turn around to head back the way you came.

5.30 Once again, take the bike/pedestrian ferry south.

8.00 You are now back on the mainland.

8.40 Cross back over Mills Point Road.

9.10 Take a left back onto Colchester Point Road.

9.40 Arrive back at the trailhead.

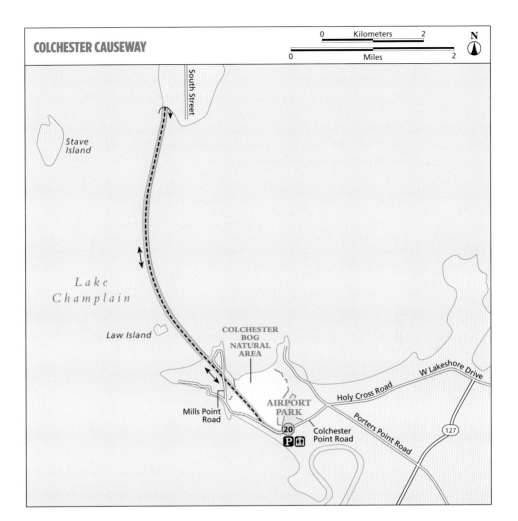

0   Kilometers   2

0   Miles   2

N

South Street

Stave Island

Lake Champlain

Law Island

COLCHESTER BOG NATURAL AREA

W Lakeshore Drive

Holy Cross Road

AIRPORT PARK

Mills Point Road

20

Colchester Point Road

Porters Point Road

127

LAKE CHAMPLAIN WILDLIFE

The Lake Champlain basin is full of diverse ecosystems that harbor many species of wildlife, including several endangered and threatened species in the region. Many bird enthusiasts flock (no pun intended) to Lake Champlain to cross bird species off their "life list." The most common birds you'll encounter on the lake include great blue herons, white egrets, Canada geese, ospreys, and turkey vultures. You might get lucky and see the rarer Merlin falcons or bald eagles.

Mammals are also in abundance on the lake, including the adorable American mink, chipmunks, squirrels, and North American beavers. Rarer are sightings of the American marten. If amphibians are more your style, the yellow-spotted salamander, leopard frog, and painted turtle are also residents of the lake. Oh, and there are a variety of bat species, including endangered/threatened species like the little brown bat, eastern small-footed bat, and more! So don't forget the binoculars on this hike, and grab some wildlife guides on your way out too.

21 OWL'S HEAD MOUNTAIN

There is a whole lot of bang for very little buck if you are lucky enough to snag a spot at the upper parking lot of Owl's Head Mountain. In just 0.25 mile, you will be greeted with sweeping views looking west into the Green Mountains. This is an ideal spot for taking in the autumn colors blanketing the tree-covered mountains that make up the bulk of Green Mountain National Forest.

Start: At the gate on Owl's Head Scenic View Road
Elevation gain: 25 to 450 feet
Distance: 0.5 to 2.2 miles
Difficulty: Easy to moderate (depending on the trailhead)
Hiking time: 1 hour if hiking from the parking lot, 2 hours if hiking from the road
Seasons/Schedule: Year-round, gravel road to the upper parking lot at the summit opens at 10:00 a.m.
Fees and permits: None
Trail contact: Groton State Forest, 1 National Life Dr., Davis 2, Montpelier, VT; (888) 409-7579; https://fpr .vermont.gov/groton-state-forest

Dog-friendly: Allowed on leash
Trail surface: Gravel and dirt
Land status: Vermont Department of Forests, Parks, and Recreation
Nearest town: Groton, VT
Other trail users: None
Water availability: None
Maps: Groton State Forest trail map
Age range: All ages
Toilets: Yes, at the summit parking lot
Stroller/Wheelchair compatibility: No
Resting benches: Yes, at the summit
Potential child hazards: Some steep drop-offs and walking on road
Gear suggestions: Trekking poles

FINDING THE TRAILHEAD

From Montpelier, take Route 2 East for 12 miles. Turn right onto VT 232 South for 5.5 miles and then turn left onto Owl's Head Scenic View Road. This road is gated from 4:00 p.m. until the following morning at 10:00. You can park next to the gate, but do not block access to the road. If the gate is open, drive up the steep gravel road to the summit parking lot. **GPS:** 44.308190 / -72.302914

THE HIKE

The first time I did this hike, I did not realize that the road going to the upper parking lot near the summit opened at 10:00 a.m., which meant I, instead, had to haul myself up a steep gravel road for the bulk of the hike. It was still well worth the effort though, so if you wanted to do an earlier hike, there is no need to wait for the gate to open at 10:00 for you to make the trek up.

You can park just outside the gate that blocks access to Owl's Head Scenic View Road. (Be sure not to block the entrance for when staff comes to open the gate, though.) However, do not park on the side of Route 232, as there is no shoulder for you to pull out on. If there is no parking outside the gate, you can head to New Discovery State Park and take the Owl's Head Mountain Trail up (it's about 3.0 miles round-trip).

Walking up the gravel road is steep and a steady ascent, so take your time. There are no views or interesting things to see as you walk up, so come prepared with games or activities to keep your kids motivated to get to the top. A favorite game I play with my

Top: At the summit looking south across the Green Mountains
Bottom left: If the gate is open, it's an easy trail up to the summit of Owl's Head.
Bottom right: The overlook where you can see Kettle Pond and the mountains beyond

A family and their dogs look out across the mountains.

son is to see how many different species of mammals he can name that might be in the area. Sometimes we go hunting for dinosaurs; unfortunately, we never find any.

You will reach the summit parking lot at just over 0.8 mile. There is a toilet up the road on your right. It is honestly one of the cleanest pit toilets I have ever experienced in my thirty years of adventuring. Even if you don't have to go, I suggest checking it out regardless—it's that nice! There is also a picnic pavilion a little farther down the road after the toilet. It's got a small view looking out onto the Green Mountains, but the better view is up at the summit.

Take the small trail on the southern side of the parking lot. From here, it is only 0.25 mile to the top and a much nicer trail. At the top there is a stone hut built in 1935 with a bench for you to sit and rest before taking in the views.

The rock outcrop that makes up the summit of Owl's Head Mountain looks west across Green Mountain National Forest. To the right, you will see Kettle Pond flanked by Kettle Mountain on its right and Hardwood Mountain on its left. In front of you, the pointier mountain is Spice Mountain, while the lake to the left is Lake Groton.

Go back the way you came when you are finished at the summit. Be careful on the way back down the road, especially if it is now after 10:00 a.m. Cars will be making their way up the road, although the speed limit is only 10 mph, so they should be going slow. The gravel on the dirt road also makes for slippery conditions, especially going down, so just be mindful of where you and your kids place your feet.

MILES AND DIRECTIONS

0.00 Start just off Route 232 at the gate on Owl's Head Scenic View Road.

0.85 Reach the summit parking lot. Head on the trail up to the summit.

1.10 The summit of Owl's Head Mountain.

1.35 Pass by the summit parking lot again.

2.20 Arrive back at the trailhead just past the gate.

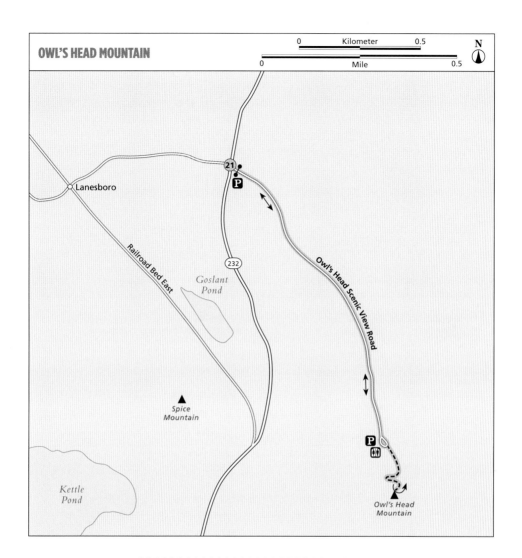

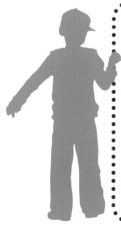

WHAT'S THE CCC?

To get the economy back up and running after the Great Depression, Franklin Roosevelt established the Civilian Conservation Corps (CCC). It essentially allowed young men to be employed by the government (and thus earn a place to sleep, steady meals, and a paycheck) while improving the public lands across the United States.

The work-relief program quickly became known as Roosevelt's "Tree Army," because they planted some 3.5 billion trees across the western United States. Seven hundred new state parks were also established during the CCC's tenure. Many of the structures built by the CCC are still in existence today, including the stone hut on top of Owl's Head Mountain and more famous places like Red Rocks Park and Amphitheater in Colorado.

22 STERLING POND TRAIL

Deep in the northern mountains of Vermont is a place where goods and livestock were once smuggled through passes to trade with Canada, which was illegal at the time. Now, the aptly named Smugglers' Notch State Park greets thousands of visitors every year. Take the short, but steep trail up to Sterling Pond to get a glimpse into the smugglers' world.

Start: At the Sterling Pond trailhead
Elevation gain: 965 feet
Distance: 2.3 miles
Difficulty: Moderate to strenuous due to steepness
Hiking time: 4 hours
Seasons/Schedule: Road usually closes from mid-October through mid-May
Fees and permits: None
Trail contact: Smugglers' Notch State Park, 6443 Mountain Rd., Stowe, VT; (802) 253-4014; https://vtstateparks.com/smugglers.html
Dog-friendly: Allowed and off-leash
Trail surface: Dirt
Land status: Vermont State Parks, Department of Forest, Parks, and Recreation

Nearest town: Stowe, VT
Other trail users: None
Water availability: Yes, at Smugglers' Notch Visitor Center
Maps: Smugglers' Notch State Park trail map
Age range: Kids in carriers or those with extensive trail experience
Toilets: Yes, at Smugglers' Notch Visitor Center
Stroller/Wheelchair compatibility: No
Resting benches: No
Potential child hazards: Lots of roots and large rocks to traverse
Gear suggestions: Trekking poles

FINDING THE TRAILHEAD

From Burlington, take I-89 South for approximately 25 miles. Take exit 10 toward Stowe. Turn left onto Route 100 North toward Stowe for 7.5 miles and then turn left onto Moscow Road. Stay on Moscow Road for 1.5 miles and then turn right onto Barrows Road for approximately 2 miles. Then turn right onto Luce Hill Road for just 0.5 mile before turning left onto Route 108 North. Stay on Route 108 North for approximately 7.5 miles. Parking for the trail is on the left and right—park wherever you can find a spot. **GPS:** 44.556625 / -72.794251

THE HIKE

Head northwest of Stowe to Smugglers' Notch State Park for a moderate hike up to Sterling Pond. The trail is steep with a continual 10 percent grade almost the entire way. There are lots of big boulders and roots to get up and over, so only kids with more trail experience should attempt this trail, or they should be carried in a child carrier the entire way.

Two miles might not seem like a very long hike, but the steady ascent up to Sterling Pond makes this a more strenuous hike than your average trail. Start the hike at the opposite side of the parking lot and information center. It doesn't matter where you park—this area is very busy, especially during the fall and on weekends, so wherever you can find a spot, take it!

Top: It's a tough ascent heading up to Sterling Pond, so make sure to pace yourself.
Bottom: A perfect sunny spot to rest and have a snack

Across the street from the main parking area is the start of Sterling Pond Trail. Almost immediately the trail quickly ascends and doesn't relent until you reach the Long Trail almost a mile in. Take your time and take plenty of breaks to make sure you or your kids do not burn out too quickly.

The trail is mostly dirt and large rocks with plenty of water cascading down. This can make for slippery and dangerous conditions, so always take heed on where you step. Trekking poles—or as my son likes to call them, "trail swords"—help tremendously during this hike, especially on the way down.

At 0.9 mile, the trail reaches the junction of the Long Trail. Vermont's 272-mile-long trail makes its way from the Massachusetts border to the Canadian border and is traveled

There are tons of rocks and roots to jump off.

by many each year. You might meet a few thru-hikers during your hike! Turn left onto the Long Trail to reach Sterling Pond.

When you reach the pond, keep an eye on the water. You might see a few newts hanging out in the shallow parts near the edge. Be mindful of anyone nearby who might be fishing. It's tempting to throw rocks in the water, but remember to be polite to others who are recreating in the area.

Now make your way back down the trail and back to your car. I cannot implore you enough to go as slow as possible. The wet trail conditions (during all months of the year) make for very slippery footing, and a fall on this steep trail could be very harmful. If you have a small child who likes to walk, bring a backup child carrier in case he or she needs assistance getting down the big rocks on the trail.

Sterling Pond is a great place to skip rocks and find newts!

A beautiful spot on a hot day

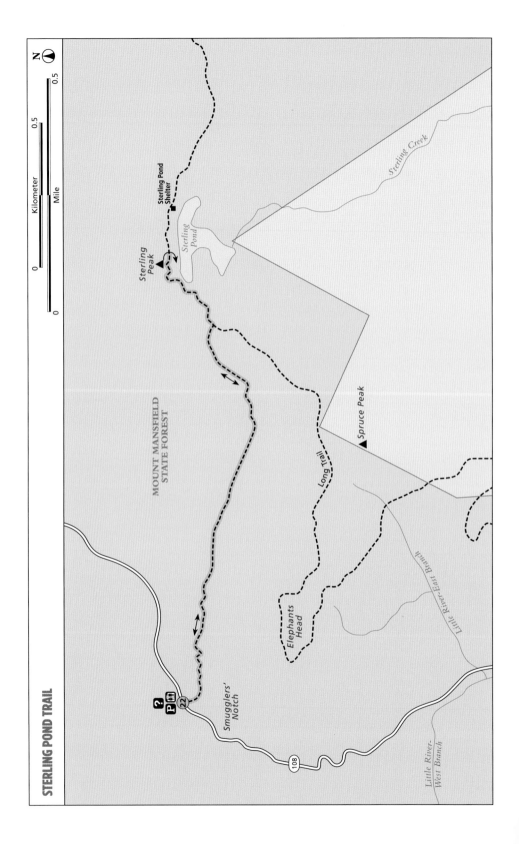

STERLING POND TRAIL

MOUNT MANSFIELD
STATE FOREST

Sterling Peak

Sterling
Pond

Sterling Pond
Shelter

Sterling Creek

Long Trail

Spruce Peak

Elephants
Head

Smugglers'
Notch

Little River-East Branch

Little River-
West Branch

108

22

N

Kilometer

0.5

0.5

Mile

0.5

0.5

A SITE EXPLODING WITH ILLEGAL ACTIVITY

Smugglers' Notch State Park has a shady history. Back in the early 1800s, President Thomas Jefferson put forth the Embargo Act of 1807, which ultimately forbade trade with both Britain and its territories. Vermonters depended heavily on trade with Canada, which was (and is still part of the Commonwealth) a territory of Britain at the time.

The Embargo Act forced Vermonters to start smuggling goods and herding cattle across the mountain pass that is now called Smugglers' Notch. The difficult terrain and assortment of caves in the area made it easy for tradesmen to smuggle things across the border. Even fugitive enslaved people used this route to make their way to freedom into Canada. The route was eventually improved to allow cars to pass through, which helped greatly during Prohibition, when alcohol became illegal. The caves were used to store the alcohol waiting to cross the border when it was safe to do so. Now Smugglers' Notch is home to hikers and outdoor enthusiasts.

When you get back to your car and back down the mountain, pop by Smugglers' Notch Resort, where you can partake in one of the many activities there. In summer make use of their water park, or take a mountain bike ride in autumn. Or simply pop by for lunch and maybe a scoop of the famed Ben & Jerry's ice cream.

MILES AND DIRECTIONS

0.00   Start at the Sterling Pond trailhead.

0.90   Hit the Long Trail and turn left.

1.00   Reach Sterling Pond, but continue down the trail for more views.

1.15   Reach the northern side of the pond. Take in the views and then head back the way you came.

1.30   Take in one last view of the pond before heading back down.

1.40   Take a right to veer off the Long Trail and back on the Sterling Pond Trail.

2.30   Arrive back at the trailhead.

23 BROUSSEAU MOUNTAIN

It does not get much more north than the trailhead for Brousseau Mountain. At the most northern edge of Vermont (you can basically reach out and touch Canada) lies a less-trafficked area than most places in this guide. Most visitors won't make the trek up here, but it would be a mistake to miss out on this place just because of its distance from civilization. For a fairly quick jaunt up a trail, you are greeted with sweeping vistas that dazzle any time of year, but especially in fall.

Start: At the Brosseau Mountain trailhead
Elevation gain: 650 feet
Distance: 2.2 miles
Difficulty: Moderate due to steepness
Hiking time: 3 hours
Seasons/Schedule: Year-round, except from March 15 to August 1, when the trail is closed for nesting peregrine falcons
Fees and permits: None
Trail contact: Vermont Fish & Wildlife Department, 1 National Life Dr., Davis 2, Montpelier, VT; (802) 828-1000; https://fpr.vermont.gov/bill-sladyk-wildlife-management-area
Dog-friendly: Not allowed

Trail surface: Dirt
Land status: Vermont Fish and Wildlife Department
Nearest town: Norton, VT
Other trail users: None
Water availability: None
Maps: Bill Sladyk Wildlife Management Area trail map
Age range: All ages
Toilets: No
Stroller/Wheelchair compatibility: No
Resting benches: None
Potential child hazards: Steep drop-offs at cliffs
Gear suggestions: Trekking poles and binoculars

FINDING THE TRAILHEAD

From Montpelier, take I-91 North for 6.5 miles and then take exit 23 toward US 5. Turn right onto US 5 North for 2 miles and then continue straight onto VT 114 North. Stay on VT 114 North for approximately 19 miles and then turn right onto Brousseau Mountain Road. End at the small parking lot where the road ends.
GPS: 44.976996 / -71.741130

THE HIKE

Out of all the hikes in this guide, this one up Brousseau Mountain is likely my favorite. There are not many places left in New England where you won't see others on the trail on any given day. But due to its rural-ness, the trail up to Brousseau Mountain is far less visited than many others.

Although most people tend to get outside in spring and summer, save this trail for a late-summer or autumn hike. The trail is closed from March 15 until August 1 every year for nesting peregrine falcons. Please adhere to trail closures, because these birds of prey are federally protected under the Migratory Bird Treaty Act.

Start your hike at the end of Brousseau Mountain Road. There are parking spots for maybe a half-dozen cars. Start the hike by heading up the wide path where the road ends. About 0.1 mile up, there is a sign showing you the way to Brousseau Mountain by taking

A misty autumn morning sends gloomy vibes along the trail.

a narrow path to your left. From here on out it's a steady but gradual ascent up to the cliffs on Brousseau Mountain.

This is a typical New England trail with beautiful hardwood and softwood trees flanking the sides and lots of roots sticking out of the ground. If there is even the tiniest bit of moisture, roots can be very slippery, so try not to step on them, or you'll likely end up face-first in the dirt. You'll know you are getting close to the cliffs when you see a

Top left: The sun finally starts to peak through the trees.
Top right: The trail mostly consists of dirt, but in the fall there are many fallen dead leaves making for slippery conditions.
Bottom: A dramatic view to breathe in all the fall colors

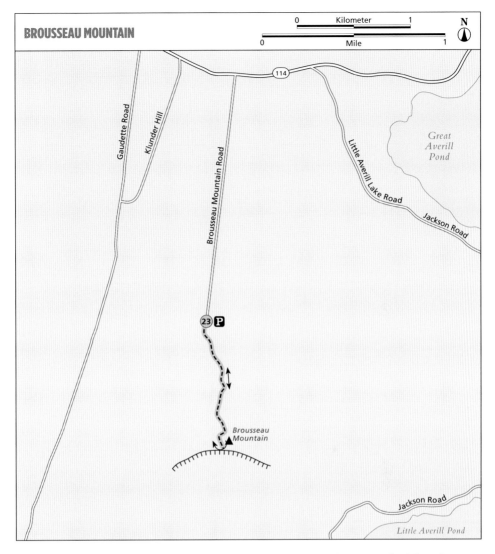

Gaudette Road

Klunder Hill

Brousseau Mountain Road

114

Little Averill Lake Road

Great Averill Pond

Jackson Road

23 P

Brousseau Mountain

Jackson Road

Little Averill Pond

sign that says, "Cliff access closed beyond this sign." If you happen to be hiking between March 15 and August 1, you'll have to turn around here and forgo the views. If you're hiking outside those times, though, proceed forward.

The cliffs offer immense vistas looking toward Little Averill Pond and the trees that cover every inch of the area. In autumn all colors along the spectrum pop on even the gloomiest of days. From the red of the oaks, the oranges of the maples, and the yellows of the cottonwoods, vibrant colors abound from every direction.

Keep an eye on your kids around the cliffs, as there are some steep drop-offs. Several of the cliffs have ledges just below them, so the photos look scarier than they are, but you should still take caution. Take your time soaking in all the views, as you will likely be the only people on the trail, especially if you go on a weekday.

When the kids start to get antsy, head back down the trail. If you want another beautiful and quick hike in the area to see a slightly different view, you can head over to Averill

The cliffs below are prime habitat for nesting peregrine falcons.

Mountain. Take a right onto Route 114 and travel about a mile. When you see the pond on your right, pull over and the trailhead will be across the road. It's a quick 0.5 mile up Averill Mountain with incredible views.

MILES AND DIRECTIONS

0.00 Start at the small parking lot at the end of Brousseau Mountain Road.

0.10 Veer left on the narrower path toward the summit.

1.10 Reach the cliffs overlooking Little Averill Pond.

2.10 Take a right to get back on the wide path to head back to your car.

2.20 Arrive back at the trailhead.

IT'S A BIRD, IT'S A PLANE! NO, WAIT, IT'S A BIRD

Although you likely won't see any peregrine falcons on this trail, they are still exquisite creatures to learn about. Historically, peregrine falcons were critically endangered and completely extinct in the eastern United States. They do not have many predators other than other birds of prey. Their biggest threat has always been, and still is, humans.

Thankfully, after DDT (which was a widely used pesticide) was outlawed in 1972 and peregrine falcons were added to the Endangered Species List, these incredible birds started making a comeback thanks to a variety of projects across the country. Nonprofits and government organizations worked in tandem to breed peregrine falcons in captivity and then release them into the wild. Due to these efforts, peregrine falcons have now been declassified from the Endangered Species List—a huge feat!

Peregrine falcons are beautiful birds of prey that rely on cliffs to nest and feed. They mate for life and almost always return to their nesting sites year after year. This is why the cliffs on Brousseau Mountain are so protected during those months of the year. Peregrine falcons also have killer eyesight and are the fastest known animal, clocking in at 242 mph when diving for prey.

24 TEXAS FALLS RECREATION AREA LOOP

Leave your Stetsons and cowboy boots at home, because this isn't Texas, folks. Instead, Texas Falls Recreation Area is home to several cascading waterfalls that flow along the Hancock Branch and Texas Brook (hence, the name). The stunning, aqua-blue waters are so clear, you can see every fish swimming around the pools. This short nature trail is perfect for kids and adults of any age.

Start: At the Texas Falls Nature trailhead
Elevation gain: 215 feet
Distance: 1.0 mile
Difficulty: Easy
Hiking time: 1 hour
Seasons/Schedule: Year-round
Fees and permits: None
Trail contact: Texas Falls Recreation Area, 99 Ranger Rd., Rochester, VT; (802) 767-4261; www.fs.usda.gov/recarea/gmfl/recreation/hiking/recarea/?recid=64953&actid=50
Dog-friendly: Allowed on leash

Trail surface: Pavement, gravel, and dirt
Land status: US Forest Service
Nearest town: Rochester, VT
Other trail users: Snowshoers
Water availability: None
Maps: Texas Falls Recreation Area trail map
Age range: All ages
Toilets: Yes, at the trailhead
Stroller/Wheelchair compatibility: No
Resting benches: None
Potential child hazards: None
Gear suggestions: None

FINDING THE TRAILHEAD

From Montpelier, follow Route 2 West for approximately 4 miles and then turn left onto VT 100B South. Travel on VT 100B South for about 33 miles and then turn right onto Route 125 West for 3 miles. Turn right onto Texas Falls Road and park at the first parking lot on your left. **GPS:** 43.935298 / -72.902141

THE HIKE

If you are looking for an easy trail on a hot summer day, the nature loop around Texas Falls Recreation Area is the trail for you. It is situated in the heart of Green Mountain National Forest off the Scenic Byway of Route 125.

The ease of access to this spot allows for an abundant amount of people to frequent the area, so do not expect to be alone on this trail. However, if you choose to come on a weekday earlier in the morning, you likely won't see too many others on the trail.

Start the trail across the road from where you parked. Cross the wide bridge to get over Hancock Branch and onthe nature trail. Enjoy some of the small trails off the main trail to take in the views of the waterfalls. Take a left when you get over the bridge to head northwest around the loop. For the first bit, you will parallel the creek and see many views of the cascading waterfalls.

As you reach the northern end of the nature loop, you will veer away from the stream and into a forested trail reminiscent of a fairy tale. Mosses, ferns, and lichens cover the ground and trees as if adding a protective layer to the delicate surface. Keep an eye out

Top: One of the many bridges throughout Texas Falls Recreation Area
Bottom: There are several lookouts for the falls.

for any fairies or trolls that might be in the area. Hopefully you brought some change in case a troll asks for money to grant you passage back across the bridge.

Even without any imagination, this area has an ethereal feel to it, and it is easy to get lost in the sounds and wonders of the forest around you. Make up a fairy tale with your kids as you work your way around the southern portion of the nature loop before you meet back up with the stream.

If you haven't already, take some of the many overlook trails to view the waterfalls and the plunging pools of crystal-clear water. See if you or your kids can count how many fish are in each of the pools. You can also talk about the geology of the gorge that makes up the cascading falls. Way back in the ice age, the melting ice carved through the

The falls cascade into crystal-clear, teal-colored pools.

bedrock that now flanks the Hancock Branch. There's even a large glacial pothole that you can see as you cross back over the bridge back to your car.

A picnic area lies just north of where you parked. You can take the kids closer to the stream while the other adults cook up some hot dogs and burgers on the grills provided at the site. These are available on a first-come, first-served basis for free. Please pack out what you pack in, as there are no garbage services at the recreation area.

The loop is shaded for its entirety.

FIDDLEHEADS

It is not a musical instrument that comes to mind when the term fiddlehead is brought up in nature. Out in the wilderness, fiddleheads are highly sought-after plants to serve in classy (and often pricey) restaurants. In actuality, fiddleheads are simply the younger parts of certain types of ferns.

Before they mature, ferns look a lot like fiddleheads—the coiled part of the stringed instrument. They are harvested in spring, before they completely unfurl their fronds. You might see a bunch of these fiddlehead ferns along the trail at Texas Falls Recreation Area, but do not pick them. For one, you should practice Leave No Trace principles and refrain from disturbing plant life when possible. Secondly, only certain ferns can be used for consumption and can be difficult for the layperson to identify. So leave it to the professionals and enjoy the fiddleheads with your eyes only. If you truly need to try one, head to one of the many local farmers' markets in the area during summer.

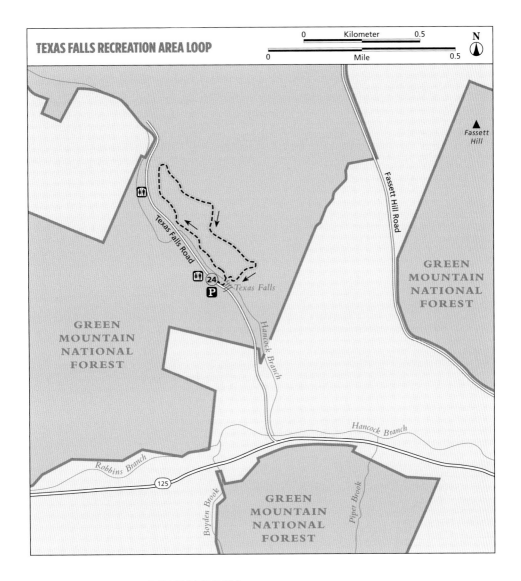

MILES AND DIRECTIONS

0.00 Start at the parking lot across from the waterfalls.

0.05 Walk over the bridge to get some great views of the waterfalls.

0.10 Take a left on the Texas Falls Recreation Area Nature Trail.

0.40 Reach the northern tip of the Nature Loop. Continue on the trail around the bend.

0.80 Reach the southern tip of the Nature Loop. Continue on the trail to head back to your car.

0.95 Go back over the bridge to return to your car.

1.00 Arrive back at the trailhead.

25 MOUNT OLGA TRAIL

Take in the big views atop a fire tower deep in the trees of Green Mountain National Forest. There are only sixteen fire towers left standing in the state; the others were allowed to go into disrepair as the state went for cheaper options to scout wildfires. Mount Olga is one of those sixteen still left standing, albeit a little precariously. But it's got 360-degree views, so well worth the climb if you can brave the stairs to get up there.

Start: At the Mount Olga trailhead
Elevation gain: 515 feet
Distance: 1.8 miles
Difficulty: Moderate
Hiking time: 2 hours
Seasons/Schedule: Year-round
Fees and permits: Fee required
Trail contact: Molly Stark State Park, 705 Route 9 E., Wilmington, VT; (802) 464-5460; https://vtstateparks .com/mollystark.html
Dog-friendly: Allowed on leash
Trail surface: Gravel and dirt
Land status: Vermont Department of Forests, Parks, and Recreation
Nearest town: Wilmington, VT

Other trail users: Cross-country skiers and snowshoers
Water availability: None
Maps: Molly Stark State Park trail map
Age range: All ages
Toilets: Yes, at the campground
Stroller/Wheelchair compatibility: No
Resting benches: No
Potential child hazards: Fire tower stairs are loose and potentially dangerous
Gear suggestions: Trekking poles and binoculars

FINDING THE TRAILHEAD

From Brattleboro, Vermont, follow VT 9 West/Western Avenue for approximately 16 miles. Turn left into the state park and park at the main parking area outside the ranger station. **GPS:** 42.852593 / -72.814615

THE HIKE

The hike up to the Mount Olga Fire Tower starts next to the ranger station within Molly Stark State Park. The trail takes you through a shaded path perfect for hot days in the summer. After you descend the dirt stairs to get on Mount Olga Trail, you will come to a small bridge over a small creek that feeds into Beaver Brook. Sometimes this creek is raging, especially during spring snowmelt or autumn rainstorms.

Continue on the trail through the spruces and hardwoods that make up the majority of Green Mountain National Forest. Ferns line most of the understory and keep small critters like mice and squirrels from being someone else's dinner. Stop every once in a while to listen to the sounds of scurrying feet and chatter from the small mammals that call Molly Stark home.

Molly Stark State Park is named after Elizabeth "Molly" Paige Stark, wife of John Stark, who was a respected general during the Revolutionary War. He fought hard for the Continental Army, but so did his wife. She recruited many men to fight for the cause and turned part of her home into an infirmary for wounded soldiers on both sides, all

Top: It's only 0.75 mile to the Mount Olga Fire Tower and summit.
Bottom: The trail has shade the entire way until you reach the fire tower.

while raising eleven children. She was quite a strong and independent woman—especially considering the time.

When you reach a T-intersection, stay to the left to head up to the fire tower. There is no view at the summit, unless you brave the five flights of stairs up to the platform. I will not lie and say this is an easy climb. Those with a fear of heights might find this part hard to do. The payoff at the top, though, is worth any butterflies in your stomach.

Unlike other fire towers, the Mount Olga Fire Tower is not as closed in on the stairs up the tower. This means that there is a higher likelihood of small children (or big ones for that matter) easily falling from the stairs. Either forgo heading up the stairs or be sure

It's a tall fire tower and has some sketchy steps—only you and your kiddos can decide if it's something you can climb.

to tell your kid to hang on to the railing the entire way—and watch them to be sure they do.

The view from the top is unprecedented. There are unobstructed vistas the entire way around. You can view the abandoned ski hills at Hogback Ski Area, which is now a backcountry ski site. If you head up here in summer, you'll be greeted by a blanket of green trees and endless blue sky. In autumn, though, the trees turn into a sea of orange, red, and purple hues as the fall foliage peaks.

THE HISTORY OF FIRE TOWERS

Back in the early 1900s, devastating wildfires decimated the western United States (as well as a few million acres in the Northeast). Early detection became a high priority for government officials so that the mistakes of the past would not be made again. Earlier you learned about the Civilian Conservation Corps (CCC) being known as Roosevelt's "Tree Army," but the CCC also built many of the fire lookouts still standing to this day.

Fire towers were used extensively over the following decades to catch the first glimpses of any wildfires that broke out over the large swaths of forests across the United States. Each fire tower was manned by federal or state government staff or volunteers who were trained at spotting wildfires. There are still several active fire towers within the country, but many (including those in Vermont) have either been decommissioned or have fallen into disrepair.

As technology improved, the use of small planes, the general public, and satellites have proven that fire towers are not needed as much as they used to be. What is their loss is now a hiker's gain, allowing 360-degree views on the summits where they are still standing.

Thrilling 360-degree views greet you if you're brave enough to head up the stairs to the top.

Never will you see more green
than this area in Vermont.

Head back down the tower, and be very careful on the way down. If kids get scared on the way down (it is actually scarier on the way down), have them go down the stairs backward. Basically, face the way you would going up but go down—it takes most of the fear out of them. If you want to return to your car, head back the way you came. However, if you want to add a bit more mileage onto your hike, walk the 0.5 mile down the Tower Trail to grab a glass of bourbon or moonshine at Vermont Distillers!

From the fire tower, head back the way you originally came and then turn left at the T-intersection. This brings you down a more gradual trail that loops back to the campground in the state park. When you hit the road (which is the campground loop), go right to find your way back to your car.

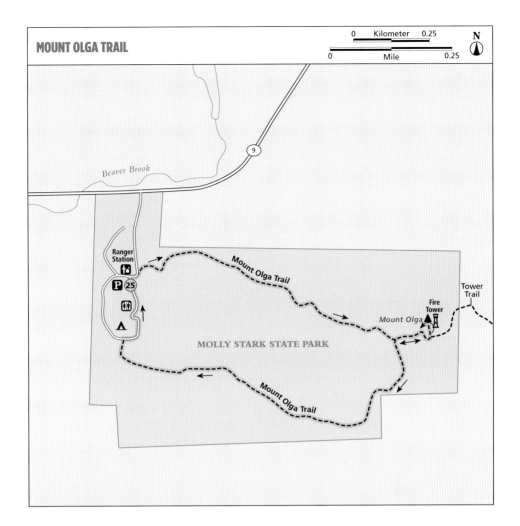

MILES AND DIRECTIONS

0.00 Start at the parking lot and head down the road until you see the trail to Mount Olga on the right.

0.10 Cross the road and a small bridge to continue on the trail.

0.60 At the junction, take a left to head toward the fire tower.

0.75 Reach the fire tower.

0.90 At the junction, go left to head down the loop.

1.70 Reach the campground loop. Head right on the road to get back to your car.

1.80 Arrive back at the trailhead.

26 PUTNEY MOUNTAIN

Head on up the unmaintained dirt road for the very short hike to Putney Mountain. It is a perfect hike in autumn to see migratory birds start making their way south for the winter or to simply take in autumn colors across the landscape. Whether you are a bird nerd, geology expert, or a simple lover of the outdoors, the short path up to the wide summit of Putney Mountain is well worth the precarious road that leads you up there.

Start: At the Putney Mountain trailhead
Elevation gain: 180 feet
Distance: 1.3 miles
Difficulty: Easy
Hiking time: 2 hours
Seasons/Schedule: Road to trailhead is not maintained in winter
Fees and permits: None
Trail contact: Putney Town Forest, 443 Putney Mountain Rd., Putney, VT; (802) 387-5862; www.putneyvt .org. Putney Mountain Association, PO Box 953, Putney, VT; www.putney mountain.org

Dog-friendly: Allowed on leash
Trail surface: Dirt
Land status: Town of Putney
Nearest town: Newfane, VT
Other trail users: Mountain bikers
Water availability: None
Maps: Putney Mountain–Pinnacle trail map
Age range: All ages
Toilets: No
Stroller/Wheelchair compatibility: No
Resting benches: No
Potential child hazards: None
Gear suggestions: Binoculars

FINDING THE TRAILHEAD

From Brattleboro, head north on VT 30 for approximately 12 miles. Turn right onto Radway Hill Road for just under 0.5 mile, which turns into Brookline Road/Grassy Brook Road. Continue for another mile and then turn right onto Putney Mountain Road. This is an unmaintained dirt road, so be careful if you don't have AWD/4WD or a high-clearance vehicle. Passenger cars can make it to the trailhead though. Continue on this road for approximately 2.3 miles until you see a small parking lot on your left. **GPS:** 42.996863 / -72.599030

THE HIKE

There are so many good things to say about Putney Mountain. You won't find many people on the trail of this southern Vermont mountain, and I have not figured out a reason why that is. Sure, the road to get there might be a little sketchy, but it's by no means dangerous. The parking area is large enough to fit a couple dozen cars, and it does usually fill up on autumn weekends, but that's about as busy as it gets.

Make your way to the large kiosk at the start of the trail to see if there are any announcements that you should pay attention to. The trail can be a little tricky to follow, as there are many social trails that have been created over the years. Try to stay on the trail as best as possible, but even if you lose your way, most trails end up at the summit, so it is hard to get lost.

As you traverse the trail, every so often there are signs off to the side describing things that you might find along the way. One sign discusses the importance of pileated

Top: It's only a half-mile to the summit of Putney Mountain.
Bottom: Random rock walls are scattered throughout most of New England.

woodpeckers, while another describes the types of trees in the area. One even describes the rocks that you are standing on, which are called a sheepback ledge. These are the leftover evidence that massive ice sheets moved south and gouged large glacial striations into the rock, showing the direction in which they moved.

After just over 0.5 mile, you will reach the summit of Putney Mountain. It is a large clearing where you can take in the views from the northwest and southeast. If you happen to be hiking between September 1 and November 15, you may see a few people standing around with binoculars and clipboards. A local group of bird monitors take watch on the mountain during those ten weeks to count the number of migratory birds

There's not a whole lot of
walking to get to mega views.

Top: This is a great place to watch the migration of hawks every September through November.
Bottom: Bring a picnic lunch to enjoy at the summit on a beautiful summer day.

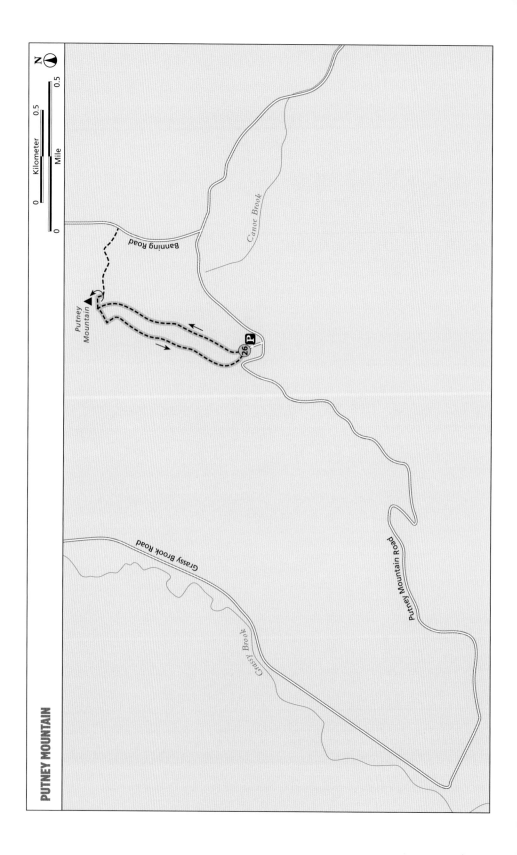

PUTNEY MOUNTAIN

N

0 Kilometer 0.5

0 Mile 0.5

Canoe Brook

Banning Road

Putney Mountain

26 P

Grassy Brook Road

Grassy Brook

Putney Mountain Road

making their way south. They are very friendly and knowledgeable; they only ask that you never stand in front of someone who is doing a count—this is a big no-no.

Head down through the clearing after you have gotten your fill of raptor-viewing and go left to head back to the trailhead. Again, there are several social trails that have popped up throughout the years, so try your best to stay on the main path. The trail is not well marked, so pay attention as best as possible.

If you are in the mood to check out more information about birds, drive about an hour north to the Vermont Institute of Natural Science to do the Forest Canopy Walk and learn more about the birds of prey within the state.

MILES AND DIRECTIONS

0.00 Start at the kiosk on the northern side of the parking lot.

0.05 Stay to the right at the fork to continue on the Nature/Ridgeline Trail.

0.65 Reach the summit of Putney Mountain and a clearing to take in the views. Head back on the West Cliff Trail on the western side of the loop.

1.25 Get back on the short trail back to the kiosk and the parking area.

1.30 Arrive back at the trailhead.

RAPTOR MIGRATION ON PUTNEY MOUNTAIN

Putney Mountain has been the site of a yearly migration by raptors for decades. Local volunteers keep a constant presence on the mountain from September 1 until November 15 to record the number of raptor sightings every year. Raptors include Cooper's hawks, American kestrels, ospreys, goshawks, northern harriers, and even a few peregrine falcons. This is the only raptor migration watch monitored full-time in the state of Vermont.

Some years they only count a few thousand over the course of ten weeks but other years, like in 2021, they counted more than 18,000 birds and had one day where the count was 6,000. Even the regular raptor monitors were in awe! If you happen to be hiking this time of year around the area, you will likely meet up with one of the many volunteers. They are very knowledgeable and friendly, so feel free to ask questions if they don't seem too busy.

27 QUECHEE GORGE—
DEWEY POND LOOP

Come experience Vermont's deepest gorge at Quechee Gorge State Park. Thousands of visitors enjoy the stunning scenery and drastic, vertical rock walls that flank the gorge every year. Heading out on the trail that towers above the Ottauqechee River offers a bit of relief from the crowds, though. The deep gorge is best viewed from the water's edge on the southern part of the state park and can only be accessed by walking.

Start: At the Quechee Gorge trailhead behind the visitor center
Elevation gain: 200 feet
Distance: 2.8 miles
Difficulty: Easy to moderate
Hiking time: 3 hours
Seasons/Schedule: Year-round, sunrise to sunset
Fees and permits: Fee required
Trail contact: Quechee State Park, 5800 Woodstock Rd., Hartford, VT; (802) 295-2990; https://vtstateparks .com/quechee.html
Dog-friendly: Allowed on leash
Trail surface: Gravel and dirt

Land status: Vermont Department of Forests, Parks, and Recreation
Nearest town: Hartford, VT
Other trail users: None
Water availability: Yes, at the visitor center
Maps: Quechee State Park geology and trail map
Age range: All ages
Toilets: Yes, at the visitor center
Stroller/Wheelchair compatibility: No
Resting benches: Yes, along the trail
Potential child hazards: Water can rise quickly if storms pass through
Gear suggestions: Trekking poles

FINDING THE TRAILHEAD

From Lebanon, take I-89 North for approximately 6 miles. Take exit 1 for US 4/ Woodstock Road toward Rutland/Quechee. Turn left onto US 4 West for approximately 3 miles. The entrance to the state park is on the left. Park at the visitor center. **GPS:** 43.636665 / -72.405653

THE HIKE

Start the hike behind the visitor center off Route 4 by descending down the concrete stairs. The trail starts out wide and under the cover of large hemlock and pine trees. The trail is covered with pine needles long since fallen from the towering trees above.

The wooden fence on your right helps keep your kids on the right path and from falling over the small drop-offs to the trail below. The trail levels off and it is an easy few tenths of a mile until you reach a T-intersection. Go left here to continue down the path toward the river access. The path is wide, and a metal fence borders the right side of the trail so there are no accidental slips down the rock walls of the gorge.

From here, the trail descends quickly and levels off once again when you reach a junction in the trail. Stay straight/to the right to continue down toward the river. You will see a few trails off to your right to head down to the river. Depending on the time of year and if there have been any recent storms, the river may be swiftly moving and at dangerously high levels. If that is the case, do not attempt to head down to the river.

The trail traverses a few switchbacks at the beginning to get down to the river.

Signs along the trail indicate that water can rise very quickly due to the gorge itself plus a dam upstream. Please take heed if there have been recent storms with a high amount of precipitation.

If the water is at manageable levels and not moving too quickly, feel free to romp around on the rocks. Depending on the water level, many pools will have filled up between the rocks. They're reminiscent of tide pools that you see at the ocean, but

Top: Careful on a rainy day—water rises fast!
Bottom: Lots of fish and tadpoles in the water equals one excited kiddo.

instead of starfish the pools are filled with tadpoles! Do not forget to look upstream to where you can see Quechee Gorge in all its glory.

After enjoying the coolness of the water and the beauty of the gorge, head back up on the trail and continue right to round the southern tip of the trail. Eventually, you will meet back up again with the trail you descended earlier. When you reach the trail on the right to bring you back to the visitor center, continue straight toward Dewey's Pond. You'll go under the Quechee Gorge Bridge and pass between the Ottauquechee River on your left and Dewey's Pond on your right.

The pond, which was once an oxbow of the Ottauquechee River, has turtles, frogs, and several waterfowl greeting its water, so be on the lookout. Turn around the way you came to make your way back to the bridge. Just after the bridge, hang a left to head back to the visitor center.

MILES AND DIRECTIONS

0.00   Start behind the visitor center at the Quechee Gorge trailhead.

0.20   Turn left to head down the gorge.

0.40   Stay right on the Quechee Gorge Trail to head down to the river. If the water is high, do not attempt to go in the river. Then continue on the trail.

0.80   Complete the loop of the southern portion of the trail and head back north toward the bridge.

1.10   Continue straight to go under the Quechee Gorge Bridge and head toward Dewey's Pond.

1.40   Reach the southern edge of Dewey's Pond. Walk on a wide, grassy path in between Dewey's Pond and the Ottauquechee River.

1.80   Reach the parking lot for Dewey's Pond. Turn back around to head back to the bridge.

2.60   Go back under the Quechee Gorge Bridge and then make an immediate left to head back to the visitor center.

2.80   Arrive back at the trailhead.

Quechee Gorge with the bridge overhead

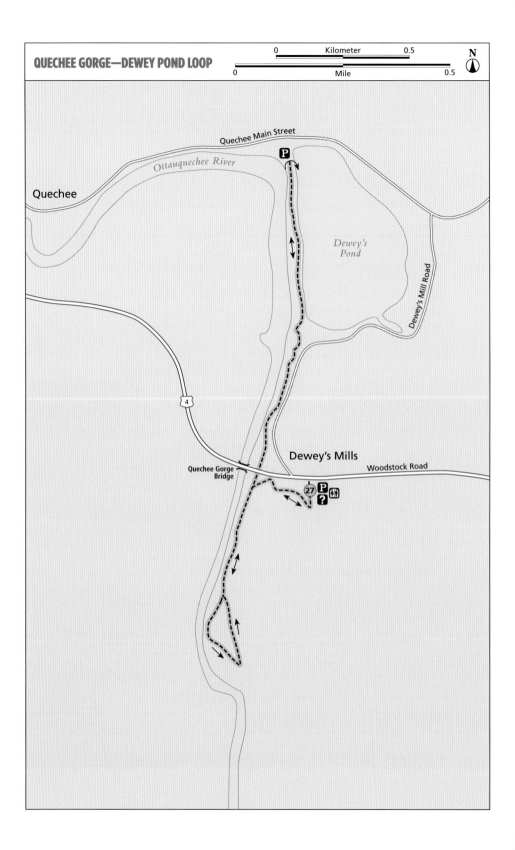

QUECHEE GORGE—DEWEY POND LOOP

0 ——— Kilometer ——— 0.5
0 ——— Mile ——— 0.5

N

Quechee Main Street

Ottauquechee River

Quechee

Dewey's
Pond

Dewey's Mill Road

4

Dewey's Mills

Quechee Gorge
Bridge

Woodstock Road

27
P
?

WHAT MAKES THAT "DUNK-DUNK" SOUND?

When you are visiting Dewey's Pond, you might hear a *dunk-dunk* sound. You might be surprised to learn that it is the advertisement call of the common green frog. This critter is sometimes known as the "banjo frog" due to its sharp, deep twang that sounds an awful lot like a banjo strum.

Even though Quechee Gorge is beautiful, do not miss out on Dewey's Pond, which is filled with all different types of sounds from a variety of wildlife. Painted turtles might be sunning themselves, while dragonflies hover above the water's surface hoping to snag an insect for lunch. Unfortunately, Dewey's Pond has slowly started to deteriorate with both an abundance of silt as well as a drastic attack of the invasive Eurasian water-milfoil. This fast-growing plant takes over the shallower sections of a waterbody, which blocks sunlight that is needed for native aquatic plants to thrive. In the coming decades, the wildlife that has called this pond home may need to move on to other places.

Water lilies on Dewey's Pond

NEW HAMPSHIRE HIKES

Looking down the boardwalk through the Flume Gorge in Franconia Notch State Park

28 ZEALAND FALLS HUT

The trail to Zealand Falls Hut is a leisurely walk through the woods that parallels several wetland areas. Keep an eye out for moose and other large mammals that might be using the trail to find food. Although this trail is one of the longer ones in this guide, the minimal elevation gain makes this a moderate walk for most kids and adults. Plus, yummy food awaits anyone who has cash when you reach the Appalachian Mountain Club (AMC) hut!

Start: The Zealand Falls trailhead
Elevation gain: 600 feet
Distance: 5.4 miles
Difficulty: Moderate
Hiking time: 6 hours
Seasons/Schedule: Road to trailhead is closed in winter
Fees and permits: Fee required
Trail contact: White Mountain National Forest, 71 White Mountain Dr., Campton, NH; (603) 536-6100; www.fs.usda.gov/whitemountain. Appalachian Mountain Club, 10 City Square, Boston, MA; (603) 466-2727; www.outdoors.org/destinations/massachusetts-and-new-hampshire/zealand-falls-hut
Dog-friendly: Allowed on leash

Trail surface: Gravel and dirt
Land status: US Forest Service
Nearest town: Bretton Woods, NH
Other trail users: None
Water availability: Yes, at the hut
Maps: White Mountains—Franconia to Pemigewasset trail map
Age range: Kids in carriers or those with extensive trail experience
Toilets: Yes, at the hut
Stroller/Wheelchair compatibility: No
Resting benches: Yes, at the hut
Potential child hazards: Slippery rocks near waterfalls
Gear suggestions: Trekking poles and insect repellent

FINDING THE TRAILHEAD

From Concord, take I-93 North for approximately 75 miles. Take exit 35 for Route 3 North toward Lancaster/Twin Mountain. Continue on Route 3 North for approximately 10 miles and then turn right on Route 302 East. After 2 miles, turn right onto Zealand Road when you see the signs for Zealand Recreation Area. Take the road for 3.5 miles, until you reach the end. Park in the large lot or anywhere along the road. **GPS:** 44.224839 / -71.478596

THE HIKE

You might feel a little queasy after bumping along the dirt road to the Zealand Falls trailhead, but the gradual walk up to the falls will make all your nausea subside. Start at the trailhead in the parking lot and head south along the trail that runs parallel to the Zealand River.

The first 2.5 miles of this trail are a pleasant ascent and allow plenty of opportunity for kids to get some energy out. The path is wide for most of the hike, allowing enough room for hikers to easily pass slower groups. Take a few breaks when the trail opens to the wetland areas surrounding the Zealand River. If you are hiking in late May or early June, you might get to witness all the pink lady's–slippers that flank the trail. They are one of the most beautiful (and easily identifiable) plants; the flower looks exact like a pink slipper.

Top: A raised boardwalk to meander through the wetlands along the trail
Bottom left: The cascades of the Zealand River
Bottom right: You can stay the night here for a fee, which grants you dinner, a bunk bed, and breakfast the next morning.

In parts of the trail, you will traverse raised boardwalks to minimize the effect of hikers on the wetland areas. These boardwalks don't have railings on either side, so keep a closer eye on your kids as you cross over these sections.

The wetlands along the Zealand River are ideal habitat for moose, so check your surroundings as you rest along the trail. Moose are fairly erratic creatures (much more so than the black bears in the area) and can change their mood quickly. Always be on the lookout for changes in wildlife's behavior and turn around if something does not feel safe.

At the 2.5-mile mark, the trail will start to ascend quickly to the falls and the Zealand Falls Hut just beyond. You can see Zealand Falls by taking a quick side trail on your left to the rocks at the base of the waterfalls. Depending on the time of year, water could be pouring over these rocks at a hefty pace, so please take caution here. Other times of the year, the wide rocks are a great spot for a picnic with Zealand Falls as your background.

Once you have experienced the falls, head back on the trail and up to the Zealand Falls Hut. Here you can use the toilets or even buy some hot food. Usually the staff there will have made some kind of soup of the day as well as sweets of some sort (chocolate cake anyone?). You can also grab a coffee, tea, or hot cocoa to boost your energy for the hike back to the car.

Head back down the trail to return to your car. The 2.5 miles back to the trailhead might seem a bit long, so make sure to keep your kids motivated. My go-to motivational

The view from Zealand Falls AMC Hut

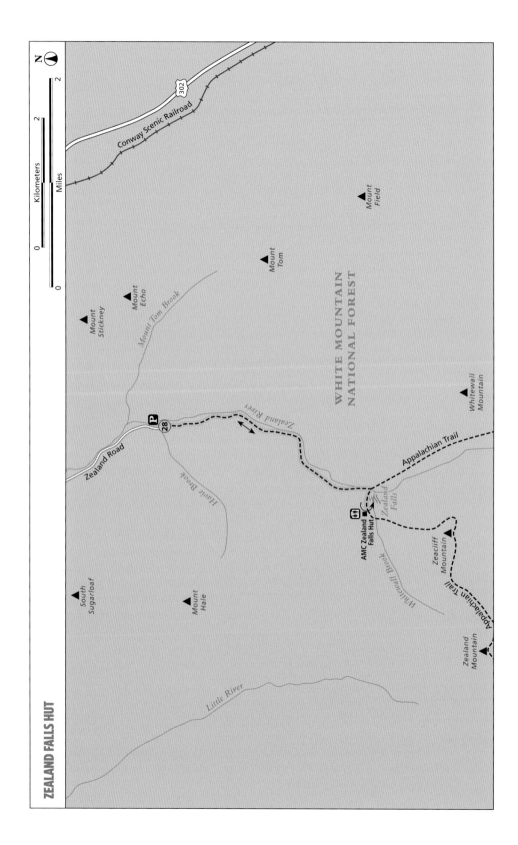

ZEALAND FALLS HUT

N

Kilometers
0   2
0   2
Miles

Conway Scenic Railroad

302

Mount
Field

Mount
Tom

Mount
Echo

Mount
Stickney

Mount Tom Brook

Zealand River

WHITE MOUNTAIN
NATIONAL FOREST

Whitewall
Mountain

Zealand Road

28

P

Haute Brook

South
Sugarloaf

Mount
Hale

Little River

Whitewall Brook

AMC Zealand
Falls Hut

Zealand
Falls

Appalachian Trail

Zeacliff
Mountain

Appalachian Trail

Zealand
Mountain

choice for this trail is to see who can count the most pink lady's-slippers (when in season). Not only is it educational, but it keeps my kiddo moving along the trail.

Before you know it, you will have made it back to the trailhead—albeit a little sorer but with a full heart. Next time, use this trail for an overnight experience. Zealand Falls Hut, along with all other AMC huts in the White Mountains, are a great introduction to the world of backpacking without having to bring a tent, stove, or dinner/breakfast food.

The price for an overnight stay in the huts can be high, but you get a bed, dinner, and breakfast the next day with each night's stay. There are usually great skits and nature talks from the staff who host each of the huts. The huts are easy ways to introduce your kid to backpacking without the added stress of carrying a ton of gear/food.

MILES AND DIRECTIONS

0.00 Start at the Zealand Falls trailhead.

2.50 Begin the steeper ascent.

2.65 Zealand Falls will be off to your left.

2.70 Reach Zealand Falls Hut, which is run by the Appalachian Mountain Club.

2.75 Take one last look at Zealand Falls.

2.90 Begin the gradual descent back to the trailhead.

5.40 Arrive back at the trailhead.

THE ONE VENOMOUS SNAKE IN NEW HAMPSHIRE

It would be quite a day if you walked along a trail in New Hampshire and witnessed the state's only venomous snake. Not only are timber rattlesnakes extremely rare (so much so that they are protected by law in the state), but they are also docile and highly unlikely to bite you. There are a total of eleven species of snake that call the Granite State home; the most common is the garter snake.

Garter snakes are found throughout most of the state, even at higher elevations like at Zealand Falls Hut. They are relatively harmless and eat nuisance creatures like insects and mice. Most of the time you will not notice a snake on the trail. They are usually found in the grasses that border a trail and are more afraid of you than you are of them. Every so often you will find a snake sunning itself on the trail. If you can't safely get around it, turn around and come back to this trail another day. Otherwise, give it a wide berth and continue on your way.

A garter snake sunning itself on the warm rocks just outside the hut

29 CANNON MOUNTAIN

Cannon Mountain is one of New Hampshire's 4,000-footers and the only one found in this guide. The hike up Kinsman Ridge is not for the faint of heart and very strenuous for most kids. However, what's nice about this hike is that you can take the Cannon Mountain Aerial Tramway up to the top and do the short Rim Trail around the summit. You can still get all the views without having to burn your muscles or your lungs to get there. With that said, there is something truly satisfying about getting up to the summit on your own two feet.

Start: At the Kinsman Ridge trailhead
Elevation gain: 2,190 feet
Distance: 3.5 miles
Difficulty: Very strenuous (unless you take the tram and only do the Rim Trail)
Hiking time: 6 hours
Seasons/Schedule: Trail is closed in winter for ski season
Fees and permits: Fee required if you want to take the tram
Trail contact: Franconia Notch State Park, 260 Tramway Dr., Franconia, NH; (603) 823-8800; www.nhstateparks.org/visit/state-parks/franconia-notch-state-park. White Mountain National Forest, 71 White Mountain Dr., Campton, NH; (603) 536-6100; www.fs.usda.gov/whitemountain

Dog-friendly: Allowed on leash
Trail surface: Gravel, dirt, and solid rock
Land status: US Forest Service
Nearest town: Franconia, NH
Other trail users: None
Water availability: Yes, at the hut
Maps: White Mountains—Franconia to Pemigewasset trail map
Age range: Kids in carriers or those with extensive trail experience
Toilets: Yes, at the visitor center
Stroller/Wheelchair compatibility: No, but you can take the tram up to see the view
Resting benches: Yes, at the visitor center and the summit restaurant
Potential child hazards: Massive cliff drop-offs
Gear suggestions: Trekking poles and insect repellent

FINDING THE TRAILHEAD

From Concord, take I-93 North for approximately 72 miles. Take exit 34B toward Cannon Mountain Aerial Tramway. Turn left onto Tramway Drive and head up to the aerial tramway parking lot. **GPS:** 44.169028 / -71.687078

THE HIKE

The drive along Highway 93 and Franconia Notch Parkway is one of the most scenic drives in the state. In autumn thousands of visitors (residents of New Hampshire like to call them "leaf peepers") make their way to this part of the state to view the incredible colors for which New England is famous..

So if seclusion is what you are after, this is not the place for you. The trailhead for Cannon Mountain starts to the left of the aerial tramway. This trail is steep enough that it is worth saying again that this trail should only be attempted by those with plenty of trail experience, including parents who are carrying their kids in carriers. If, for any reason, you do not think you or your kid can do this hike, opt for taking the Cannon Mountain

Top: You can get to the Rim Trail from the difficult hike up Cannon, or you can take the Cannon Mountain Aerial Tramway.
Bottom: The views are breathtaking throughout the entire loop.

aerial tramway up to the summit of Cannon Mountain. This cuts the bulk of your trail and leaves only the Rim Trail for you to do at the top.

If you choose to take the Kinsman Ridge Trail, do so carefully while also keeping in mind your pace and the weather. The trail is narrow, extremely steep (a consistent 12 percent grade), and full of large rocks to climb over. There is no shame in just taking the tramway up. The bulk of the ascent happens within the first mile when you reach tree line, and the views are endless.

At the 1.2-mile mark, check out the overlook just ahead to get your first glimpses of Mount Lafayette, Mount Truman, Mount Lincoln, Little Haystack, and Mount Liberty.

Top: Careful of the huge drop-offs—there are many along the trail.
Bottom: Most of the travel is dirt and gravel with some solid granite as well.

Continue up the trail to head toward the summit of Cannon Mountain. At 1.7 miles, you will reach the summit of Cannon Mountain and the tramway station at the top.

There is food and drinks to purchase at the top as well as toilets. Take a breather here until you are ready to do the Rim Trail. If you have taken the tramway, it will drop you off at the Mountain Station, where you can connect with the Rim Trail that brings you around the summit to get endless views of some of the mountains that make up the Presidential Range.

The Rim Trail traverses the summit of Cannon Mountain and has some hefty drop-offs, so never let your kids run along this trail by themselves. Keep your body between

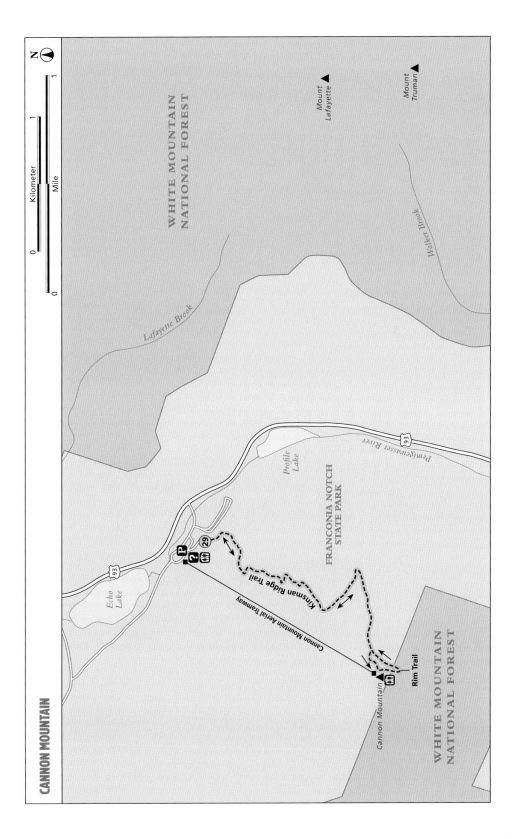

CANNON MOUNTAIN

N

0   Kilometer   1

0   Mile   1

WHITE MOUNTAIN
NATIONAL FOREST

Mount
Lafayette ▲

Mount
Truman ▲

Lafayette Brook

Walker Brook

Profile
Lake

93

Pemigewasset River

FRANCONIA NOTCH
STATE PARK

Echo
Lake

93

P
29

Cannon Mountain Aerial Tramway

Kinsman Ridge Trail

Cannon Mountain

Rim Trail

WHITE MOUNTAIN
NATIONAL FOREST

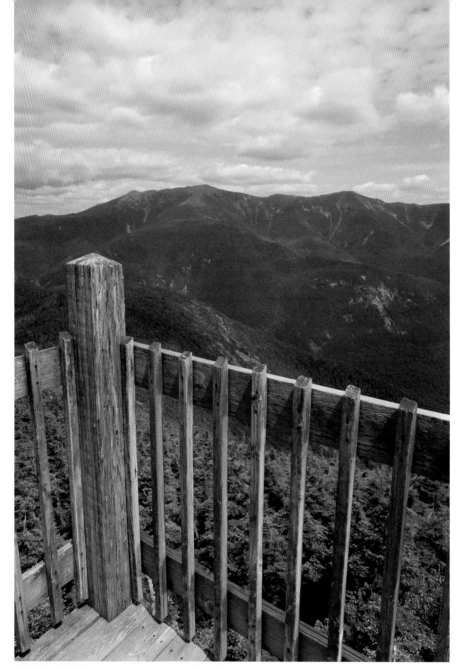

An observation tower gives you even better views!

them and the cliffs. Your kids will love all the views, especially up at the weather station. Grab some fries and a hot dog or two when you make it back to the Mountain Station.

If you have made the trek up the mountain but want to take the aerial tramway down, you will need to reserve tickets ahead of time and pay for a round-trip ticket (they no longer do one-way tickets). You can also choose to take the tramway up and then hike back down, although this will be killer on your knees regardless of how good they are.

NEW HAMPSHIRE'S FAMED FORTY-EIGHT

New Hampshire is home to forty-eight total 4,000-footers. These are mountains considered to be more than 4,000 feet above sea level and to have a minimum prominence of 200 feet. This means that some mountains that are more than 4,000 feet might not be included in the forty-eight listed mountains, because they are too close in height to the mountains around them.

Most of the 4,000-footers can be found in the White Mountains, where there are some of the most beautiful ridgelines in the world (like Franconia Ridge). Outdoor enthusiasts have been traversing New Hampshire's forty-eight 4,000-footers for decades. Some spend their whole lives trying to bag all the peaks, while others have tried to do it all in one year. Some have even done it all in one go; the fastest known time is three days, eight hours, and fifty-six minutes. Now that is fast!

Heading down Kinsman Ridge will be slow, so keep that in mind as you check the weather. Storms in the summer roll in usually in the afternoon, and thunderstorms are no joke when you are above tree line. Take your time heading back to the trailhead and enjoy the views on the way down.

MILES AND DIRECTIONS

0.00   Start to the left of the Tram Valley Station and immediately start the steep ascent up the mountain. Or take the Cannon Mountain Aerial Tramway up.

1.10   Keep right to stay on Kinsman Ridge Trail.

1.60   Take a right onto the Rim Trail.

1.65   Take a much-deserved breather at the Mountain Station and the summit restaurant. Then continue on the trail along the rim.

1.90   Get back on the Kinsman Ridge Trail by taking a right, or continue straight to take the aerial tramway back down the mountain if you have reserved tickets.

2.40   Take a left to stay on the Kinsman Ridge Trail.

3.50   Arrive back at the trailhead.

The second Appalachian Mountain Club (AMC) hut hike in this guide is the one to Lonesome Lake. The views from the hut are similar to ones from the previous hike up Cannon Mountain but with a gorgeous high-altitude lake to boot. The hike up to the hut is steadily uphill but littler legs can do it if they have experience on the trail. Lonesome Lake is a great trail to do any time of year, but I would argue the best time to go is in winter. There are way fewer people on the trail, but the views are just as big.

Start: At the Lonesome Lake trailhead
Elevation gain: 1,025 feet
Distance: 3.1 miles
Difficulty: Strenuous (due to steepness)
Hiking time: 4 hours
Seasons/Schedule: Year-round
Fees and permits: None
Trail contact: Franconia Notch State Park, 260 Tramway Dr., Franconia, NH; (603) 823-8800; www.nhstateparks.org/visit/state -parks/franconia-notch-state-park. Appalachian Mountain Club, 10 City Square, Boston, MA; (603) 466-2727; www.outdoors.org/ destinations/massachusetts-and -new-hampshire/lonesome-lake-hut

Dog-friendly: Allowed on leash
Trail surface: Dirt and solid rock
Land status: US Forest Service and New Hampshire State Parks
Nearest town: Franconia, NH
Other trail users: None
Water availability: Yes, at the hut
Maps: White Mountains—Franconia to Pemigewasset trail map
Age range: Kids in carriers or those with extensive trail experience
Toilets: Yes, at the hut
Stroller/Wheelchair compatibility: No
Resting benches: Yes, at the hut
Potential child hazards: None
Gear suggestions: Trekking poles and insect repellent

FINDING THE TRAILHEAD

From Concord, take I-93 North for approximately 72 miles. Take exit 34B toward Cannon Mountain Aerial Tramway. Turn left onto Tramway Drive and then turn left to get back on I-93 South for 2.2 miles. Take the exit into Lafayette Place Campground and turn left to the parking lot for Lonesome Lake. **GPS:** 44.142059 / -71.684246

THE HIKE

This has quickly become one of my favorite hikes to do in winter, but it's beautiful no matter what time of year you go. The hike to Lonesome Lake is a steady ascent with jaw-dropping views of the surrounding 4,000-footers.

The hike starts at the Lonesome Lake trailhead at Lafayette Place Campground. The parking lot is off to the left, although overflow parking is on the right. This place can get very busy, so if there is no parking, you will either have to wait or come back another time, as there is no parking on the sides of the roads. Head over the small bridge and through the campground to stay on the trail. You will have to cross some roads within the campground, so use caution with kids when you cross.

Top: Walking across the bridge at the trailhead
Bottom: The views are worth all the climbing.

This hike is considered strenuous due to the elevation gain in such a short distance. With that said, my son (4 years old at the time) made it up to the hut on his own two legs, so those who have a bit more trail experience can do this hike, even if they are young and walking on their own.

There are several places along the steep trail that might be difficult for smaller legs to climb. They may need some help to climb over the roots and rocks jutting out through the trail's surface. Like I said, though, small legs can do this if they have a bit of experience.

Around the 1.0-mile mark, the trail starts to level off to give you and your kids a bit of reprieve before the final push to the lake and hut. In fact, the trail descends slightly right before you reach Lonesome Lake. You arrive at the lake around 1.2 miles. If you look out

The trail is full of lots of rocks and roots—a typical New Hampshire hike!

across the water slightly to your left, you can see the hut tucked in the trees. Turn left when you reach Lonesome Lake to head straight to the hut.

This section of the trail has some raised boardwalks, but they are very rustic and some are even rotted through. Try to walk on them when you can to help prevent more soil erosion. After 0.25 mile you will hit the Appalachian Mountain Club's Lonesome Lake Hut. Just like the Zealand Falls Hut, staff run the hut all summer long and provide the meals for overnight guests.

You can also buy the food they have cooked up for the day even if you are there just for a day hike. The few times my son and I have done this trip, there's been potato leek soup, chocolate cake (even gluten-free), and muffins for purchase. They almost always have hot cocoa, tea, and coffee for those wanting to partake in some caffeine before they head back out on the trail. Unfortunately the huts are not open in winter.

There's a great wooden dock down at the lake in front of the hut. From there you can see east to all the 4,000-footers, including Mount Lafayette, Mount Lincoln, and Little Haystack Mountain. The view can truly take your breath away—especially if you have just huffed and puffed your way up the 1,000 feet of vertical elevation gain to get there.

Once you have inhaled the chocolate cake from the hut and feel refreshed, head back around the western side of the lake. The loop will bring you back around to where you first encountered the lake. Turn left to get back on that trail and make your steady descent back to your car. Do not forget that the trail was steep on the way up and can look and feel steeper on the way down. Take as much time as you need to make it back to the trailhead safely.

One last look at the beautiful view of Little Haystack, Mount Lincoln, and Mount Lafayette

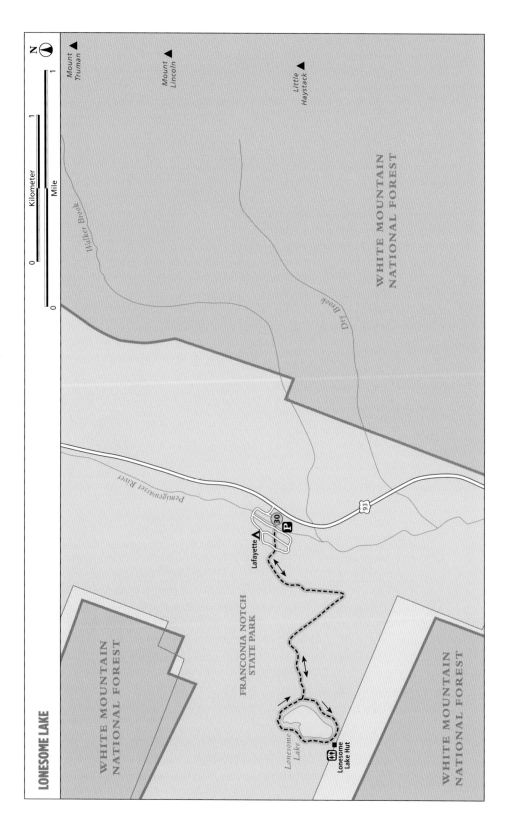

LONESOME LAKE

WHITE MOUNTAIN NATIONAL FOREST

WHITE MOUNTAIN NATIONAL FOREST

WHITE MOUNTAIN NATIONAL FOREST

FRANCONIA NOTCH STATE PARK

Pemigewasset River

Walker Brook

Dry Brook

Lonesome Lake

Lonesome Lake Hut

Lafayette

Mount Truman

Mount Lincoln

Little Haystack

Kilometer

Mile

0   1

N

MILES AND DIRECTIONS

0.00 Start on the western side of the parking lot.

0.40 Keep straight to stay on the Lonesome Lake Trail. Do not turn right.

1.20 Reach the lake. Turn left to head toward the Lonesome Lake Hut.

1.50 Reach the Lonesome Lake Hut. Continue north on the loop around the lake.

1.90 Meet back up with the Lonesome Lake Trail and head back down to the trailhead.

2.70 Stay straight to head back to your car.

3.10 Arrive back at the trailhead.

THE APPALACHIAN MOUNTAIN CLUB HUT SYSTEM

The Appalachian Mountain Club (AMC) has many responsibilities. The organization has been around since 1876 and has always had a mission of "protecting the mountains, forests, waters, and trails" along the Mid-Atlantic and northeast United States. But it also maintains and staffs a handful of mountain huts in both New Hampshire and Massachusetts.

The huts in New Hampshire are the most famous and for good reason. The dozen or so mountain huts include ones along the trails to Mount Washington and others along the Presidential Range. The most famous of the huts is the Lakes of the Clouds Hut, which sits on the saddle just below Mount Washington at more than 5,000 feet above sea level. The lakes for which the hut is named sit not too far away and earned their name because they always seem to be sitting above the clouds.

These huts are a great way for kids to experience these higher altitudes and bigger peaks without having to backpack or cram it into a long day hike. Instead, you pack some overnight clothes, a sleeping bag, and a good attitude, and the hut staff takes care of the rest!

Chocolate cake, hot cocoa, and coffee are available at the Lonesome Lake AMC Hut to keep you energized.

31 **MOUNT WILLARD**

The White Mountains are highly sought after in the autumn months when the fall colors are at their peak. Cars line the roads and trailheads to get a glimpse of the beauty and wonder of the changing leaves. Mount Willard is a very popular destination during this time, with its gradual climb up to a picturesque (and wide) summit.

Start: At the Mount Willard trailhead behind Crawford Train Station
Elevation gain: 900 feet
Distance: 3.1 miles
Difficulty: Moderate
Hiking time: 3 hours
Seasons/Schedule: Year-round
Fees and permits: None
Trail contact: White Mountain National Forest, 71 White Mountain Dr., Campton, NH; (603) 536-6100; www.fs.usda.gov/whitemountain and Crawford Notch State Park
Dog-friendly: Allowed on leash
Trail surface: Gravel, dirt, and solid rock
Land status: US Forest Service

Nearest town: Bretton Woods, NH
Other trail users: None
Water availability: Yes, at the trailhead
Maps: Crawford Notch State Park trail map
Age range: All ages
Toilets: Yes, at the trailhead
Stroller/Wheelchair compatibility: No
Resting benches: Yes, at the Crawford Train Station
Potential child hazards: Massive cliff drop-offs and crossing railroad tracks
Gear suggestions: Trekking poles and insect repellent

FINDING THE TRAILHEAD

From Concord, take I-93 North for approximately 75 miles. Take exit 35 for Route 3 North toward Lancaster/Twin Mountain. Continue on Route 3 North for approximately 10 miles and then turn right on Route 302 East. After 8.5 miles, you will see the Appalachian Mountain Club (AMC) Highland Center on your right. Parking for the Mount Willard trailhead is on the right side of the road, next to Crawford Train Station. **GPS:** 44.217830 / -71.410789

THE HIKE

If you were to search the internet for "best hikes to do in New Hampshire to see the fall colors," the hike up Mount Willard would likely be at the top of everyone's list. This 3.0-mile hike is not only easily done by most hikers, including little ones, but has one of the most scenic views at its summit.

Start your hike up Mount Willard at Crawford Train Station. This is an active train station that operates out of North Conway. The Conway Scenic Railroad has three types of excursions from which to choose. The Mountaineer excursion brings visitors up to Crawford Notch through a scenic track.

Cross the tracks to get to the start of the Mount Willard Trail. There will be a trail to the left indicating the way to Mount Willard. Going straight here would bring you up to Mount Avalon, a 3,000-footer. There are a few stream crossings after you take the left onto the Mount Willard Trail, but either they are easily crossed or bridges are there to help.

Top: Just below the summit, there are a few "tree tunnels" that simply look magical.
Bottom: The Crawford Train Station—take Conway Scenic Railroad's Mountaineer train here for a special occasion.

The trail then takes a sharp turn right, and the true ascent of the hike begins. The trail has several steeper sections and also sections of reprieve so you're never going up all the time—there are breaks in between. Around the 1.2-mile mark, the trail starts to level out. Here you will encounter one of my favorite sections on any trail I have ever hiked. Spruce and bird trees flank the trail, while moss blankets the surrounding understory and naturally creates a "tree tunnel" for those who are paying attention. The trail does this for about 0.25 mile, so enjoy it while it lasts.

Finally the trail ends at the summit of Mount Willard, which is a wide outcrop that allows views to the south looking down at Crawford Notch Road. The valley is fringed

Top: A beautiful spring day at the summit
Bottom: Spring is in full bloom outside the AMC Highland Center.

with Mount Webster on the left and Mount Whitney on the right. Soak in the views and then head back down the trail to get back to your car.

Tom Crawford—who came from a well-known family in this region for being early innkeepers and opening the trail system here (Crawford Notch State Park is named for the family)—was an avid hiker and mountaineer. He created the path that is used for Mount Willard to this day. But he named the mountain after his climbing companion, Joseph Willard.

If you want to stay in the area, look no further than the AMC's Highland Center. It's just next door to Crawford Train Station, and makes a perfect basecamp for a Mount

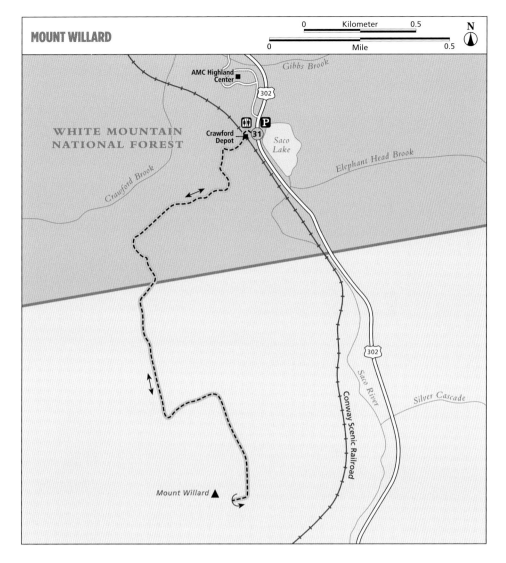

Willard climb. In spring the fields surrounding the Highland Center are filled with lupines and other wildflowers that sway with the wind.

MILES AND DIRECTIONS

0.00 Start across the train tracks behind Crawford Train Station.

0.10 Turn left to head on the Mount Willard Trail.

1.55 Reach the summit of Mount Willard. Hang out for as long as you like along the wide, rocky summit. Then head back the way you came.

3.00 Turn right to head back to the trailhead.

3.10 Cross the train tracks and arrive back at Crawford Train Station.

A hazy fall day at the summit. The fall colors are glorious on this trail.

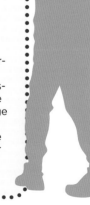

DID YOU KNOW LEAVES DON'T CHANGE COLOR IN AUTUMN?

It's true. Leaves *don't* actually change color in the autumn; in fact, the color was there all along! As you might well know, chlorophyll is what creates the green color of a leaf. This is a big factor in how trees survive (photosynthesis anyone?). Chlorophyll absorbs energy through sunlight to transform carbon dioxide and water into carbohydrates that trees use to stay healthy and strong.

There are also other chemicals within a leaf, but they are masked by the huge amount of chlorophyll. Two of these chemicals are carotene and xanthophyll, which give off yellow and orange pigments, respectively. On top of that, most trees have now evolved to produce yet another chemical, called anthocyanins, that has a reddish tint. This chemical is what gives a blueberry its color.

The mixture of these colors is what makes up a leaf and what eventually gets revealed as chlorophyll starts to break down throughout the autumn months. As daylight shortens and temperatures drop, trees stop the food-making process and chlorophyll breaks down. As the chlorophyll breaks down, the green color disappears to allow other colors to shine through. Depending on the amount of other chemicals in a tree's system, leaf colors can range from purple to orange to yellow.

So now when someone says they can't wait for trees to change color, you can say: "Actually a leaf doesn't change color, the color has been there all along! The chlorophyll's strength masked the other colors."

32 MIDDLE SUGARLOAF MOUNTAIN

If you're looking for the most iconic New England autumn adventure with your family, look no further than the trail up to Middle Sugarloaf Mountain. You'll get a whole lot of bang for very minimal buck, which also means the trail can be quite popular. The trail wanders through typical New England forests, including trees of the birch, maple, aspen, and oak varieties. The abundance and assortment of trees also means there is a mix of colors come autumn. You can witness the sea of oranges, reds, yellows, and even some purples from the sprawling rocky summit.

Start: At the Sugarloaf trailhead
Elevation gain: 885 feet
Distance: 2.6 miles
Difficulty: Moderate
Hiking time: 3 hours
Seasons/Schedule: The road to the trailhead is closed in winter.
Fees and permits: None
Trail contact: White Mountain National Forest, 71 White Mountain Dr., Campton, NH; (603) 536-6100; www.fs.usda.gov/whitemountain
Dog-friendly: Allowed on leash
Trail surface: Gravel, dirt, and solid rock
Land status: US Forest Service

Nearest town: Bretton Woods, NH
Other trail users: None
Water availability: None
Maps: White Mountains—Franconia to Pemigewasset trail map
Age range: All ages
Toilets: None
Stroller/Wheelchair compatibility: No
Resting benches: None
Potential child hazards: Large drop-offs at the summit and a steep ladder
Gear suggestions: Trekking poles and insect repellent

FINDING THE TRAILHEAD

From Concord, take I-93 North for approximately 75 miles. Take exit 35 for Route 3 North toward Lancaster/Twin Mountain. Continue on Route 3 North for approximately 10 miles and then turn right onto Route 302 East. After 2 miles, turn right onto Zealand Road when you see the signs for Zealand Recreation Area. Follow Zealand Road for 1 mile. Park in the small parking lot to your right before the bridge and the road turns to dirt. **GPS:** 44.254836 / -71.503937

THE HIKE

Hiking up Middle Sugarloaf Mountain can be done any time of year. Hiking in winter adds on another 2.0 miles to this hike, because you start in the snowmobile parking lot and have to walk to the summer trailhead a mile up Zealand Road. But the absolute best time of year to make this trip is during peak foliage season.

The problem, though, is that everyone else knows this is the best time for a visit, so expect a crowded trail on weekends. The parking area has room for only ten or so cars. Luckily, the trail isn't very long, so people tend to come and go from the parking area often. I recommend arriving earlier than 8:00 a.m. or after 5:00 p.m. on weekends for the best chances of snagging a parking spot.

Top left: There are boulders around the half-mile mark for kiddos to explore.
Top right: Before the last push to the summit, you'll need to climb a steep ladder, so keep an eye on walking kiddos.
Bottom: The view is breathtaking on the wide summit, with plenty of room to spread out.

I'M LICHEN THIS TRAIL

Let's face it, kids love to climb things, which can be very nerve-wracking for parents on the trail. This trail has some huge boulders where kids can wrack every parent's last nerve. Instead, have them play around the boulders; some are so close together that it looks like you're going through a narrow canyon. And then make sure to give your kids a lesson in nature and check out the things that grow on these hard surfaces.

This trail has a plethora of lichens called rock tripe, which blankets many of the granite slabs that make up the majority of the White Mountains. It is supposedly edible (only when boiled, though, so don't try this on the trail), but I'm not sure it's especially fun to eat. Apparently, rock tripe saved the lives of George Washington and his troops in the winter of 1777 at Valley Forge when they ran out of other things to eat.

The trail starts out at the kiosk, which warns visitors of wildlife in the area. Black bears are frequent visitors, so always use caution and make noise along the trail—although if you're with children, you likely won't have a problem making sure bears are aware of your presence.

For the bulk of the hike, you'll travel along dirt paths that cross over several perennial streams that small legs can easily jump over. Let out your inner child and splash around in the water too. Just make sure to bring extra socks if your boots aren't waterproof. The forests that surround you come alive with the cackling laughs of red squirrels and the beautiful melodies of veeries (a native songbird).

Autumn is a must-see in New England, and this is an ideal trail to take it all in.

The author taking in the views to the west with her son

As you start your gradual ascent, dirt paths turn to granite slabs. The White Mountains get their name from the white color of the granite that blankets the majority of New Hampshire. Be careful on rainy days or when the ground is wet on this trail, as granite can become slick under the slightest bit of moisture.

You'll eventually meet a T-junction at just under a mile that will take you to either North or Middle Sugarloaf Mountain. You can do both in a day if you choose, but the views are basically the same. Middle Sugarloaf Mountain has the bonus of having a large summit, so even when the trail has a lot of hikers, you can still get away from the crowds.

To get to Middle Sugarloaf Mountain, take a left at this junction and continue straight up. A few steep sections appear past this point, with larger rock slabs that might be somewhat difficult for little feet to maneuver. Right before the crest of the summit, you reach a steep wooden staircase with no handrails.

Please do not go around the stairs, as this can create trail erosion. If kids need help, just hold their hands on the way up and down.

Just after the steps, the forest will open up to the expansive summit. There are almost 270-degree views at the top. Grab your jaw off the ground as you take in the impressive views. There are multiple places for you to sit and relax while hanging out on the summit. Stay on the rock surfaces to protect the sensitive plants that grow in the cracks. Once you've had your fill, turn around the same way you came and make your way back down to your car.

MILES AND DIRECTIONS

0.00 Begin at the trailhead on the southwestern side of the parking area. Elevation is 1,569 feet. Make sure to check for alerts or announcements on the large kiosk at the start.

0.05 Follow the road to cross over the Zealand River and turn right just after the bridge to stay on the trail.

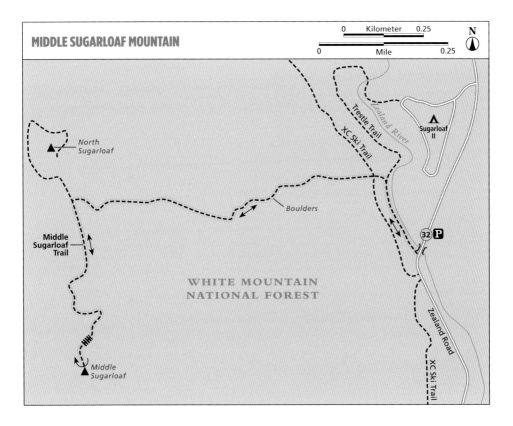

0   Kilometer   0.25

0   Mile   0.25

N

North Sugarloaf

Trestle Trail

Zealand River

XC Ski Trail

Sugarloaf II

Boulders

Middle Sugarloaf Trail

32 P

WHITE MOUNTAIN
NATIONAL FOREST

Zealand Road

XC Ski Trail

Middle Sugarloaf

0.10 Cross over a small gully; kids may need help crossing a seasonal stream.

0.20 Come to the intersection of the Sugarloaf and Trestle Trails. Take the left fork to stay on the Sugarloaf Trail. You should be veering away from the Zealand River at this point. The trail steadily ascends starting from here.

0.40 This is a great spot to take a small break if you or the kids are needing it. There are two large granite boulders that create a fun place to play around.

0.90 Reach the junction of the Middle Sugarloaf and North Sugarloaf Trails. You can opt to add on North Sugarloaf Mountain, but the views are basically the same and Middle Sugarloaf Mountain has a better summit. To make your way to Middle Sugarloaf Mountain, take a left here.

1.20 Arrive at the base of a steep wooden staircase. Kids may need help here. When it's wet, the steps can be very slippery—so be careful.

1.30 Reach the large and sprawling summit of Middle Sugarloaf Mountain. There are multiple places to take a long break while also taking in the views.

1.40 Head back down the steep steps; remember to help kids down.

1.70 Reach the junction of the North Sugarloaf and Middle Sugarloaf Trails. To continue back to the parking area, take a right. Continue downhill.

2.40 Reach the junction of the Sugarloaf and Trestle Trails. Take a slight right to stay on the Sugarloaf Trail, which will lead back to the parking lot. The Zealand River should now be on your left.

2.60 Arrive back at the parking lot by crossing back over the bridge.

33 BLACK CAP

The trail up to Black Cap provides one of the most scenic views of the White Mountains and beyond, including the iconic Mount Washington. This is one of the few trails that little legs can easily traverse to get incredible views. Cloud inversions tend to pop up around this area, so you might get lucky and see one so you can, quite literally, be hiking above the clouds.

Start: At the Black Cap trailhead
Elevation gain: 610 feet
Distance: 2.3 miles
Difficulty: Moderate
Hiking time: 3 hours
Seasons/Schedule: The road to the trailhead is closed in winter.
Fees and permits: None
Trail contact: Green Hills Preserve, 252 Thompson Rd., North Conway, NH; (802) 295-2990; www.nature .org/en-us/get-involved/how-to-help/places-we-protect/green-hills-preserve
Dog-friendly: Allowed on leash
Trail surface: Dirt and solid rock

Land status: The Nature Conservancy
Nearest town: North Conway, NH
Other trail users: Mountain bikers
Water availability: None
Maps: Green Hills Preserve trail map
Age range: All ages
Toilets: No
Stroller/Wheelchair compatibility: No
Resting benches: No
Potential child hazards: Slippery granite rocks
Gear suggestions: Trekking poles and insect repellent

FINDING THE TRAILHEAD

From Portsmouth, take Route 16 North/Route 202 East for approximately 17 miles. The road turns into just Route 16 North. Keep on this road for approximately 55 miles, until you reach the town of Conway. Keep left to stay on Route 16 North for another 3 miles. Then turn right onto Mountain Valley Boulevard; at the traffic circle, take the third exit onto North–South Road (this road bypasses the busy downtown of North Conway). Follow this road until you reach the end (approximately 2.5 miles) and then turn right onto Kearsarge Road. After 0.3 mile, turn left to stay on Kearsarge Road for another 1.6 miles. Turn right onto Hurricane Mountain Road, which cannot accommodate large RVs or trailers. Follow this road for 2.6 miles and pull into the trailhead parking lot on your right. **GPS:** 44.068438 / -71.071801

THE HIKE

The trail up to Black Cap is by no means secluded. A typical weekend will see hundreds of hiking enthusiasts coming up and down the mountain. However, hiking during the week or even earlier in the morning will allow you to relish in the beauty of the surrounding nature without having to share the mountain with anyone else.

For most of the hike, the trail is mostly covered in typical New England fashion: lots of dirt, rocks, and roots.

There are some more-difficult spots with large rocks along the trail. I like to watch my son problem-solve as he figures out how to manage his way around the rocks. Most of the time he successfully problem-solves and is rewarded with a lot of pride in his heart.

When you get above tree line, trail blazes are marked on the granite rocks.

The rest of the trail becomes obvious when you inch out of the trees and onto solid granite rock. If it has rained recently or if dew has fallen, these rocks can be quite slippery, so make sure to wear proper footwear that has grippy soles. This is where the trail gets significantly steeper, but only for a short amount of time.

Red blazes dot the rock surface to show you where the trail ascends the summit of Black Cap. Please stay on the trail regardless of what other people have done. There are several lichens, mosses, and other sensitive species that live between the rocks and could be irreparably harmed if stepped on.

Just below the summit is a pillar with a circular disk on top with instructions from The Nature Conservancy to be a citizen scientist. The nonprofit organization is monitoring the health of the forest around Green Hills Preserve and needs hikers, like you, to send in their photos. They give you clear instructions on what to do and where to send the photos using a QR code. Let's all do our part to help protect these beautiful spaces.

Once you have taken your photos, continue on the loop around the summit and then make your way back down the granite slabs to the dirt path. Head back to your car at the trailhead the same way you came up.

The majority of the trail is forested, with lots of rocks to hop over.

Top: Lots of lichens and other sensitive species cover the area above tree line, so make sure to stay on the rocks.
Bottom: Heading up to the summit with Mount Washington in the background

MILES AND DIRECTIONS

0.00 Start at the southern end of the parking lot.

0.60 Stay straight on the Black Cap Trail. Do not turn right onto the Cranmore Trail.

0.70 Keep left at the fork.

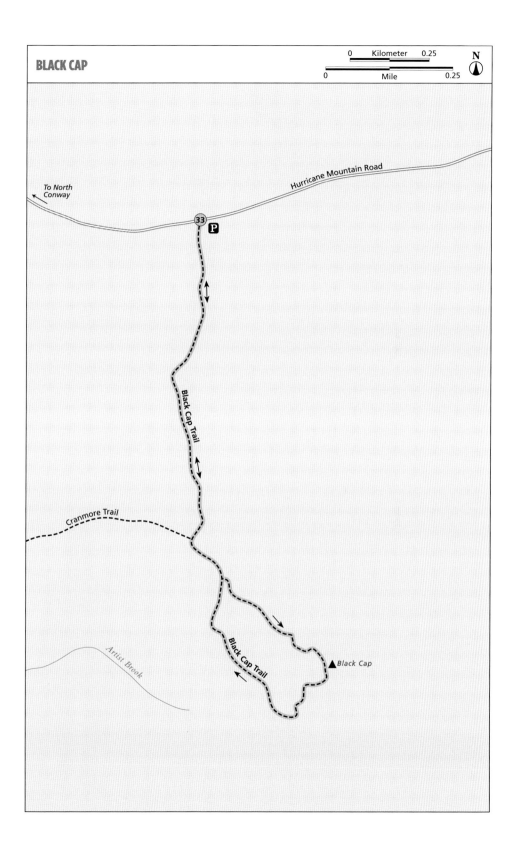

BLACK CAP

Hurricane Mountain Road

To North Conway

33

P

Black Cap Trail

Cranmore Trail

Artist Brook

Black Cap Trail

Black Cap

A perfect day with a perfect adventure buddy

1.00   Reach the summit of Black Cap. Keep straight to continue the loop around the summit.

1.20   Keep straight/right to continue the loop. Do not take the trail to your left.

1.60   Meet back up with the trail you took up to Black Cap. Head down the mountain.

1.70   Stay straight/right. Do not take the Cranmore Trail to your left.

2.30   Arrive back at the trailhead.

THE DEADLIEST MOUNTAIN IN THE UNITED STATES

When you think of the deadliest mountains in the world, you might think of K2, Mount Everest, or even Mount Denali. But would you believe that the deadliest mountain in the United States is in New Hampshire?

Mount Washington has been attracting tourists for decades, and with its Auto Road completely paved up to the summit, almost anyone can enjoy the views from above 6,000 feet. Because of its "easy" access, the highest mountain in New England also lays claim to having the most lives lost. The first recorded summit of Mount Washington was in the mid-1600s, and the first recorded death was in 1849. Since that day, more than 130 people have died on the mountain—more than on any other mountain in the United States.

Not only are more inexperienced hikers thinking they can easily climb the 6,288-foot mountain, but Mount Washington is also home to some of the most dangerous weather on Earth. This includes one of the highest-recorded wind speeds of 231 mph at the summit. Imagine trying to hold on when a gust that strong knocks you down!

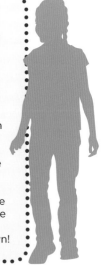

34 FLUME GORGE

Enter a land full of whimsy and fairy tales when you visit the Flume Gorge in Franconia Notch State Park. It is one of the most-visited attractions in White Mountain National Forest, but it is something every New Englander should experience. Kids will love the different spots along the trail, including the flume itself and the narrow caves of the Wolf Den. It's easy to become a kid again along this trail.

Start: At the Flume Gorge trailhead
Elevation gain: 490 feet
Distance: 2.1 miles
Difficulty: Moderate
Hiking time: 3 hours
Seasons/Schedule: Year-round, but the boardwalk is closed in winter.
Fees and permits: Fee required
Trail contact: Franconia Notch State Park, 260 Tramway Dr., Franconia, NH; (603) 823-8800; www.nhstateparks.org/visit/state-parks/franconia-notch-state-park. White Mountain National Forest, 71 White Mountain Dr., Campton, NH; (603) 536-6100; www.fs.usda.gov/whitemountain.
Dog-friendly: Not allowed

Trail surface: Dirt, gravel, and boardwalk
Land status: New Hampshire State Parks
Nearest town: Franconia, NH
Other trail users: None
Water availability: Yes, at the visitor center
Maps: Flume Gorge trail map
Age range: All ages
Toilets: Yes, at the visitor center
Stroller/Wheelchair compatibility: No
Resting benches: Yes, throughout the trail
Potential child hazards: Raised boardwalk is slippery from waterfalls.
Gear suggestions: Trekking poles and insect repellent

FINDING THE TRAILHEAD

From Concord, take I-93 North for approximately 66 miles. Take exit 34A to merge onto Route 3 North toward the Flume Gorge/Park Information Center. Take your first right into the Flume Gorge parking lot. Park anywhere in the large lot west of the visitor center. **GPS:** 44.097264 / -71.681113

THE HIKE

The Flume Gorge is one of the busiest spots in White Mountain National Forest. That's because nothing compares to it. Due to its popularity, reservations are needed during the spring, summer, and autumn months, when the boardwalk through the flume is open.

The trail starts to the left of the visitor center, where you can check in with your reserved time. To beat the crowds, go during the week and first thing in the morning. If you go on the weekend or later in the day, trails get busy with tourists as well as school groups.

The first bit of the trail meanders along a paved path until it crosses the staff road and becomes dirt. Before turning right to head down the trail, check out the Great Boulder on your left. It is huge, so you cannot miss it. Then head down the trail with several switchbacks to quickly descend toward the Pemigewasset River. The trail levels out as you approach the covered bridge. Do not attempt to cross under the bridge, as it is closed for pedestrian use. Instead, follow the trail to the left of the covered bridge to cross the river.

Top: Entering the Flume Gorge
Bottom: This is the spot where the raised boardwalk starts; it is closed in the wintertime.

Start the ascent toward Boulder Cabin on your right (sometimes open in the summer with refreshments and toilets) and Table Rock in the middle of Flume Brook on your left. After that, it is only another 0.1 mile to get to the start of the raised boardwalk that traverses through the slot canyon of Flume Gorge. Take a look at the granite walls and the moss and water dripping from their sides. The power of water is truly remarkable and can be easily seen in this place. The boardwalk can be slippery from rain as well as the mist that rises from Avalanche Falls, so be careful.

Take the steps to get up and out of the gorge and make your way north to Liberty Gorge. The trail slowly descends down to Liberty Gorge. This gorge is not as drastic as Flume Gorge and not as easily seen from the trail. Do not stray from the trail to get

Make sure to look up to see the moss and lichens blanketing the cliff walls.

This is the way to the Wolf Den—a narrow, one-way passageway crawling on your hands and knees.

a better look. Instead, keep moving forward down the overlook to The Pool along the Pemigewasset River, a beautifully turquoise waterbody way at the bottom of the gorge.

Make your way back up the Overlook Trail and pass by Wolf Den on your right. This is one of the most fun attractions on the trail but can be scary for those who do not like tight or dark spaces. Take the precautions seriously, because even as a petite hiker, I had difficulty getting through the narrow passageway. Most kids can likely get through easily, but keep an eye on them as they go. You will have to crawl on your hands and knees and will get dirty, so if you don't want that, skip Wolf Den.

After crawling around in the cave, keep heading down the trail, where your next stop is at Glacial Boulders. About 25,000 years ago, an ancient ice sheet carried these boulders. As the ice sheet melted, the boulders deposited and left here, where nature has learned to thrive both on and around them.

Continue forward on the trail and make your way back to the Great Boulder and the trail you originally took down to the covered bridge. Do not turn left (unless you want to do the Flume Gorge again); instead, head straight back to the visitor center. Enjoy a walk through the gift shop before heading back to your car.

MILES AND DIRECTIONS

0.00   Start on the Flume Gorge Trail to the left of the visitor center.

0.15   Reach the Great Boulder. You will turn right to continue toward Flume Gorge.

0.30   Pass the covered bridge on your right.

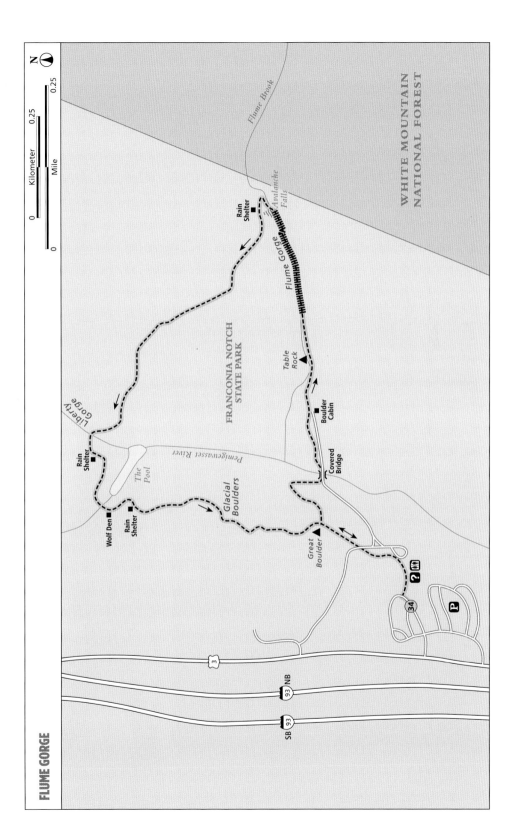

FLUME GORGE

N

Kilometer
0   0.25

Mile
0   0.25

WHITE MOUNTAIN
NATIONAL FOREST

FRANCONIA NOTCH
STATE PARK

Flume Brook

Avalanche
Falls

Rain
Shelter

Flume Gorge

Table
Rock

Boulder
Cabin

Liberty
Gorge

Rain
Shelter

The
Pool

Pemigewasset River

Covered
Bridge

Wolf Den

Rain
Shelter

Glacial
Boulders

Great
Boulder

34

P

3

93 NB

SB 93

0.40   Come to Boulder Cabin on your right.

0.50   Table Rock is on your left.

0.60   Reach the start of the raised boardwalk through Flume Gorge.

0.80   Pass by Avalanche Falls and climb out of the gorge. This is the highest point on the trail—it's all downhill from here.

1.40   Cross over Cascade Brook; Liberty Gorge is off to your right.

1.60   Take a walk (or crawl) through Wolf Den to your right.

1.80   Come to Glacial Boulders on your left.

1.95   Meet back up with the Great Boulder and the trail you took in the beginning to head to Flume Gorge. Stay straight here to go back to the visitor center.

2.10   Arrive back at the visitor center.

HOW TREES GROW ON ROCKS

The tree seen here looks as if it has grown out of a rock, but, in essence, this particular tree grew *around* the rock. Over time the tree adapted to its location by spreading its roots down the rock to seek the soil that it needs to thrive. Despite the evolution of this tree's growth, other trees can grow out of rocks.

Trees, like most plants, need soil's nutrients and the water it holds to survive. You might have seen a small tree or plants growing out of what was essentially a large rock. What you might not have seen are the tiny pockets of soil that developed over time within the rock's crevices. As more soil, dead leaves, lichens, and mosses accumulated, they provided more nutrients for other plants to survive.

The plant started to take root (literally), allowing it to send roots through the crevices of the rock to find the soil they needed deep underneath. So, really, trees are not actually growing out of rocks. It is a trick of the eye. Look closer and you will find those small pockets of organic matter that give life to the plants.

Nature always finds a way to live, doesn't it?

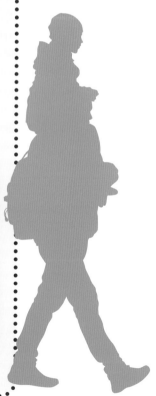

35 OLD BRIDLE PATH

Although named Old Bridle Path, you will not find any horses accompanying you on the trail up to West Rattlesnake Mountain. Don't worry about that name either—the timber rattlesnake (the only venomous snake in the state) is so rare that state biologists have said there is only a single den in the entire state. The trail still boasts some interesting features and gives an unbelievable view of Squam Lake at its summit.

Start: At the Old Bridle Path trailhead to West Rattlesnake
Elevation gain: 380 feet
Distance: 1.7 miles
Difficulty: Easy to moderate
Hiking time: 2 hours
Seasons/Schedule: Year-round
Fees and permits: None
Trail contact: West Rattlesnake Natural Area, NH Division of Forests and Lands, 172 Pembroke Rd., Concord, NH; (603) 271-2214; www.nh.gov/nhdfl
Dog-friendly: Allowed on leash
Trail surface: Dirt, stone steps, and solid rock

Land status: New Hampshire Division of Forests and Lands
Nearest town: Holderness, NH
Other trail users: None
Water availability: None
Maps: West Rattlesnake Mountain trail map
Age range: All ages
Toilets: None
Stroller/Wheelchair compatibility: No
Resting benches: None
Potential child hazards: Large drop-offs at the summit
Gear suggestions: Trekking poles

FINDING THE TRAILHEAD

From Concord, take I-93 North for approximately 36 miles. Take exit 24 for Route 3/Route 25 toward Plymouth. Keep right at the fork and merge onto Route 25 East/Route 3 South. Stay on Route 25 East/Route 3 South for approximately 4.5 miles. Turn left onto Route 113 and travel for approximately 5.5 miles. You will pass the town of Holderness as well as travel along the banks of Squam Lake before hitting the parking lot on your right. **GPS:** 43.788939 / -71.548634

THE HIKE

Old Bridle Path starts just off Route 113, past the town of Holderness. The parking lot is small considering the hike's popularity, so expect to be required to turn around if there are no spots available. There is another small parking area across the street at the Mount Morgan trailhead. Do not park on the sides of the road, as you will be ticketed and potentially towed.

The trail starts out over a series of large steps made up of wood and stone. On rainy days or if dew has fallen, the wood steps can be slippery, so take caution. Hemlock, beech, oak, and pine trees surround the trail—a typical upland forest ecosystem in this part of New England. As you head farther uphill, the trees change, and red pine takes over as the dominant species.

Almost every time I have hiked this trail with my son, he ends up finding a stick or branch on the ground to play "trail swords" with. I don't discourage the activity, as it keeps

The path is well forested until the overlook at the end.

Playing swords with the sticks on the trail is the perfect way to keep kiddos motivated.

him moving on the trail. Just remember, as I always do, to keep the branch on the trail when you are finished playing with it and don't bring it home with you.

Before you know it, you will reach the overlook on West Rattlesnake Mountain and the pink granite outcrops that make up its summit. From here you can see for miles across Squam Lake and the variety of forested islands peppered throughout it. Keep an eye out for bald eagles, as they are known to have roosts on several of the islands across the lake.

It is fun to come back to do this trail each of the four seasons. Winter allows for more solitude on the trail, as residents and visitors alike head to the ski slopes. Fall calls for crowds on the trails trying to get glimpses of the beautiful leaves, while spring brings out lush green landscapes. Summer can potentially bring a lot of bugs, so pack insect repellent. Luckily, the summit is usually windy, which keeps the bugs at bay.

Top: The beauty of Squam Lake from the overlook
Bottom: A kiddo points the way to all the beautiful views on a frigid winter day.

If you need to add more miles to your hike, you can head east along the Ridge Trail to summit East Rattlesnake. It boasts practically the same views as West Rattlesnake but with way fewer people on the summit. You will add another 2.0 miles to your round-trip length if you choose to do this part of the trail. Whichever path you take, head back the way you came to make your way back down the mountain.

After the hike, you can head to Squam Lake Science Center to partake in several activities. You can take a cruise with a naturalist and check out the loons and bald eagles that take up residence on the lake. There are several animals that call Squam Lake Science Center home and educate visitors on their behavior and need for protection. Those animals include a black bear, bobcat, coyote, red fox, river otter, and even a mountain lion!

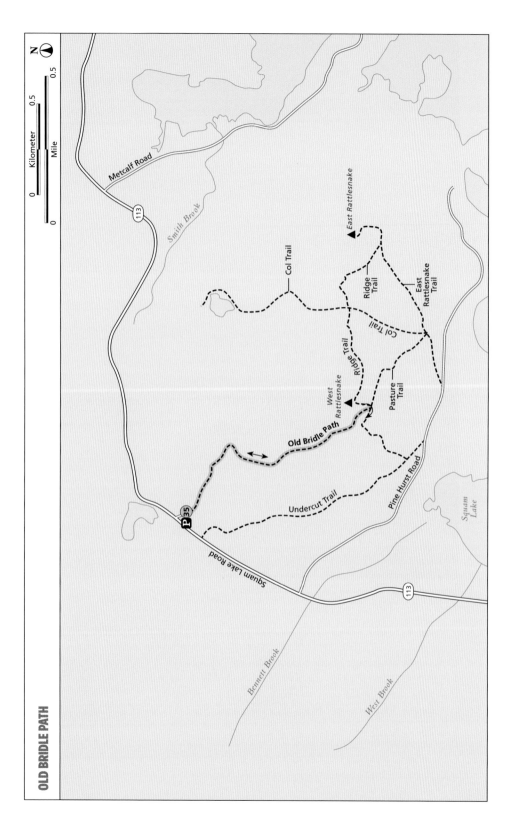

OLD BRIDLE PATH

There are huge boulders to sit on and relax while taking in the views.

MILES AND DIRECTIONS

0.00 Start at the Old Bridle Path/West Rattlesnake trailhead.

0.85 Reach the summit of West Rattlesnake Mountain.

1.70 Arrive back at the trailhead.

WHAT IS THERE TO DO AROUND SQUAM LAKE?

Squam Lake covers 6,791 acres and has 61 miles of shoreline. It is the second-largest lake in the Granite State. Many residents and visitors use the lake for recreation that includes boating, waterskiing, and more! But there's more than just water activities to do on and around the lake.

Visit Center Harbor on the other side of the lake from West Rattlesnake and walk down Main Street. Here you can shop at Squam Lake Artisans and then grab an ice-cream cone at Dewey's Ice Cream Parlor. Cap off your day at Squam Brewing, located in a quaint barn in Holderness.

Or you can head south to Meredith and the larger Lake Winnipesaukee, where the fun never ends. Whether it be boating in summer, leaf-peeping in fall, or pond hockey in winter, there is something for everyone.

If there is a more perfect trail to do with kids in New England, I have yet to hear of it. The Winnie-the-Pooh Trail located in Goodwill Conservation Area is ideal for those young kiddos (or, let's face it, anyone) who still believe books can become reality. Enter the Hundred Acre Wood to check on Winnie-the-Pooh and his friends and maybe hunt for Woozles and Heffalumps while you're romping through the forest.

Start: At the Winnie-the-Pooh trailhead	**Trail surface:** Dirt
Elevation gain: 80 feet	**Land status:** Town of Barrington
Distance: 0.75 mile	**Nearest town:** Barrington, NH
Difficulty: Easy	**Other trail users:** None
Hiking time: 1 hour	**Water availability:** None
Seasons/Schedule: Year-round	**Maps:** Goodwill Conservation Area trail map
Fees and permits: None	**Age range:** All ages
Trail contact: Barrington Conservation Commission, 333 Calef Hwy., Barrington, NH; (603) 664-5798; www.barringtonconcom.org/barringtons-conserved-lands-goodwill-conservation-area	**Toilets:** None
	Stroller/Wheelchair compatibility: No
Dog-friendly: Allowed on leash	**Resting benches:** Yes, along the trail
	Potential child hazards: None
	Gear suggestions: Insect repellent

FINDING THE TRAILHEAD

From Portsmouth, head west on Route 4 for approximately 5 miles and then take the exit (no number) toward Route 4 West. Turn left onto Route 4 for approximately 10 miles and then take the first exit at the traffic circle to head north on Route 125. Stay on Route 125 North for approximately 4.5 miles and then turn left on Route 9. Travel for about 1.5 miles. The parking lot is on your left. **GPS:** 43.214974 / -71.023339

THE HIKE

Tucked away in the quiet Southern New Hampshire town of Barrington resides a trail that transports you into a fairy tale or, at the very least, a children's book. Speaking of books—there is a mini library at the trailhead housed in a glass cabinet. Feel free to peruse the books or drop off one of your own for others to take.

The trail starts just over the bridge, where you hang a right toward Christopher Robin's house. It will be marked with a door on the tree. Better knock to see if he's home. If he isn't, keep making progress on the trail. A path leading right down toward the water's edge will bring you to Rabbit's House. Are there any carrots around the ground to indicate whether or not he's home?

When you hit a junction, Kanga, Roo, and Tigger's House is on your right. They might be hiding underneath the big rock waiting for you to leave. Next up is Owl's House, where you might see him perched on the large log. You might have to ring the bell on his door to see if he's home. Keep an eye out for Heffalumps or Woozles as you

Top: The trail is covered by pine needles and is very easy to follow.
Bottom: The Six Pine Trees from the story

head toward Piglet's House. The small door is exactly the right size for him but might be too small for any human.

Pass by the Heffalump Trap but steer clear in case any Heffalumps have been caught—best leave it for the authorities. At the intersection, Six Pine Trees is on your right, the shortcut to Pooh's House is straight ahead, but you will go left to head toward Eeyore's House. If it starts to get gloomy outside, you'll know you're close to Eeyore, as his moods always seem to disrupt the weather around here.

Head around the bend to find Winnie-the-Pooh's large cave and honey stash. Some-times Pooh will be sleeping (every so often a stuffed Winnie-the-Pooh is left by locals),

Christopher Robin's door—is anybody home? You'll also see everyone else's home from Winnie-the-Pooh.

and other times he'll be out with his friends. Go around the large outcrop and back up to Six Pine Trees before making your way back to the parking lot on the same trail.

Check to see if Christopher Robin is home once more when you pass the door to his house. If not, maybe you'll have better luck next time. Come back to the bridge over the small stream that comes out of Richardson Pond. Grab some sticks off the ground and play "Pooh Sticks." Drop the sticks in the water on one side of the bridge and see which stick makes it across the other side of the bridge first! After your hike, you can visit Barrington Public Library, where often there are story times happening outside. The librarians here are big fans of Winnie-the-Pooh and can point you in the direction of all the best stories.

Top: A heffalump trap along the trail
Bottom: The happiest of kiddos at Winnie-the-Pooh's cave

THE REAL STORY BEHIND WINNIE-THE-POOH

Did you know that Winnie-the-Pooh was named after a real bear? During World War I, Canadian soldier and veterinarian Harry Colebourn bought a bear at the train station (of all places) for twenty dollars and took her (yes, it was a "she") to London to join the war effort. He named her after the town he grew up in: Winnipeg.

Winnie, as she was nicknamed, joined Harry and his brigade, but when his troop was called to France, she couldn't go with him. So Harry loaned her to the London Zoo, which eventually became her permanent home. Here zoo-goers were allowed to ride on Winnie and feed her some of her favorite treats. She loved a mix of condensed milk and corn syrup—unlike the sweet honey that the book character loves.

One day A.A. Milne (the man behind Winnie-the-Pooh) visited the London Zoo with his son, Christopher Robin. They frequented the zoo, where Christopher fell in love with Winnie, going so far as to name his own stuffed bear Winnie. A.A. Milne simply added the name of a friend's pet to the end of his name to create the famous beloved character, Winnie-the-Pooh.

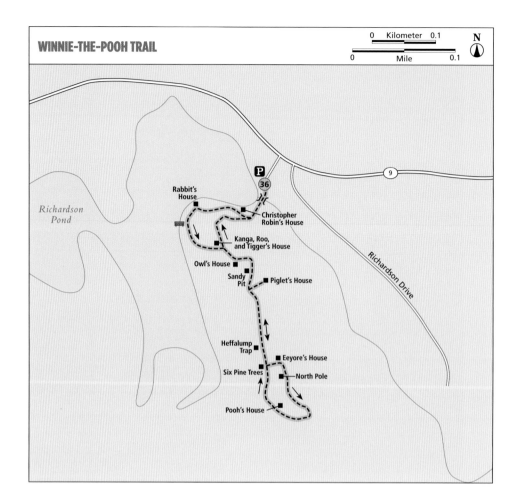

0   Kilometer   0.1

0   Mile   0.1

N

Rabbit's House

Christopher Robin's House

Richardson Pond

Kanga, Roo, and Tigger's House

Owl's House

Sandy Pit

Piglet's House

Richardson Drive

Heffalump Trap

Eeyore's House

Six Pine Trees

North Pole

Pooh's House

9

36

P

MILES AND DIRECTIONS

0.00 Start at the Winnie-the-Pooh trailhead off Route 9. Cross over the bridge and take a right to continue on the trail. Check to see if Christopher Robin is home by knocking on his door. Turn right down the path to visit Rabbit's House

0.10 Arrive at Rabbit's House. Continue on the trail.

0.20 Arrive at Kanga, Roo, and Tigger's House. Turn right to continue on the trail. You will pass by Owl's House and the Sandy Pit.

0.25 Take the small trail to the left to check if Piglet is home.

0.30 See if there are any Heffalumps in the trap on your right; then at the Six Pine Trees, take a left to head up to Eeyore's House and the North Pole.

0.35 Reach Eeyore's House and the North Pole. Continue down the trail to Pooh's House

0.45 Round the bend to come to Pooh's Cave. Pass Pooh's Cave and head up the trail back to Six Pine Trees.

0.50 Pass Six Pine Trees and the Heffalump Trap once again.

0.60 Take the trail to the right to go hunting for Woozles!

0.75 Arrive back at the trailhead.

37 DIANA'S BATHS

I do not recommend bringing soap or shampoo to take an actual bath at Diana's Baths. Instead, bring a bathing suit, picnic, and towel to enjoy a day dipping your toes in the water and enjoying the cascading falls. The cold water will be the perfect reprieve for those simmering hot and humid days that make up the bulk of any New England summer.

Start: At the Moat Mountain/Diana's Baths trailhead
Elevation gain: 260 feet
Distance: 3.0 miles
Difficulty: Easy
Hiking time: 2 to 3 hours, depending on how long you stay at the waterfalls
Seasons/Schedule: Year-round
Fees and permits: Fee required
Trail contact: White Mountain National Forest, 71 White Mountain Dr., Campton, NH; (603) 536-6100; www.fs.usda.gov/recarea/whitemountain/recreation/recarea/?recid=74963&actid=70
Dog-friendly: Allowed on leash

Trail surface: Dirt, gravel, and solid rock
Land status: US Forest Service
Nearest town: North Conway, NH
Other trail users: None
Water availability: None
Maps: White Mountains—Carter Range/Evans Notch trail map
Age range: All ages
Toilets: Yes, at the trailhead
Stroller/Wheelchair compatibility: No
Resting benches: None
Potential child hazards: Slippery rocks along the waterfalls and large drop-offs
Gear suggestions: Bathing suit, towel

FINDING THE TRAILHEAD

From Portsmouth, take Route 16 North/Route 202 East for approximately 17 miles. The road turns into just Route 16 North. Keep on Route 16 North for approximately 55 miles, until you reach the town of Conway. Take a left onto Washington Street and continue for approximately 6 miles. At the T-intersection, take a left onto West Side Road. Drive for approximately 1.5 miles, and the parking lot for Diana's Baths will be on your left. **GPS:** 44.074605 / -71.164112

THE HIKE

The Abenaki called this area home before settlers stole it from them. They referred to Lucy Brook and its small pools scattered throughout the granite that makes up the waterfalls as the "Water Fairies' Spring." The ethereal nature of the brook can still be seen today. By the 1860s the name "Diana's Baths" started appearing on maps, and the Lucy family, who owned the land, kept the name that referred to the Roman goddess of wild animals and the hunt.

The trail starts out on a level path from the parking lot, which is just north of Cathedral Ledge State Park. It takes only about 0.5 mile to get to Lucy Brook, where Diana's Baths begin. This is where the bulk of visitors go on a hot summer day and where it will be most crowded.

To get away from the hordes of hikers, keep going up the trail and find a spot to head into Diana's brook. The farther up you go, the brook provides several waterfalls and pools

The trail is mostly dirt and pine needles, but once you get up to Diana's Baths, the path becomes rocky with lots of roots.

for you to choose from. Once you have found the perfect place to take a dip, be wary of the various ledges throughout the brook. After all, this section of the brook is full of cascading waterfalls, which means they need ledges to fall from.

When you and your kids walk around the rocks, they may be slippery, especially the ones underneath the water. Algae and other things like to grow in these pools, and you can easily slip and break a bone. So walk only on the dry rocks and then scoot on your bum when you enter the pools.

It is worth noting that the water that runs through this brook is coming off snowmelt from the 4,000-footers that surround the area. This means the water could potentially be freezing cold. Even on the hottest of days, the water can throw you into shock, so keep an eye on your kids for any visual indicators of hypothermic shock.

After a day filled with lots of splashing, sore cheeks from laughing, and fun in the

There are several tiers of pools—pick the best one for you!

Crystal-clear water also means it's likely cold!

THE HARMFUL NATURE OF THE SPONGY MOTH

During my most recent visit to Diana's Baths, there was a massive infestation of spongy moth caterpillars. These caterpillars can do extensive damage to a stand of trees in just a matter of weeks. You can identify this moth by the double rows of blue and red spots along its back and the long hairs poking out of its body. If you see one on the trail, never touch it, as its hair can irritate the skin.

Oaks and aspens are the preferred tree of the spongy moth caterpillar, but in large infestations they'll feed on almost anything, including conifers (like pine trees). One spongy moth caterpillar can eat up to 1 square foot of leaves in a single day. This might not seem like a lot, but if you have an infestation, that could be thousands of leaves per day and an entire forest in a few weeks. Although eating the leaves does not outright kill a tree, it does leave it quite vulnerable to other infestations and attacks.

When my son and I were most recently here, we could hear the caterpillars pooping (their poop is called *frass*) from the trees and literally raining down on us. To say I was grossed out is an understatement. My son, however, thought being pooped on by a caterpillar was the coolest thing in the world.

sun, head back on the trail. The path is just as easy heading back to your car as it was coming in. It is what makes this trail so popular and accessible to so many people. Due to the busyness of the area, though, make sure you leave this place better than you found it. In recent years there has been a lot more trash in and around the pools. So even if the trash is not yours, feel free to pick it up (with gloves, of course) and throw it out in a receptacle when you are back home.

Pop by North Conway on your way out. This quaint mountain town is full of fun shops, good coffee, yummy restaurants, and one of the best general stores in the country. My son and I always stop at Zeb's General Store to grab some honey lollipops and then head over to the local playground to get some more energy out before heading home. The views are reason enough to stop in town, or you can hop on one of the Conway Scenic Railroad's trains.

Testing out the frigid water on a warm, summer day

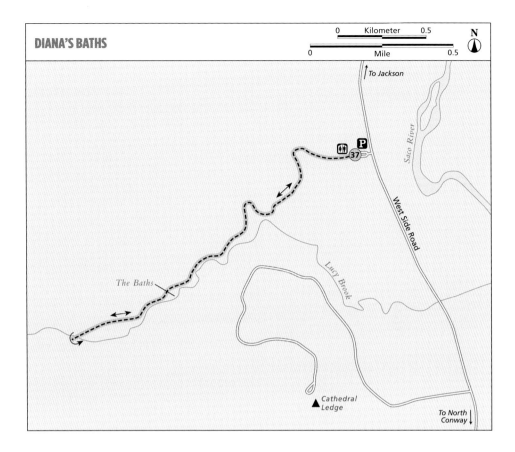

MILES AND DIRECTIONS

0.00 Start at the Moat Mountain/Diana's Baths trailhead on the western side of the parking lot.

0.50 Reach the start of the Diana's Baths Trail. For the next mile, you can choose any place to head into Lucy Brook and splash around. The farther you go on the trail, the fewer people you'll see.

1.50 Turn around to head back to the trailhead.

2.50 Veer away from Lucy Brook and back to the trailhead.

3.00 Arrive back at the trailhead.

38 SABBADAY FALLS

There are dozens of beautiful waterfalls in New Hampshire, but none are quite as photogenic as Sabbaday Falls. And due to award-worthy photographs, you will see lots of people on the short trail to the falls on any given day. The beautifully made wooden boardwalk that skirts the ledges around Sabbaday Falls makes for the perfect backdrop and an easy climb to see the raging waters flow over the edge.

Start: At the Sabbaday Falls trailhead
Elevation gain: 100 feet
Distance: 0.75 mile
Difficulty: Easy
Hiking time: 1 hour
Seasons/Schedule: Year-round
Fees and permits: Fee required
Trail contact: White Mountain National Forest, 71 White Mountain Dr., Campton, NH; (603) 536-6100; www.fs.usda .gov/recarea/whitemountain/ recarea/?recid=74927
Dog-friendly: Allowed on leash

Trail surface: Dirt, gravel, and boardwalk
Land status: US Forest Service
Nearest town: Conway, NH
Other trail users: None
Water availability: None
Maps: White Mountains—Crawford Notch/Sandwich Range trail map
Age range: All ages
Toilets: Yes, at the trailhead
Stroller/Wheelchair compatibility: No
Resting benches: None
Potential child hazards: Boardwalk can be slippery.
Gear suggestions: Insect repellent

FINDING THE TRAILHEAD

From Portsmouth, take Route 16 North/Route 202 East for approximately 17 miles. The road turns into just Route 16 North. Keep on Route 16 North for approximately 55 miles. Just before you reach the town of Conway, take a left onto Route 112/Kancamagus Highway West for approximately 15.4 miles. The large parking lot is on your left. **GPS:** 43.997368 / -71.393216

THE HIKE

My son and I were lucky on a somewhat rainy Tuesday in October when we stumbled upon Sabbaday Falls after touring around the Kancamagus Highway to see the fall colors. I had pulled into almost every overlook and trailhead to check things out, and Sabbaday Falls was one of the last pullouts of the day.

Sabbaday Falls was once called Church's Falls, named after landscape painter Frederic Church. But legend says that a group of builders who had been working on the road from Albany Intervale to Waterville decided to store their tools around the waterfalls before winter set in and ceased their work. They happened to leave on a Sunday morning and named the falls "Sabbaday Falls" after the Sabbath Day (aka Sunday). Believe it or not, the workers never returned to collect their tools—someone should have taught them about Leave No Trace principles.

Quickly we realized this was going to be a stellar hike. There was a fair amount of people in the parking lot—but not compared to what it would be like on a weekend or sunnier day. The trail is very wide and easily accessible for most trail users. My son

Top left: Walking up the short path to the falls is quick and easy.
Top right: Checking out the falls from the upper platforms
Bottom: Looking down the falls from the top

You can hop down to the stream to get a better glimpse of the viewing platforms and the falls.

stopped throughout the short hike to check out all the fungi that had sprouted up on the trail's edge.

I had to pull out some candy to get him motivated to keep going, but he eventually did. After all, the hike is only about a third of a mile from the trailhead to the falls. Nothing can prepare you for the beauty that is Sabbaday Falls. Despite how beautiful the photographs come out, nothing compares to seeing the waterfalls in real life.

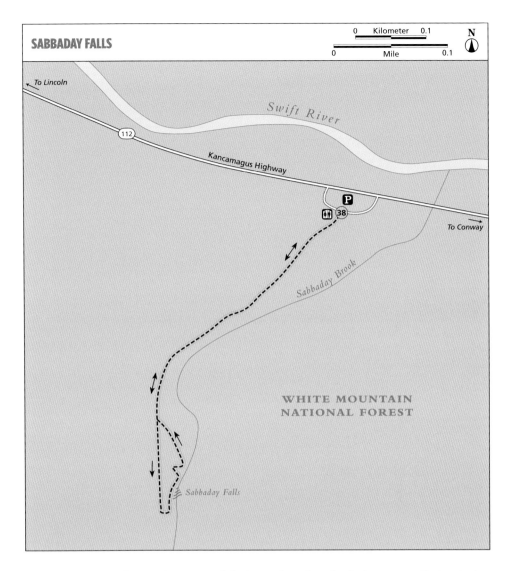

0   Kilometer   0.1

0   Mile   0.1

N

To Lincoln

Swift River

112

Kancamagus Highway

P

38

To Conway

Sabbaday Brook

WHITE MOUNTAIN
NATIONAL FOREST

Sabbaday Falls

I can see why certain poets and fiction authors have looked to nature for inspiration after seeing the fantastical elements of Sabbaday Falls. If you climb up the boardwalk's right-hand side of the waterfalls, you can view the swift-moving water from the top and watch it go crashing down into the deep pool below. The boardwalk is completely safe and fenced in so that no one, not even small bodies, can fit through its holes.

You can also view the waterfalls from their base. The waterfalls are the central focus with the boardwalk just above. The flat rocks at the bottom can be slippery from the water that somehow keeps a constant mist in the air. If you squint your eyes, you might think you are in the Pacific Northwest with how green and wet everything looks.

After you have filled your camera or phone to its maximum capacity for photograph storage, head back down the trail to your car.

Sabbaday Falls in all its glory

MILES AND DIRECTIONS

0.00 Start at the Sabbaday Falls trailhead.

0.37 Reach the falls. Turn around and head back to the trailhead.

0.75 Arrive back at the trailhead.

THE MAGIC OF THE "KANC"

The Kancamagus (pronounced kank-ah-mah-gus) Highway, lovingly nicknamed by locals as the "Kanc," is a 34-mile scenic byway connecting Conway to Lincoln, New Hampshire. It's a highly sought-after tourist destination, especially in fall. Its highest point reaches just under 3,000 feet above sea level and encompasses breathtaking overlooks of the White Mountains.

You can start on the Kanc (Route 112) on either side. There are several stops along the way, including Sabbaday Falls, Rocky Gorge, and Lower Falls. Just make sure to have enough gas (and snacks) to get you across, as there are no gas stations, restaurants, or other businesses along the road. It stays that way to this day to keep the natural beauty of the area intact.

If you are headed through here on a peak day, upward of 4,000 vehicles can be traveling the road, leaving little room for parking at all the overlooks. Luckily, most visitors don't stay very long at each spot, so all you have to do is wait a few minutes to snag a spot. Although it's only 34 miles long, give yourself plenty of time to drive the entire byway. Time can easily slip away when you are stopping at every spot, because every spot looks beautiful.

39 WHITE LEDGES TRAIL

Although many of the best trails are in the White Mountains, there are still a few outside the national forest that will give you jaw-dropping views. One such trail is the White Ledges Trail that leads to the white cliffs (hence the name) that overlook Lake Solitude within the borders of Sunapee State Park. You can shave off a big chunk of the trail if you take the chairlift up to the top of Mount Sunapee. Some might call this cheating; others call it intelligent.

Start: At the Summit trailhead
Elevation gain: 1,790 feet
Distance: 6.0 miles
Difficulty: Strenuous
Hiking time: 6 hours
Seasons/Schedule: Trail is closed in winter for ski season.
Fees and permits: Fee required
Trail contact: Sunapee State Park, 86 Beach Access Rd., Newbury, NH; (603) 763-5561; www.nhstateparks .org/visit/state-parks/mt-sunapee-state-park. Mount Sunapee Resort, 1398 Rte. 103, Newbury, NH; (603) 763-3500; www.mountsunapee.com
Dog-friendly: Allowed on leash
Trail surface: Gravel and dirt
Land status: New Hampshire State Parks and Mount Sunapee Resort

Nearest town: Sunapee, NH
Other trail users: None
Water availability: Yes, at the visitor center and summit restaurant
Maps: Sunapee State Park trail map
Age range: Kids in carriers and those with extensive trail experience
Toilets: Yes, at the visitor center and summit restaurant
Stroller/Wheelchair compatibility: No
Resting benches: Yes, at the summit restaurant
Potential child hazards: Large drop-offs at White Ledges/Lake Solitude overlook
Gear suggestions: Trekking poles

FINDING THE TRAILHEAD

From Concord, take I-89 North for approximately 6 miles and take exit 5 for Route 202 West/Route 9 toward Henniker/Keene. Merge onto Route 9 West for 7 miles. Take the exit for Route 114 toward Henniker/Bradford. Turn right onto Route 114 North for approximately 8.5 miles. Turn left onto Route 103 West and continue for approximately 9 miles. Take a slight left onto Route 103B South and immediately go straight onto Mount Sunapee Access Road. Park as close as you can get to the buildings at the resort. **GPS:** 43.330110 / -72.081320

THE HIKE

As stated prior, this trail is considered strenuous if climbed from the base of the mountain. However, in summer the chairlift up Mount Sunapee runs for visitors, so you can skip the trek up the mountain and opt for a shorter hike. It is important to note, however, that kids cannot be in child carriers (soft or framed ones) on the chairlift. Infants and kids are not allowed on a parent's lap either, so if you have kids age 2 or younger, you will have to carry your kid up the mountain the good ol' fashioned way. Otherwise, kids 4 and under ride free!

If you are making your way up the mountain on foot, start to the right of the chairlift on the Summit Trail. After 0.5 mile, turn left to continue on the Summit Trail. In 1.5

Top: Once you get up to the top of Mount Sunapee, the trail to White Ledges traverses the gravel service road for the first half.
Bottom: A father and son look out onto Lake Sunapee from one of the overlooks.

miles, you will reach the summit of Mount Sunapee and a much-deserved break at the summit restaurant. This is also where those who took the chairlift up will meet up with the trail down to Lake Solitude's overlook.

Once you have caught your breath, make your way east down the gravel road. There is a great place to look out onto Lake Sunapee to the left as you head down the steep path. Continue down the wide path until you reach a narrower path on the right.

This is the Solitude Trail. After about 0.75 mile, you will reach the White Ledges overlooking Lake Solitude. Be careful around the rocky outcrops here, as it is a huge drop-off to the forest below.

Top: Once off the service road, the tree-lined trail gets narrower.
Bottom: Overlooking Lake Solitude

Take in the beauty of Lake Solitude and then head back the way you came. Once you make it back up to the summit, take another break before your lengthy trek back down the mountain. The restaurant at the summit serves hot dogs, chicken nuggets, fries, and even beer if you are feeling so inclined. If you have chairlift tickets, lucky you—your hike is practically done. If you can't take the chairlift, head back down on the Summit Trail you took up.

Once you are back down to the visitor center, you can think about doing some of the other activities the ski resort offers in summer. Their "Play-All-Day" package includes unlimited Aerial Sky Rides (aka the chairlift), disc golf rentals, a round of miniature golf,

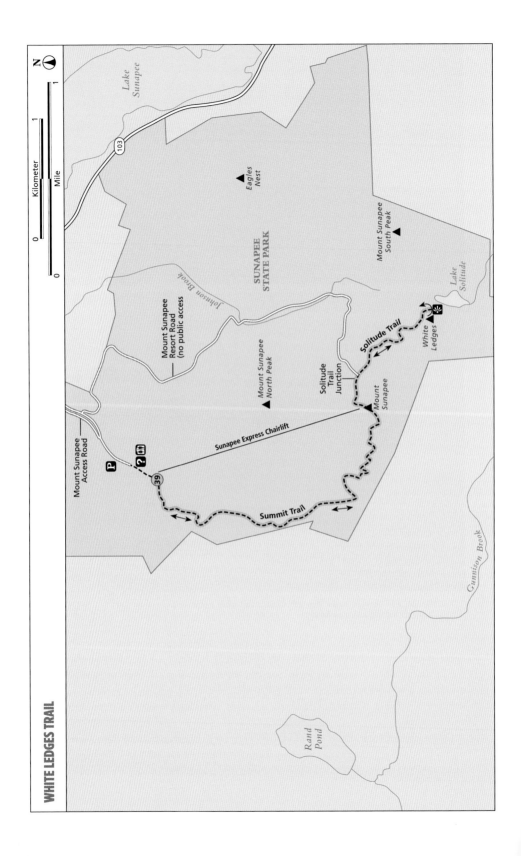

WHITE LEDGES TRAIL

N

0   Kilometer   1
0   Mile   1

Lake Sunapee

103

Eagles Nest ▲

SUNAPEE STATE PARK

Johnson Brook

Mount Sunapee Resort Road (no public access)

Mount Sunapee North Peak ▲

Mount Sunapee Access Road

P

? 🏠

39

Sunapee Express Chairlift

Solitude Trail Junction

▲ Mount Sunapee

Solitude Trail

Mount Sunapee South Peak ▲

Lake Solitude

White Ledges

Summit Trail

Rand Pond

Gunnison Brook

six climbing wall attempts, four loops along the aerial challenge course, a small bag of mining materials (they have a sluice on-site!), and access to Sunapee State Park Beach.

You can also buy individual tickets for each of the activities or play around in the sluice (it's free, but mining materials cost a small fee) at the base of the chairlift. This area is also well-known for its mountain biking trails. They are on a different mountain and different chairlift than the one you just did, so no need to worry about mountain bikers flying by you while you are hiking.

MILES AND DIRECTIONS

- **0.00** Start to the right of the chairlift on the Summit Trail.
- **0.50** Turn left to continue on the Summit Trail.
- **2.10** Reach the summit of Mount Sunapee. The Summit Trail becomes the Monadnock-Sunapee Greenway/Solitude Trail.
- **2.30** Veer right onto the narrow path off the gravel road.
- **2.95** Stay right at the fork to head toward White Ledges.
- **3.00** Reach the White Ledges overlook. Lake Solitude is in front of you. Return to the trail and head back the way you came
- **3.05** Stay left at the fork.
- **3.70** Turn left to head back toward the summit on the large gravel path.
- **3.90** Summit Mount Sunapee once again and head down the Summit Trail.
- **5.50** Turn right to head toward the parking lot.
- **6.00** Arrive back at the trailhead.

THE FUN DOESN'T END IN SUMMER

As you might have suspected, Mount Sunapee isn't just a fun place to recreate in the summer. It is also a ski resort in the winter. The same trails you walk on in summer get turned into ski trails when the snow falls, and they offer the same beautiful views you witness in summer.

While here in winter, there are plenty of other activities if the hefty price of a ski pass isn't in your budget. The towns of Sunapee, New London, and Newport have places to ice-skate and play hockey, and other offerings include the Lake Sunapee snowmobiling club, plenty of winter hikes, and dozens of cross-country ski trails.

40 WAGON HILL FARM LOOP

Take a leisurely walk along the many meadows and fields that comprise Wagon Hill Farm's 40 acres. You will also walk alongside the Oyster River, which flows out to the Atlantic Ocean, and climb on the iconic wagon that sits atop the hill here. In winter the hill where the wagon sits is a local seacoast favorite for sledding.

Start: At the trailhead south of the big white building
Elevation gain: 75 feet
Distance: 1.5 miles
Difficulty: Easy
Hiking time: 1.5 hours
Seasons/Schedule: Year-round, dawn until dusk
Fees and permits: None
Trail contact: Wagon Hill Farm, 156 Piscataqua Rd., Durham, NH; (603) 868-8034; www.ci.durham.nh.us/boc_conservation/wagon-hill-farm
Dog-friendly: Allowed on leash all the time, off-leash before 10:00 a.m.

Trail surface: Gravel and dirt
Land status: Town of Durham
Nearest town: Durham, NH
Other trail users: Cross-country skiers and snowshoers
Water availability: None
Maps: Wagon Hill Farm trail map
Age range: All ages
Toilets: Yes, at the trailhead
Stroller/Wheelchair compatibility: No
Resting benches: Yes, along the trail
Potential child hazards: Dog park on the trail
Gear suggestions: Insect repellent

FINDING THE TRAILHEAD

From Portsmouth, head west on Route 4 for approximately 5 miles and then take the exit (no number) toward Route 4 West. Turn left onto Route 4 West for approximately 1.5 miles and then turn left onto the gravel road to the Wagon Hill Farm parking lot. **GPS:** 43.129334 / -70.872588

THE HIKE

The loop that brings you around the border of Wagon Hill Farm starts at the wide gravel path next to the big white building on the property. As you start the walk, there is a section of grassland on the right that tends to be a popular spot for dog owners to have their dogs off-leash. Dogs are allowed off-leash (although under voice control) before 10:00 a.m. every day. If you or your children are afraid of dogs, I would wait until after 10:00 to start your hike.

Take a right to head toward the apple orchard after about 0.1 mile on the wide gravel path. There is a scenic view off to the left of the trail, opposite the apple orchard, as well as a bench to relax. Continue heading down the same trail and keep straight when you see a trail to your left. Go over a bridge and then stay straight on a spur trail when the main trail veers left. This spur trail will bring you to the Oyster River overlook.

During a recent visit ospreys were swooping down to catch fish along the river. My son and I must have stayed there for half an hour just watching the ospreys dive to see what they might catch. Head back to the main trail and turn right. This brings you to the beach area, picnic tables, and a scenic overlook. Some of the shoreline along Wagon Hill was recently restored to a "living shoreline."

Top: Overlooking the Oyster River, which flows into the Atlantic Ocean
Bottom: Riding in the passenger seat on the wagon

Many fields at Wagon Hill Farm are dedicated to certain species like monarchs and various birds.

THE MAGIC OF MONARCH BUTTERFLIES

The milkweed in one of the fields on Wagon Hill Farm does not get mowed to allow monarch butterflies to complete their life cycle. After traveling thousands of miles from Mexico, female monarch butterflies must lay their eggs quickly before their life cycle ends. Milkweed is the only plant that the larvae will eat, and, as such, is needed to thrive.

Monarch butterfly populations, although not technically on the Endangered Species List of the United States, have declined over the past few decades due to habitat loss through deforestation, excessive use of pesticides, and climate change. They are important pollinators due to their extensive migratory pattern from Canada to southern Mexico every year. Without their pollination, many species of plants, as well as food we humans eat, would decline significantly and be cause for concern.

The field in front of the famous wagon at Wagon Hill Farm

Over the past few decades, the shoreline along Wagon Hill Farm had deteriorated to the point where erosion was accelerating. The town of Durham decided to restore the area to protect and enhance the shoreline habitat by strategically placing plants, sand, stone, and organic materials to bring the natural shoreline back to the area. The living shoreline was built back in 2019, so there has not been enough time to see significant effects yet, but the results look promising.

Moving on from the beach area, head back up through the picnic tables to pick up the trail again. You will cross over another bridge and then veer right to head back toward the river. The trail will loop around and you will stay straight where a trail goes off to the left. Eventually, the trail turns left and the iconic wagon should come into view at that point. Make sure to stop here and climb on the wagon to get the best view. After the wagon it's just a hop, skip, and a jump back to your car.

A fun fort along the trail to explore

After your hike be sure to head across the road to the Market and Café at Emery Farm. You can grab a sandwich, pick up some local produce, or visit their petting farm complete with goats, chickens, and even a resident bunny. This is a favorite spot for locals to grab plants in spring, pumpkins in fall, and Christmas trees in December.

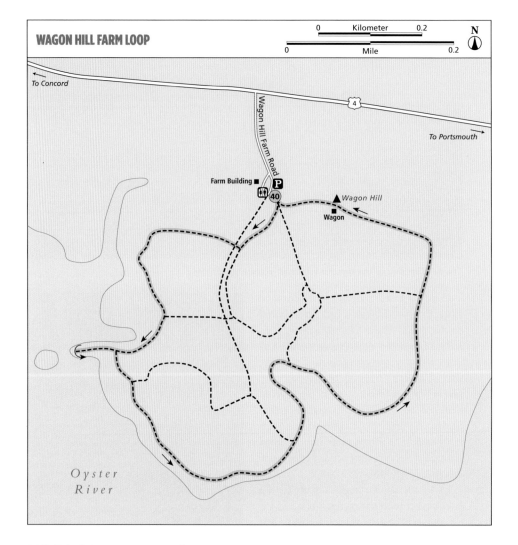

MILES AND DIRECTIONS

0.00 Start on the trail south of the big white building.

0.10 Turn right onto the trail.

0.35 Stay straight on the trail; do not turn left onto a different trail.

0.40 Take the trail to your right to go to the Oyster River overlook.

0.45 Reach the overlook. Return the way you came.

0.50 Take a right when you hit the intersection again. Stay right at the next fork.

0.80 Stay straight to continue on the trail. Do not take the trail to the left.

1.20 Stay straight to continue on the trail.

1.40 Reach the wagon and climb on board. Continue on the trail to head back to the parking lot.

1.50 Arrive back at the trailhead.

MAINE HIKES

A pebble beach at the Wells National
Estuarine Research Reserve

41 COASTAL MAINE BOTANICAL GARDENS LOOP

Some might not want to call this a hike, but you would be missing out if you skipped this gem of a place. The Coastal Maine Botanical Gardens. sits along the shorelines of the Back River, which drains directly into the Atlantic Ocean. You can smell the sea air even over all the fragrant scents of the flowers that inhabit the property. What makes this place truly magical, though, are the giant Guardians of the Seeds (read giant wooden sculptures) that are found throughout the gardens.

Start: Behind the visitor center
Elevation gain: 125 feet
Distance: 2.1 miles
Difficulty: Easy
Hiking time: 2 hours
Seasons/Schedule: May 1 through October 23, daily 9:00 a.m. to 5:00 p.m.
Fees and permits: Fee required
Trail contact: Coastal Maine Botanical Gardens, 105 Botanical Gardens Dr., Boothbay, ME; (207) 633-8000; www.mainegardens.org
Dog-friendly: Not allowed
Trail surface: Gravel, dirt, and pavement

Land status: Coastal Maine Botanical Gardens
Nearest town: Boothbay, ME
Other trail users: None
Water availability: Yes, at the visitor center, education center, and café
Maps: Coastal Maine Botanical Gardens trail map
Age range: All ages
Toilets: Yes, at the visitor center and café
Stroller/Wheelchair compatibility: Yes, on some of the trails but not all
Resting benches: Yes, along the trail
Potential child hazards: Lots of pollinators on the flowers
Gear suggestions: Insect repellent

FINDING THE TRAILHEAD

From Portland, take I-295 for approximately 23 miles. Use the right two lanes to take exit 28 to merge onto Route 1 North toward Coastal Route/Brunswick/Bath. Follow signs for Route 1 North for approximately 22 miles. Turn right onto Route 27 South for about 10 miles and then take the first exit at the traffic circle onto Corey Lane. After 0.3 mile turn right onto Barters Island Road for 1 mile. The entrance to the Coastal Maine Botanical Gardens will be on your left. Park anywhere in the large parking lot. **GPS:** 43.872004 / -69.659060

THE HIKE

Even if there were no giant trolls hidden in the forests that surround the Coastal Maine Botanical Gardens, it still would be worth a trip. The thousands of different flowers and plant species that are lovingly cared for bring a whole new meaning to "life in nature."

A huge draw to this place, however, are the Guardians of the Seeds. There are five of these mammoth-size wooden sculptures found throughout the gardens. Each troll represents a different part of a plant, such as the roots, leaves, and flowers, while they all hold (and therefore protect) a seed—hence, the name "Guardians of the Seeds."

Top: Lupines are just one of the hundreds of plant species at Coastal Maine Botanical Gardens.
Bottom: Gro is the wandering troll who represents the leaves of the tree. She disappears every autumn but also returns every spring.

There is no wrong way to visit the gardens. The trail I describe here is just one way to visit all the trolls and the sights around the property, but feel free to head on your own path too. I highly recommend grabbing a trail map at the visitor center before heading out as it shows all the details of where to find everything within the garden boundary. Either way, start your hike behind the visitor center and by crossing the Heafitz Wetland Bridge. All the attractions and trails will be to your right, so head that way to continue the trail.

If you head north (or right), you will be able to see the first Guardian of the Seed: Roskva. This gigantic guardian stands for the trunks, like the one she holds with her left hand. She is considered the heaviest and strongest of the trolls and has a memory like an elephant.

Soren is another troll and Guardian of the Seeds. He represents the branches of a tree and likes to dance in the wind.

Next head through the Bosarge Family Education Center to continue down the wide gravel path. There is a shuttle for visitors, but it will not bring you to every troll on the property. Turn down the first path on the right and then a quick left onto the narrower path of Maine Woods Trail. When you reach the intersection of another trail, turn right to head toward Giles Rhododendron and Perennial Garden.

Zigzag your way up the gardens to visit Gro, the next troll on your hike. Gro represents the leaves of a tree and is a wanderer among her people. She is always leaving to find

Birk is one of the Guardians of the Seeds and is the wisest and most mysterious of them. He holds the roots of the tree.

new sources of sunlight to produce more trees and more food for her forest friends. She disappears every fall to rejuvenate and returns in spring ready to grow again.

After saying bye to Gro, head up the North Trail and then take a left onto the main path. Soren will be on your left. He represents the branches of a tree and, just like a branch, is always searching for higher places to reach. He knows that he is home to many woodland creatures and holds strong for them to thrive.

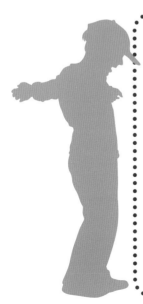

THE ARTIST BEHIND THE TROLLS

The trolls at Coastal Maine Botanical Gardens might look familiar to you, especially if you have visited Isak Heartstone in Breckenridge, Colorado, or Mama Mimi in Jackson Hole, Wyoming. All these sculptures have been imagined and designed by the same artist: Thomas Dambo.

Dambo was born in Denmark and lives in Copenhagen to this day, building and creating these amazing sculptures. He calls himself a "recycle art activist," as his art is meant to decompose as anything in nature would.

He uses his art to incite knowledge about our natural landscapes and the importance of saving these areas for future generations. He connects with people throughout the world with his work. Currently he has sculptures across the United States, South Korea, China, Belgium, Puerto Rico, and, of course, in his home country. Have you seen more than one of these mesmerizing sculptures? Which one is on your list to see next?

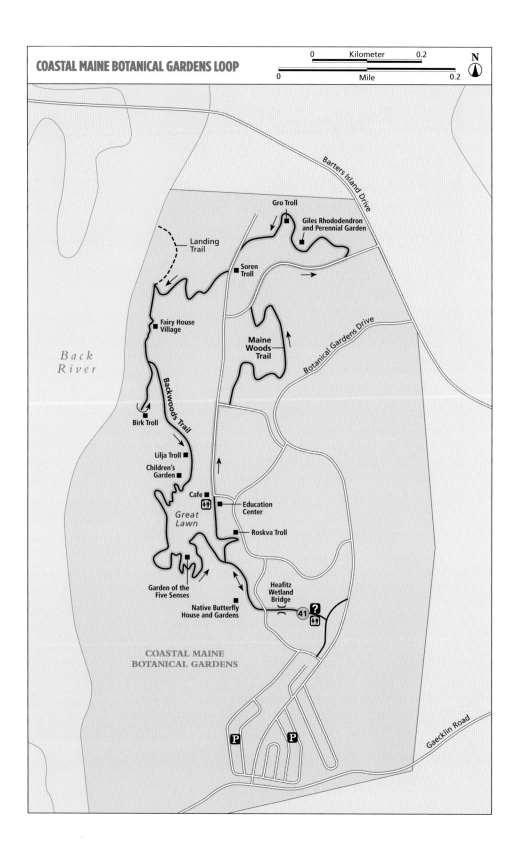

Kilometer

Mile

N

Barters Island Drive

Gro Troll

Giles Rhododendron
and Perennial Garden

Landing
Trail

Soren
Troll

Fairy House
Village

Maine
Woods
Trail

Botanical Gardens Drive

Back
River

Backwoods Trail

Birk Troll

Lilja Troll

Children's
Garden

Cafe

Great
Lawn

Education
Center

Roskva Troll

Garden of the
Five Senses

Heafitz
Wetland
Bridge

Native Butterfly
House and Gardens

41

COASTAL MAINE
BOTANICAL GARDENS

P

P

Gaecklin Road

Head down the Maine Woods Trail across from Soren and then left at the next junction. A few steps down the trail brings you to the Fairy House Village where you and your kids can make some of your own fairy houses using the natural materials around the area.

Then get back on the trail to meet up with Birk, the holder of the roots of the tree. Just like roots, Birk listens to the soil and connects with everything around him. This is why he is considered to be the wisest among his people.

Return the way you came and take a right onto the Backwoods Trail after the pinecone sculpture. This trail will bring you right to the last Guardian of the Seeds: Lilja. She is the youngest of the trolls and holds the scent of the flowers of the tree. Her unabated whimsy makes her a joy to be around.

A fairy house built with natural materials by visitors at the Fairy Village

After Lilja, head to the Children's Garden where you can romp around in the treetops or make your own music on the instruments scattered throughout. Stop by the small buildings within the Children's Garden to see if there are any story times happening during your visit. Once you've had your fill, take one last stroll through the Great Lawn and the Garden of the Five Senses and then make your way back to the visitor center.

MILES AND DIRECTIONS

0.00   Start on the path behind the visitor center.

0.20   Stay right to head over a bridge. Reach the Roskva Troll just after the bridge.

0.30   Go straight through the Bosarge Family Education Center and out the other side to continue on the gravel path.

0.40   Take the first right down another gravel path and then an immediate left onto Maine Woods Trail.

0.70   Take a right onto the gravel path and head toward the Giles Rhododendron and Perennial Garden area. Wind your way through until you reach the top.

0.90   Reach the Gro Troll and then continue down the path. Take a left when you get to the junction just after the troll.

1.00   Reach the Soren Troll, then turn right down the Maine Woods Trail.

1.20   Take a left onto the Landing Trail.

1.25   Explore the Fairy House Village on your left. Then continue on the trail and stay straight.

1.30   Reach the Birk Troll. Turn back the way you came and turn right on the Backwoods Trail just after the pinecone sculpture.

1.50   Reach the Lilja Troll. Continue on the path to head toward the Children's Garden.

1.80   Meander around the Great Lawn through the Arbor Garden, Slater Forest Pond, and Garden of the Five Senses. Head back to the visitor center

2.10   Arrive back at the trailhead.

Take a long drive up to the great wilderness of Northern Maine and head up to Baxter State Park. As home to Mount Katahdin and the end of the Appalachian Trail, Baxter State Park sees thousands of visitors every year despite its remote location. But as everyone is heading up the 5,000-footer, I suggest you try out the short (but beautiful) trail along Blueberry Ledges.

Start: East of Abol Bridge Campground and Store at the Appalachian trailhead
Elevation gain: 340 feet
Distance: 3.8 miles
Difficulty: Moderate
Hiking time: 4 hours
Seasons/Schedule: The road is closed in winter.
Fees and permits: Fee required
Trail contact: Baxter State Park, Maine State Parks, Bureau of Parks and Lands, 22 State House Station, Augusta, ME; (207) 723-5140; https://baxterstatepark.org
Dog-friendly: Not allowed
Trail surface: Gravel and dirt

Land status: Maine Bureau of Parks and Lands
Nearest town: Millinocket, ME
Other trail users: None
Water availability: Yes, at the campground store
Maps: Baxter State Park trail map
Age range: All ages
Toilets: Yes, at the campground store
Stroller/Wheelchair compatibility: No
Resting benches: None
Potential child hazards: Well-established black bear habitat
Gear suggestions: Trekking poles, bear spray, and insect repellent

FINDING THE TRAILHEAD

From Bangor, take I-95 North for approximately 58 miles. Take the exit toward Route 157 West. Turn left and drive on Route 157 West for 11 miles and then turn right onto Katahdin Avenue. Take an immediate left at the second cross street onto Bates Street for just under a mile. Continue on Millinocket Road for about 6 miles, which then turns into Millinocket Lake Road for a mile. Continue on Baxter Park Road for 3 miles and turn left and then an immediate right onto Golden Road. Parking will be on your left before you hit the Abol Bridge Campground and Store.
GPS: 45.835019 / -68.959121

THE HIKE

You might think you are going the wrong way when you hit the dirt road to get to the trailhead for Blueberry Ledges, but I swear you are headed to the right place. Unfortunately the road to the trailhead closes in winter, so this is a trail you can enjoy only in summer months.

That works out great, considering its name is "Blueberry Ledges" and blueberries don't grow in the winter. Start the trail by walking along the road that goes away from the Abol Bridge Campground and Store. If you need to stock up on any snacks or water, do so here. Turn left down a forest road. You will see a sign that states you are on the Appalachian Trail and 0.2 mile from the boundary of Baxter State Park.

At the small parking area at the end of this forest road, continue straight to stay on the Appalachian Trail and follow the signs for Blueberry Ledges. Cross over a small stream

The start of the hike gives you a clear view of the park's grandest feature: Mount Katahdin.

and take a look to your right where the majestic Mount Katahdin stands prominently. When the trail forks, stay right to get off the Appalachian Trail and onto the Abol Pond Trail.

Stay left at the next fork to get on the official trail for Blueberry Ledges and slowly make your way up the gradual ascent. When I did this hike, there was not a single person on the trail. Most times I enjoy having solitude on the trail, but I will admit that being alone on this trail had me wary. I popped into the campground store before the hike and the staff member there informed me that bears were commonly seen in the area and on the trail. I had my bear spray handy (and you should too) in case of an encounter.

Top: A trail sign steers you in the right direction toward Blueberry Ledges.
Bottom: The trail's edges are peppered with dozens of birch trees.

I meandered through the forest and passed by several fresh clumps of bear scat complete with berries and seeds from the surrounding forest. This put me on high alert and reminded me that I should ask my son what we do in case of a bear encounter. The best thing for your kids to do is to slowly walk to a parent if they see a bear on the trail. It is also a good idea to keep your kids from running ahead of you if wildlife is frequently encountered on the trail. My son and I like to sing to keep curious wildlife at bay. A favorite is "Let It Go" from *Frozen*, which we sing at the top of our lungs so no bears (or moose) will be surprised by our presence.

Just after a mile from the last fork, you will reach a large rock cairn that indicates a turn in the trail. Head left to make your way down to the waterfalls that make up Blueberry

Top: When you reach Blueberry Ledges, grab a seat along the water's edge and watch the cascading falls descend.
Bottom: The reason this area is called Blueberry Ledges: blueberry bushes galore!

Ledges. Stay on the rock face and do not trample any of the sensitive plants and lichens that grow within the crevices. The rocks and river edges are covered in blueberry bushes. Luckily I went prior to when the blueberries were in season, so no bears or other creatures were in my company while I sat and ate a snack on the river's edge.

I likely would have stayed longer if I hadn't been so nervous about an encounter with a wild animal. After I quickly scarfed down my snack, I made my way back up the trail to head down and away from any wildlife that might have wanted to say hello. Luckily, I encountered no bears or moose on the trail, but be careful when you do this hike with your kids. Fortunately kids are not exactly quiet on the trail and will likely scare off any wildlife that might be in the area just by being kids.

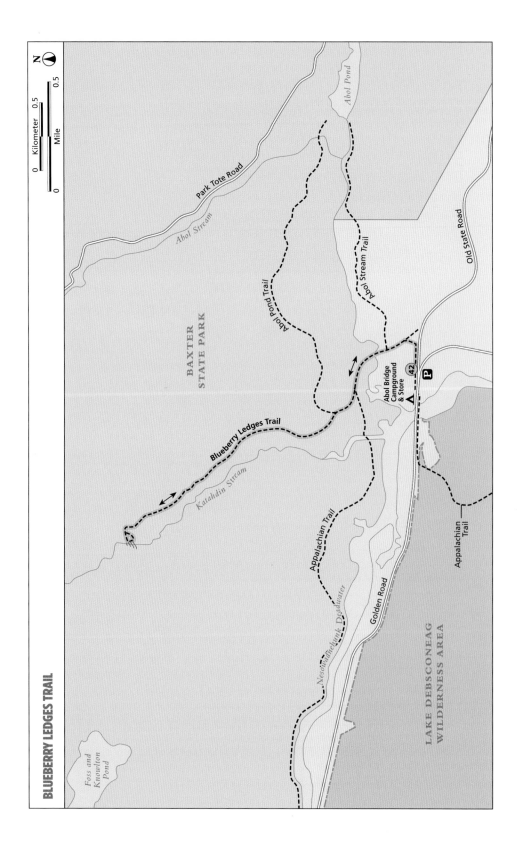

BLUEBERRY LEDGES TRAIL

N

0   Kilometer   0.5

0   Mile   0.5

Foss and
Knowlton
Pond

Park Tote Road

Abol Stream

Abol Pond

BAXTER
STATE PARK

Abol Pond Trail

Abol Stream Trail

Blueberry Ledges Trail

Katahdin Stream

Abol Bridge
Campground
& Store

P

42

Old State Road

Appalachian Trail

Nesowadnehunk Deadwater

Golden Road

Appalachian
Trail

LAKE DEBSCONEAG
WILDERNESS AREA

WHAT TO DO IN CASE OF A BEAR ENCOUNTER

Due to the higher likelihood of encountering a bear on this trail than other trails, here is a rundown of what to do if you see a black bear on the trail. (Grizzlies do not live in Maine or in the northeastern United States.) Prior to any hike, talk to your kids about the wildlife you might encounter and teach them what to do in different situations.

1. Stay calm and say hello to the bear in a calm, but strong voice. Try not to startle it.
2. Say something like, "Hey bear, I'm just passing through—I don't mean you any harm."
3. If they haven't come to you already, have your kids walk slowly over to you. Make sure they do not run.
4. Check your deterrent and have it handy in case things go sour.
5. If you are downhill from a bear, try to find a spot that has higher ground. Make yourself look as big as possible.
6. If the bear is stationary and not walking away, simply back away slowly. Do so sideways (to avoid tripping) and have your kids do the same.
7. If the bear starts to walk toward you, stop moving and stand your ground. Start yelling and waving your hands and trekking poles. If it continues to move forward, you are welcome to throw things at it.
8. Whatever you do, do *not* run and do *not* climb up a tree—black bears will chase you and can easily climb trees.

Although extremely rare, if you get attacked by a black bear:

1. Use your bear spray when it charges you. Wait until it is close enough for it to be a deterrent.
2. Do not play dead. Contrary to popular belief, playing dead will not save you in the case of a black bear attack.
3. Protect your kid as much as you can and fight back focusing your blows to the face and muzzle. Do not stop fighting for as long as you can.

Keep in mind: In recorded history, no one has ever been killed by a black bear in Maine.

MILES AND DIRECTIONS

0.00 Head right along the gravel road across from the parking area (away from the store). Turn left onto the Appalachian Trail, which starts on a forest road.

0.20 Look to your right to take in the views of Mount Katahdin.

0.40 Veer right at the fork to head on the Abol Stream Trail.

0.60 Take a left at the fork to get on the Blueberry Ledges Trail.

1.80 Take a left to head down to Blueberry Ledges.

1.90 Reach Blueberry Ledges and the cascading river.

2.00 Take a right to head back along the Blueberry Ledges Trail.

3.20 Stay straight to get back on the Abol Stream Trail.

3.40 Stay straight to get back on the Appalachian Trail.

3.80 Arrive back at the trailhead.

43 MOUNT KINEO

As the only trail in this guide where you have to take a boat to get to the trailhead, the hike up Mount Kineo will definitely be one to remember. This short but steep hike lies on the shores of Moosehead Lake, New England's second-largest lake. In this region of Maine, moose outnumber people three to one, so keep an eye on the road to the boat launch.

Start: At the Carriage trailhead—accessible only by boat
Elevation gain: 905 feet
Distance: 3.4 miles
Difficulty: Moderate to strenuous
Hiking time: 3.5 hours
Seasons/Schedule: Year-round, 9:00 a.m. to sunset
Fees and permits: Fee required
Trail contact: Mount Kineo State Park, Maine State Parks, Bureau of Parks and Lands, 106 Hogan Rd., Ste. 7, Bangor, ME; (207) 941-4014; www.maine.gov/mountkineo
Dog-friendly: Not allowed
Trail surface: Gravel and dirt
Land status: Maine Bureau of Parks and Lands

Nearest town: Rockwood, ME
Other trail users: None
Water availability: Yes, at golf course restaurant
Maps: Mount Kineo State Park trail map
Age range: All ages
Toilets: Yes, at the boat launch parking
Stroller/Wheelchair compatibility: No
Resting benches: Yes, at boat launch
Potential child hazards: Steep trail with large drop-offs
Gear suggestions: Trekking poles and insect repellent

FINDING THE TRAILHEAD

Mount Kineo is accessible by water only, with the nearest public boat launch site in Rockwood. From Bangor, take Route 15 North for approximately 36 miles, until you reach Dover Foxcroft. Take a left on Route 6 (also Route 15) West for approximately 53 miles. Turn right onto Village Road toward the Town Landing. A commercial boat shuttle (fee charged) to Mount Kineo leaves routinely from Rockwood in summer months. **GPS:** 45.691253 / -69.733486

THE HIKE

There are no accessible roads that lead to the trailhead of Mount Kineo. Instead, you must take a passenger ferry from the Rockwood Town Landing/Boat Launch to the start of the trail just across Moosehead Lake.

The ferry runs from May through October and varies in its schedule depending on the month. Usually the ferry leaves every hour on the hour from around 9:00 a.m. to 4:00 p.m. Again, double-check the ferry schedule prior to your departure. The ferry takes only cash, so come prepared to pay the fee for all passengers in your party.

Take note of when the last shuttle brings visitors back across the lake. If you miss that last ferry, you will be stuck on the island and will have to wait until the next morning to take the shuttle back. Once you make it across the lake, begin the hike by taking a left on the Carriage Trail. After just over 0.5 mile, turn right to head up the Indian Trail. This is a slightly quicker, but much steeper, way to get up the mountain.

Top: The junction of the Bridle and Carriage Road Trails—the Bridle Trail is the steeper way to hike up Mount Kineo.
Bottom: Looking out across Moosehead Lake

This trail should be attempted only as an ascent. It is too steep and has too many slippery rocks, roots, and leaves to be safe as a descent. Those with little kids who insist on walking on their own might need to take the Bridle Trail up and back and forgo the Indian Trail altogether.

There are several spots to look out across the lake as you make your way up on the Indian Trail. You will likely need the rest as you climb more than 600 feet in under 0.5 mile—that's a consistent 12 percent grade and no easy feat. Eventually you will see the Bridle Trail off to your left, but continue straight to head toward the observation tower. Another almost 0.5 mile brings you to the base of the observation tower, where 360-degree views greet you at the top.

The stairs to get up the observation tower can be a little scary. The fencing and railings have large holes in them that can easily fit a small child, so please be extra careful with your little ones. If you don't feel safe heading up the observation tower, do not attempt it. The views that you see coming up the trail are almost as good as the ones at the top, so you won't miss out on much.

When you have soaked up enough views of the lake, head back down the observation tower and back down the Indian Trail. When you reach the junction of the the Bridle and Bridle Trails, turn right to head down the Bridle Trail. Again, do **not** attempt to descend on the Indian Trail—it will be very dangerous. The path down the Bridle Trail is much more gradual and easier on your knees, but there are no views of the lake from this side.

Eventually you will meet back up with the Carriage Trail. Turn left and continue on the flat path that will bring you back to the boat launch. Wait however long you need to for the ferry to carry you back to your car. If you need a snack or some ice cream while you wait, you can head over to the golf course restaurant, which is happy to serve the day-use hikers at the park.

Left: The trail is steep going up, with lots of roots and rocks, so be careful!
Right: The tail of a maritime garter snake slithers off into the grass next to the trail.

Dozens of islands dot the landscape across Moosehead Lake.

WHY IS IT CALLED MOOSEHEAD LAKE?

Sure, you might see moose along the shores of Moosehead Lake, but these resident ungulates are not the reason it's called Moosehead Lake. The lake derives its name from what it looks like from a bird's-eye view. Show your kids a map of the lake and ask them what animals it reminds them of. After they have made their guesses (hint: do not tell them the name of the lake), hold up a photo of a moose with antlers and see if they think they are similar.

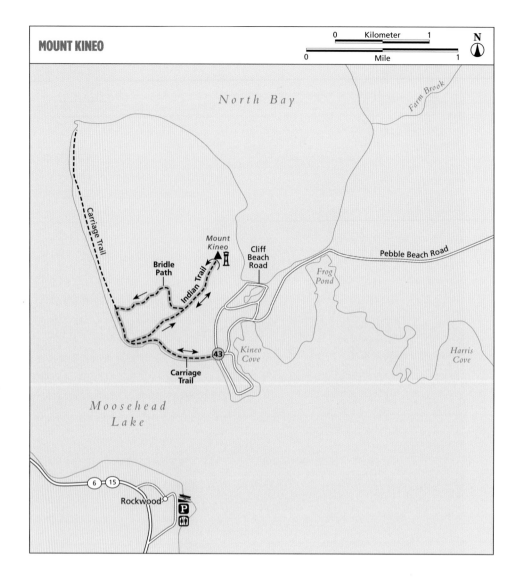

MILES AND DIRECTIONS

0.00 Start on the level Carriage Trail by taking a left from the boat launch (away from the golf course).

0.60 Turn right onto the Indian Trail.

1.10 Stay straight to head toward the summit.

1.50 Reach the summit. Go back the way you came.

1.90 Veer right to head down the Bridle Trail.

2.50 Take a left to head back on the Carriage Trail toward the boat launch.

3.40 Arrive back at the trailhead.

44 BLUE HILL MOUNTAIN

Originally called Awanadjo, meaning "small, misty mountain," by the Abenaki, Blue Hill Mountain has become an adored local landmark. European settlers called the mountain "Blue Hill" after the blue-gray granite that sits atop its summit. But if you go at the right time of year, you might see another reason to call it Blue Hill. Each June the hayfields along the trail are blanketed with hundreds of blooming blue lupines.

Start: At the trailhead at the hayfields off Mountain Road
Elevation gain: 600 feet
Distance: 1.8 miles
Difficulty: Easy to moderate
Hiking time: 2 hours
Seasons/Schedule: Year-round, dawn until dusk
Fees and permits: None
Trail contact: Blue Hill Heritage Trust, 157 Hinckley Ridge Rd., Blue Hill, ME; (207) 374-5118; htpps://bluehillheritagetrust.org/blue-hill-mountain
Dog-friendly: Allowed on leash
Trail surface: Dirt and solid rock

Land status: Blue Hill Heritage Trust
Nearest town: Blue Hill, ME
Other trail users: None
Water availability: None
Maps: Blue Hill Heritage Trust trail map
Age range: All ages
Toilets: None
Stroller/Wheelchair compatibility: No
Resting benches: Yes, at the summit
Potential child hazards: Crossing a road to get to the trailhead and brown-tail moths
Gear suggestions: Insect repellent

FINDING THE TRAILHEAD

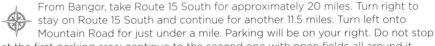

From Bangor, take Route 15 South for approximately 20 miles. Turn right to stay on Route 15 South and continue for another 11.5 miles. Turn left onto Mountain Road for just under a mile. Parking will be on your right. Do not stop at the first parking area; continue to the second one with open fields all around it.
GPS: 44.429152 / -68.582883

THE HIKE

The loop around Blue Hill Mountain, within a town of the same name, lies just northwest of Acadia National Park. This small town might not have a bustling economy like Bar Harbor, but the town does have this beautiful mountain overlooking the bay toward Mount Desert Island.

Start the hike at the trailhead along Mountain Road. If you come from Bangor, make sure to park at the second parking lot at the top of the road where it opens into a large swath of hayfields. The first parking lot brings you to another trail that is not in the parameters of this hike. Once parked in the correct parking lot, cross the road to start your hike.

If you go at the right time of year (early June), you will immediately be greeted with fields upon fields of wild lupines blooming with violet, blue, white, and pink flowers. As enticing as the blooms may be, stay on the trail when taking photos of these gorgeous plants so as not to encourage anyone else to trample off the trail.

Blue Hill Mountain is known for its lupines.

Head straight up the hayfields, but remember to look back and take in the views of the bay. Turn left at the fork and then right to get on Hayes Trail. This is a narrow trail with lots of stone steps. The stones can get slippery, especially in the early morning hours prior to the sun drying the dew that has fallen throughout the night. Take a left when you reach the junction with the Osgood Trail to make your way up to the summit.

At the summit there is a bench looking out across the bay to Mount Desert Island. If you squint, you might be able to see the hordes of tourists traversing their way around the

A WOLF OF A PLANT

As part of the legume (think pea) family, lupines share genetics with green beans, wisteria, and clovers. Lupines are named after the Latin word for wolf, *lupus*. Wolves do not eat lupines, and lupines do not look anything like a wolf—so why is the name associated with this canine? It's because of the way people viewed lupines as sucking up all of the nutrients in the soil; in essence, they felt lupines "wolfed down" the nutrients.

In reality lupines (along with most others in the pea family) are nitrogen fixers. These plants absorb nitrogen from the air and adhere the nutrient to its roots. Eventually the nitrogen is released into the soil and provides essential nutrients to the ground for other plants to use. Even today, farmers use plants from the legume family to ready the soil for other crops instead of adding costly fertilizer or other chemicals to the soil.

Pink, purple, and blue lupines line the fields up to Blue Hill Mountain.

Top: Looking southeast toward Mount Desert Island and Acadia National Park
Bottom: At the summit looking southeast

trails in Acadia National Park. Keep along the Osgood Trail until you find the letterbox. Blue Hill Heritage Trust has several letterboxes placed on its properties. There is a stamp in every letterbox that you use in your "Passport to the Trails" booklet (you can pick one up at the Blue Hill Heritage Trust office in town). Collect all the stamps and you can get a prize! This is a great incentive to keep kids interested in hiking.

Take a left at the next junction to stay on the Osgood Trail. You will leave the Osgood Trail at the next junction by taking a left onto the South Face Trail. If you went down Osgood Trail, this would bring you to that first parking lot along Mountain Road. South Face Trail will link you back up with the Hayes Trail and then back down through the hayfields.

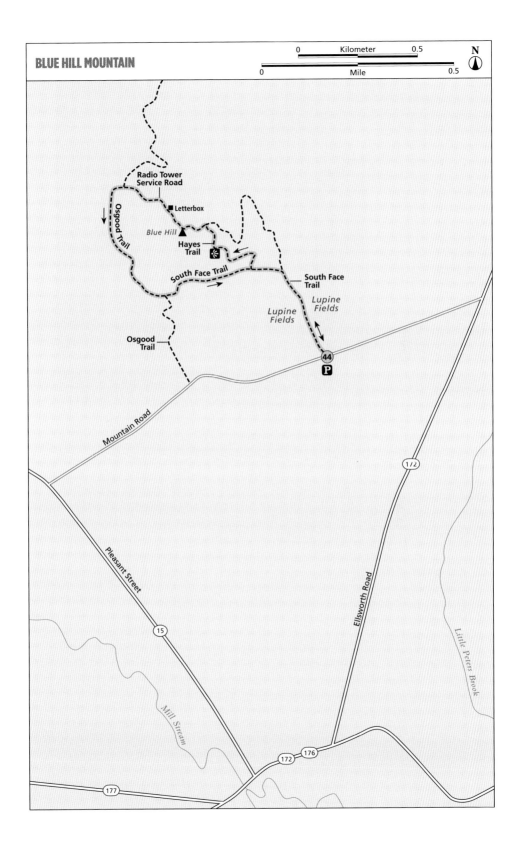

Kilometer

Mile

N

Radio Tower
Service Road

Osgood Trail

Letterbox

Blue Hill

Hayes
Trail

South Face Trail

South Face
Trail

Lupine
Fields

Lupine
Fields

Osgood
Trail

44

P

Mountain Road

1/2

Pleasant Street

15

Ellsworth Road

Little Peters Brook

Mill Stream

172   176

177

The tree that holds one of Blue Hill Heritage Trust's letterboxes. Collect all the stamps!

Keep an eye on the lupines as the sun crests overhead. Lots of pollinators, such as bees, butterflies, and hummingbirds, will be shifting from plant to plant to get all the juicy nectar they can. Head back over Mountain Road to get back to your car and on to your next adventure.

MILES AND DIRECTIONS

0.00 Start on the trail across the road leading up a large hayfield.

0.20 Turn left at the fork.

0.30 Turn right to head up the Hayes Trail.

0.50 Take a left onto the Osgood Trail.

0.60 Reach the summit.

0.70 The letterbox is found here. Stop and stamp your passport.

0.80 Keep straight to stay on the Osgood Trail.

1.20 Take a left to head on the South Face Trail.

1.50 Connect back up at the junction of Hayes Trail and the trail heading down the hay-fields. Take a right to head back down to your car.

1.80 Arrive back at the trailhead.

There are many trails ideal for families in Acadia National Park. You honestly cannot go wrong with any of them. Jordan Pond Loop is the first of two hikes I chose in Acadia National Park due to its easy path and yummy treats at the end of the hike. As with any trail in Acadia, don't expect to be alone. However, it seems most visitors walk only a short distance on either side of Jordan Pond and never make the full loop. The farther you make it out from Jordan Pond House, the less likely you will encounter others on the trail.

Start: At the Jordan Pond trailhead
Elevation gain: 75 feet
Distance: 3.1 miles
Difficulty: Easy
Hiking time: 3 hours
Seasons/Schedule: Year-round
Fees and permits: Fee required
Trail contact: Acadia National Park, PO Box 177, Bar Harbor, ME; (207) 288-3338; www.nps.gov/acad
Dog-friendly: Allowed on leash
Trail surface: Gravel, dirt, and raised boardwalk
Land status: National Park Service
Nearest town: Bar Harbor, ME

Other trail users: None
Water availability: Yes, at Jordan Pond House
Maps: Acadia National Park trail map
Age range: All ages
Toilets: Yes, at the Jordan Pond House
Stroller/Wheelchair compatibility: No
Resting benches: None
Potential child hazards: Trail gets close to water's edge and brown-tail moths
Gear suggestions: Insect repellent and binoculars

FINDING THE TRAILHEAD

From Bangor, take Route 1A East for approximately 27 miles. When you hit Ellsworth, continue straight on Route 3 East. Follow Route 3 East for about 16 miles and then turn right onto Paradise Hill Road for 3 miles. This turns into Park Loop Road; follow it for approximately 4.4 miles to parking for Jordan Pond House. **GPS:** 44.321177 / -68.252048

THE HIKE

The parking lot at Jordan Pond House is huge. Thousands of visitors head here daily to glimpse the crystal-clear waters of Jordan Pond. Normal visibility in the waters of the pond are usually around 40 or so feet, but records show that up to 60 feet of visibility has been seen on occasion.

Start your trek from whatever parking lot you end up in. The key to parking in Acadia National Park, especially during the peak summer and autumn months, is to be opportunistic. If you see a spot, grab it. Wherever you park around here will still lead you to the same trail. Make your way to Jordan Pond House and head around the back—do not fret, you'll grab some food on the way out.

Head along the western bank of the pond; this will be on your left if your back is to Jordan Pond House. There will be lots of people on the trail, but most will turn around shortly before the raised boardwalk starts. Take some time to check out any wildlife that

Top: Looking north from Jordan Pond House across the pond to The Bubbles in the distance.
Bottom: The raised boardwalk traverses a large portion of the western side of the loop.

might be on the pond. My last excursion here had me sitting and watching a pair of loons for 45 minutes!

Around the 0.5-mile mark, the raised boardwalk begins. This was put in years ago to keep erosion along the banks of the pond to a minimum. As you traverse this single-file boardwalk, keep an eye out for those traveling the other way. Two people cannot pass each other easily on the boardwalk, so small pullouts were built into the boardwalk to fix this problem. Anticipate where you can pull out so you don't damage any plant life trying to recover around the boardwalk.

At just under a mile in, the raised boardwalk ends, and you're walking on a dirt path. Loop around the northern tip of the pond. Then make your way down the eastern side of

Again, looking north across
Jordan Pond to The Bubbles

it to head back to Jordan Pond House. Around the 2.0-mile mark, there is a small beach area on your right. Feel free to dip your feet in if they are feeling a bit sore from the hike.

The trail will get busier the closer you get to Jordan Pond House. As I mentioned, most visitors don't go more than a 0.5 mile on either side of the pond from the Jordan Pond House. Make your way back up to the restaurant and order up some of their famed popovers. The house has been serving tea and popovers since the late 1800s, and stopping here has become a favorite activity for those visiting the national park.

I would argue that even if you are not hungry, grab some popovers to go—they are just that good. They're served with Maine-made strawberry jam and butter (although you can get blueberry jam if you prefer). They will melt in your mouth, and you will be begging for more before you even finish the first one.

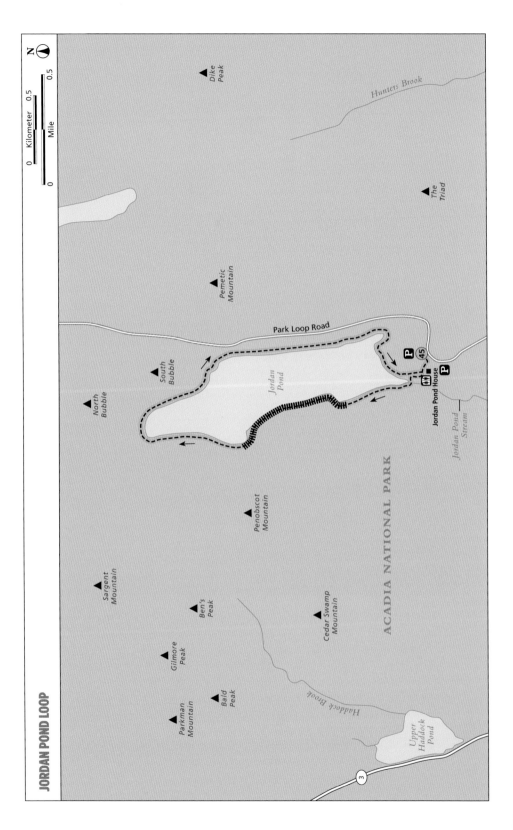

JORDAN POND LOOP

N

0   Kilometer   0.5

0   Mile   0.5

Dike Peak

Hunters Brook

The Triad

Pemetic Mountain

South Bubble

North Bubble

Park Loop Road

Jordan Pond

P

45

P

Jordan Pond House

Jordan Pond Stream

Penobscot Mountain

ACADIA NATIONAL PARK

Sargent Mountain

Ben's Peak

Cedar Swamp Mountain

Gilmore Peak

Bald Peak

Parkman Mountain

Haddock Brook

Upper Haddock Pond

3

The raised boardwalk has several spots where you can move to the side to let others pass without destroying the surrounding vegetation.

MILES AND DIRECTIONS

0.00 Start on the trail behind Jordan Pond House.

0.40 The raised boardwalk begins.

0.90 The raised boardwalk ends.

1.40 Round the northern tip of Jordan Pond.

1.90 Reach a small beach area.

3.10 Arrive back at the trailhead.

LOONS ARE EXCELLENT DIVERS

You might get lucky and witness the resident loons out on the pond catching some fish. Every now and then they disappear under the water only to pop back up a few hundred feet away. Loons swim underwater to catch (and eat!) fish with their sharp beaks. They have backward-facing projections on the roof of their mouths/beaks that help keep prey in place once it's caught. Part of what makes loons excellent swimmers is that they

A loon swims in Jordan Pond.

have solid bones, unlike most birds that have hollow bones. This makes them heavier and better equipped to dive after prey. Loons are also well-known for their haunting call, usually heard at dusk and dawn. They use it to locate their partners and chicks that might have gotten lost or separated from the flock.

46 JESUP PATH TO DORR MOUNTAIN

Many trails in Acadia National Park are geared toward families so are, subsequently, shorter and have less elevation gain. I wanted to include a trail that provides a bit more endurance for those with older kids wanting more of a challenge. You can also skip Dorr Mountain and opt for an easier walk around the grounds of Jesup Path through the wild gardens and the Abbe Museum.

Start: At the Jesup Path trailhead off Route 3
Elevation gain: 1,200 feet
Distance: 3.75 miles
Difficulty: Strenuous
Hiking time: 5 hours
Seasons/Schedule: Year-round
Fees and permits: Fee required
Trail contact: Acadia National Park, PO Box 177, Bar Harbor, ME; (207) 288-3338; www.nps.gov/acad
Dog-friendly: Allowed on leash on Jesup Path; not allowed up Dorr Mountain
Trail surface: Gravel, dirt, and stone steps

Land status: National Park Service
Nearest town: Bar Harbor, ME
Other trail users: None
Water availability: Yes, at the Nature Center
Maps: Acadia National Park trail map
Age range: Kids in carriers and those with extensive trail experience
Toilets: Yes, at the Nature Center
Stroller/Wheelchair compatibility: No
Resting benches: None
Potential child hazards: Brown-tail moths
Gear suggestions: Trekking poles and insect repellent

FINDING THE TRAILHEAD

From Bangor, take Route 1A East for approximately 27 miles. When you hit Ellsworth, continue straight on Route 3 East. Follow Route 3 East for about 18.5 miles and then turn left onto Mount Desert Street for 0.5 mile. Turn right onto Main Street/Route 3 East and continue for another 2.2 miles. Parking for the trailhead will be on your right. **GPS:** 44.358930 / -68.206000

THE HIKE

This hike either could be a leisurely stroll through some beautiful gardens and a stop at the Nature Center or could get your blood pumping for an extended adventure up one of the many mountains within the park. Choose wisely depending on your and your kid's abilities.

If you want to do just Jesup Path and walk around the Nature Center and Wild Gardens of Acadia, there will be minimal elevation gain, and most children can easily do this. Stop by the Abbe Museum (if it's open), which focuses on Native American culture in the park. It showcases thousands of archaeological objects of the Wabanaki ("People of the Dawn").

For those wanting to do the bigger, more challenging hike up Dorr Mountain, start out on the same path. You will skirt The Tarn (the body of water to the south of you) by hopping over some large rocks in the small creek draining from the lake. Go straight at the junction to head up Kurt Diederichs Climb. You will ascend about 500 feet in about

Lupines line the pond at the start of the hike along Jesup Path.

Top: The entrance to the Wild Gardens of Acadia
Bottom: A view looking south toward Huguenot Head

Top: A large portion of the trail has wide, rocky steps.
Bottom: A rocky path between the trees heading up to the summit of Dorr Mountain

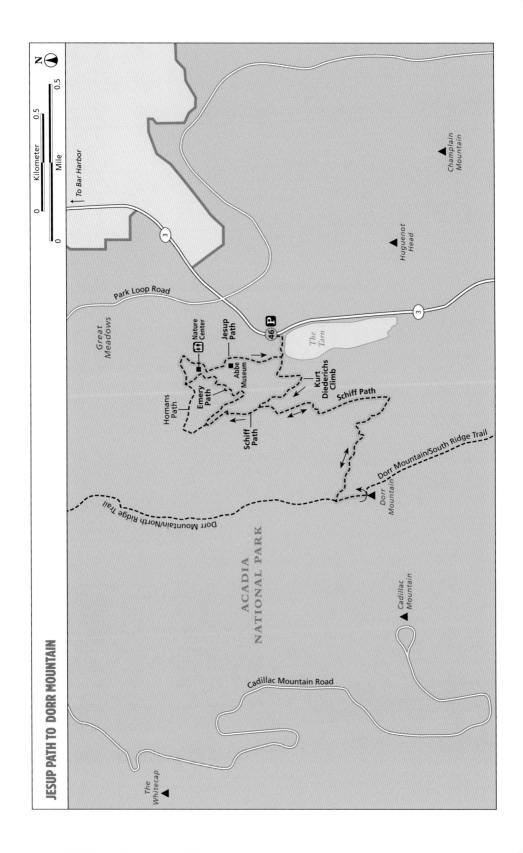

JESUP PATH TO DORR MOUNTAIN

N

Kilometer
0   0.5

Mile
0   0.5

To Bar Harbor

Great Meadows

Park Loop Road

Nature Center

Jesup Path

Abbe Museum

Homans Path

Emery Path

Schiff Path

Schiff Path

Kurt Diederichs Climb

The Tarn

Huguenot Head

Champlain Mountain

ACADIA NATIONAL PARK

Dorr Mountain/North Ridge Trail

Dorr Mountain/South Ridge Trail

Dorr Mountain

Cadillac Mountain

Cadillac Mountain Road

The Whitecap

0.5 mile, making for a steep and steady climb up. Take the sharp left turn to head up Schiff Path and continue your ascent.

Another 0.5 mile up (with only about half the elevation of the previous section) will bring you to another junction. Stay right to continue on Schiff Path. The next 0.5 mile is even more gradual and eventually brings you to a four-way junction. Take a sharp left turn to follow the Dorr Mountain/South Ridge Trail and make your final ascent to the mountain.

After taking in the views, head back the way you came down the South Ridge Trail and then take a sharp right back onto Schiff Path. At the junction where you first encountered Schiff Path with Kurt Diederichs Climb, continue straight on Schiff Path. Do not turn back down Kurt Diederichs Climb. At the fork, take a right to follow Emery Path. You will traverse one of the many historical "memorial trails" within the park. Many trails in the Sieur de Monts portion of Acadia are considered memorial trails—trails financed by an individual, who then can name the trail after whomever they want, often someone they want to honor.

The trail down Emery Path has large, steep stone slabs as steps, so be careful as you head down the trail here. You will meet up with Jesup Path on the left, which leads you to the left of the Wild Gardens and Nature Center. Take a right onto Homans Path to learn everything you can about the wildflowers in Acadia at the Wild Gardens, then head south on Jesup Path and past the Abbe Museum on your right to get back to the trailhead.

MILES AND DIRECTIONS

0.00 Start on the trailhead to the south of the parking lot and then turn right.

0.10 Cross over the stream using the rocks provided to you. Stay straight when you reach the other side and head up Kurt Diederichs Climb.

0.40 At the junction, take a sharp left onto Schiff Path.

1.00 Continue right on Schiff Path at the next junction.

1.40 Take a left onto the Dorr Mountain/South Ridge Trail at the four-way junction.

1.50 Reach the summit of Dorr Mountain. Head back the way you came.

1.60 Take a sharp right onto Schiff Path.

2.00 Stay left to continue on Schiff Path.

2.60 Continue straight to stay on Schiff Path.

2.70 Go right onto Emery Path.

3.00 Take a left onto Jesup Path. Stay left at the next junction.

3.10 Take a right onto Homans Path and go through the Wild Gardens of Acadia. You'll end up at the Nature Center.

3.40 Take a left onto Jesup Path once again.

3.60 Take a left to head back to the trailhead.

3.75 Arrive back at the trailhead.

47 BARRIER BEACH TRAIL

The fun and educational experience you and your kids will receive at Wells National Estuarine Research Reserve will live with you for some time. Its headquarters is listed on the National Register of Historic Places, and its accolades don't stop there. There are dozens of projects and several visiting scientists at any given time here. The sheer number of educational walks and summer day camps will keep you coming back for more.

Start: At the trailhead next to the gift shop and visitor center
Elevation gain: 75 feet
Distance: 1.5 miles
Difficulty: Easy
Hiking time: 1.5 hours
Seasons/Schedule: Year-round, 7:00 a.m. to sunset
Fees and permits: Fee required
Trail contact: Wells National Estuarine Research Reserve, 342 Laudholm Farm Rd., Wells, ME; (207) 646-1555; www.wellsreserve.org
Dog-friendly: Not allowed
Trail surface: Gravel, dirt, and sand
Land status: US Fish and Wildlife Service

Nearest town: Wells, ME
Other trail users: None
Water availability: Yes, at the trailhead
Maps: Wells National Estuarine Research Reserve trail map
Age range: All ages
Toilets: Yes, at the trailhead
Stroller/Wheelchair compatibility: No
Resting benches: Yes, along the trail
Potential child hazards: Trail crosses part of a resident-only road
Gear suggestions: Beach accessories such as sunscreen, sun hat, and a picnic lunch

FINDING THE TRAILHEAD

From Portsmouth, New Hampshire, take I-95 North for approximately 20 miles. Take exit 19 for NH 9/Route 109 toward Wells. Turn left onto Route 109 and continue for 1.5 miles. Turn left onto Route 1 North for 1.5 miles. Turn right onto Laudholm Farm Road and then left onto Skinner Mill Road. Turn right to head into the reserve's entrance and park in the large parking lot. **GPS:** 43.338257 / -70.550938

THE HIKE

The southern coastal town of Wells, Maine, is home to several beautiful places, including a handful of beaches, the Rachel Carson Wildlife Refuge, and the Wells National Estuarine Research Reserve. Parents love this place as an educational opportunity for themselves and their kids. Children love this place because of its diverse wildlife, hands-on activities, and long stretch of beach at its shore.

Start your hike from the parking lot and head southeast toward the restrooms. These are the only toilets on the property, so use them now if you have to go. Walk between the building that houses the toilets and the gift shop and visitor center on the right. After you pass the teaching lab on your left, continue left down the trail.

If you're curious, pop into the gift shop and visitor center to see what educational programs are happening that day. Many weekends provide visitors with bird/shore walks, bird-banding demonstrations, story walks, yoga, and even painting classes. There is, quite literally, something for everyone here.

Top: The bulk of the trail is on a wide, gravelly path with minimal elevation gain.
Bottom: The boardwalk to access Laudholm Beach

The trail naturally drifts right and follows a wide, gravelly path down to the beach. The path is smooth enough for an off-road stroller or a beach wagon but is not equipped for wheelchairs. After passing a large body of water to your left around the 0.6-mile mark, head down the dirt road to the boardwalk. The dirt road is used by the residents along the shore, so keep hold of your children as you walk along here.

Cross the boardwalk to get to the beach and then take a left. Walk along the beach for as long or as little as you like. Oyster- mussel-, and clamshells line the beach and can be easily used as shovels if you forgot to bring your beach accessories. You can also use them to adorn any sandcastles you might create. Get lost in the many colors of the rocks along Barrier Beach and feel how smooth they are from being constantly battered by the waves.

Top: Come at low tide and you'll be able to check out all the shells that are unearthed.
Bottom: Shoveling sand is the best pastime!

WHAT IS AN ESTUARY?

By definition an estuary is simply a place where a large river meets the ocean. Fresh and salt water mix together for a unique eco-system where diversity thrives. In addition to both fresh and salt water, estuaries are home to mudflats, tidal pools, and beaches, creating different types of micro-ecosystems for a variety of wildlife. Dozens of different species of shorebirds—such as great blue herons, great egrets, and migrating Canada geese—and more than thirty species of mammals—including white-tailed deer, red foxes, and harbor seals—call this area home.

Rocks of all different shades await
you at Laudholm Beach.

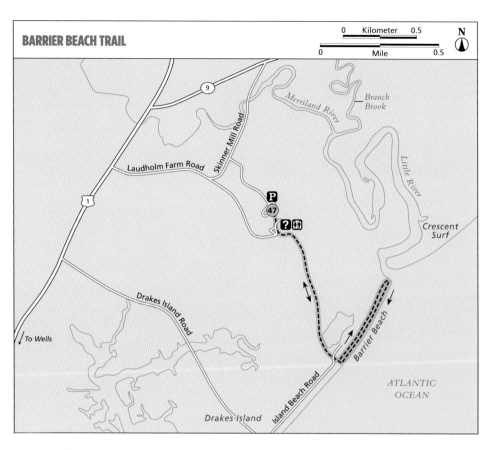

After you've enjoyed the beach and watched the gulls feed on unsuspecting fish, pack up your stuff and head back the way you came. The walk back can seem long, because it's all uphill, but at least it's only a 0.75-mile hike back to your car.

MILES AND DIRECTIONS

0.00 Start from the parking lot.

0.10 Walk between the building that houses the toilets and the gift shop and visitor center on the right.

0.15 Take a left to head down the Barrier Beach Trail.

0.60 Pass a large body of water to your left.

0.75 Arrive at the beach. Feel free to walk the long stretch of beach as far as you desire. Return the way you came when you are finished.

1.35 Turn right to head back to the parking lot.

1.50 Arrive back at the trailhead.

48 MACKWORTH ISLAND LOOP

Take a stroll along the loop around Mackworth Island and enjoy the never-ending views of the Atlantic Ocean. The 100-acre island might be one of the smallest state parks in Maine, but what it lacks in size, it makes up for in personality. Not only is there a fairy village that your kids can add to, there is also a pet cemetery (not the Stephen King version) complete with tombstones and everything.

Start: At the Mackworth Island trailhead
Elevation gain: 50 feet
Distance: 1.4 miles
Difficulty: Easy
Hiking time: 1.5 hours
Seasons/Schedule: Year-round, 9:00 a.m. to sunset
Fees and permits: Fee required
Trail contact: Mackworth Island State Park, Andrews Avenue off Route 1, Falmouth, ME; (207) 781-6279; apps.web.maine.gov/mackworthisland
Dog-friendly: Allowed on leash
Trail surface: Gravel, dirt, and sand

Land status: Maine Bureau of Parks and Lands
Nearest town: Falmouth, ME
Other trail users: None
Water availability: None
Maps: Mackworth Island State Park trail map
Age range: All ages
Toilets: Yes, at the trailhead
Stroller/Wheelchair compatibility: Yes, if you stay on the main loop
Resting benches: Yes, along the trail
Potential child hazards: Large drop-offs at some overlooks
Gear suggestions: Insect repellent

FINDING THE TRAILHEAD

From Portsmouth, New Hampshire, go north on I-95 for approximately 44 miles. Keep right at the fork to head north on I-295 for 7 miles. Take exit 9 for Route 1 North toward Falmouth. Merge onto Route 1 North/Veranda Street for 1 mile and then turn right onto Andrews Avenue. Take the causeway over to the entrance of the state park. Take a right into the parking lot. **GPS:** 43.689148 / -70.235274

THE HIKE

I remember the exact internet search I was doing when I first learned about Mackworth Island State Park. I typed in "where can I find fairy houses along the seacoast?" My kid was going through a fairy-loving phase, and I put in my best effort (including creating a fairy garden at my own home) to make his dreams come true. The first thing that popped up on my computer screen was this small state park just north of Portland. I figured we would give it a try, and it turned out to be such a joyful hike that we've gone back dozens of times.

The trail starts just after you cross the causeway and drive into the park. Start south on the trail (away from the entrance station) and make your way around the border of the island. There are several social trails that head down to the beach below. If it's low tide, feel free to walk along the beach for the entire hike.

As you traverse the edges of the island, there are several benches to sit on and take in the views from every angle imaginable. There is even a swing that you and your kids can lounge on over on the eastern side of the island. As you continue north, turn left down

Top: A wide, dirt path leads around the perimeter of the island and is perfect for strollers.
Bottom: Check out the sweet (and maybe creepy) Percival Baxter Pet Cemetery.

a small social trail to get to Percival Baxter's Pet Cemetery. Here is where several canine companions of Maine's former governor, Percival Baxter, are laid to rest.

Get back on the main trail to reach the fairy village. Tucked among the towering pine trees you will find an array of fairy houses built by visitors like yourself. Garlands of twigs and paths made of seashells adorn the ground at the fairy village.

Feel free to spend some time here making new fairy houses and adding to those already constructed. This is likely one of the only times that all those rocks and twigs your kids like to pick up on the trail will actually go to some good (or, at the very least, creative) use. Head down to the beach and grab some seashells to help beautify the fairy houses you create. Use only natural materials and preferably ones that you have found along the trail. Then head back on the trail to complete the loop around the other side. Stop whenever you can to take in the views, as there are many places to do so.

One of the many beaches along the island that you can explore

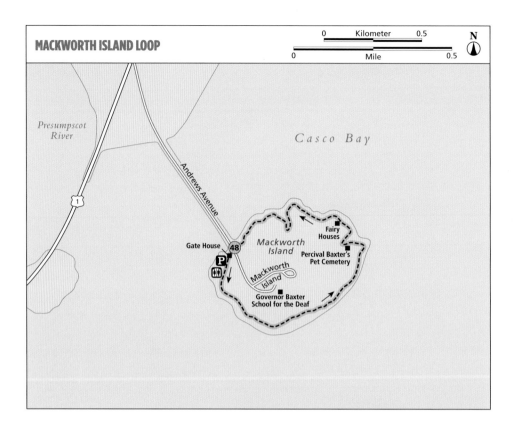

A beautiful view and resting spot to take in the fresh, salty breeze

MILES AND DIRECTIONS

0.00 Start on the Mackworth Island trailhead to the right of the entrance station.

0.50 A small overlook juts out into the ocean on your right.

0.70 Reach Percival Baxter's Pet Cemetery.

0.80 Reach the fairy village.

1.40 Arrive back at the trailhead.

FOR THE LOVE OF FAIRIES

Fairies have always been a part of childhood, and today it's no different. No single culture or religion can lay claim to the origin of fairies, but, instead, they are more of a collection of folk beliefs from way back in ancient times.

Fairies are often known for their magical powers and fondness for trickery. Over the years humans have thought they needed to repel fairies, as they were bringers of doom and evil. To ward them off, people did silly things like wear their clothes inside-out and wear four-leaf clover charms. I tend to think that fairies are just misunderstood. They're full of whimsy and enchantment (the good kind), and I like my kid to think that too.

Fairies guard their small village that resides on the island.

49 MOUNT BATTIE

Several trails can take you up Mount Battie, including the park road to the summit that you can take by car. The one described here is a more gradual climb up and more easily done if you have kiddos with you. The trail traverses an old carriage road that pops you out onto the road that heads up the mountain. The views of the bay from the top of the observation tower are unparalleled in the area.

Start: At the Carriage trailhead
Elevation gain: 525 feet
Distance: 2.4 miles
Difficulty: Moderate
Hiking time: 3 hours
Seasons/Schedule: Year-round, 9:00 a.m. to sunset
Fees and permits: Fee required
Trail contact: Camden Hills State Park, 280 Belfast Rd., Camden, ME; (207) 236-3109; https://apps.web .maine.gov/camdenhills
Dog-friendly: Allowed on leash
Trail surface: Gravel, dirt, and pavement
Land status: Maine Bureau of Parks and Lands

Nearest town: Camden, ME
Other trail users: None
Water availability: None
Maps: Camden Hills State Park trail map
Age range: Most ages, except those who have just started to walk and do not like being in a carrier
Toilets: Yes, at the summit
Stroller/Wheelchair compatibility: No
Resting benches: Yes, at the summit
Potential child hazards: The stairs up the tower (which can be scary) and brown-tail moths
Gear suggestions: Trekking poles and insect repellent

FINDING THE TRAILHEAD

From Augusta, take Route 17 East for approximately 32 miles. Turn left onto Pushaw Road for 0.5 mile. Turn right onto Hope Street and then take an immediate left onto Gillette Road. Travel 1.6 miles and then turn right onto Barnestown Road for 1.5 miles. Turn left onto Molyneaux Road for approximately 3 miles and then turn right onto Route 52 South. Drive for about 0.5 mile and the parking will be on the left. Make sure to pull off entirely within the white lines depicting where the shoulder of the road is. Do not drive up the carriage road. **GPS:** 44.227026 / -69.078341

THE HIKE

If your kids are big fans of castles and medieval stories, look no further than the trail up Mount Battie. The iconic Stone Tower that sits atop its summit was built to memorialize soldiers from World War I, but it might as well be a castle tower awaiting a siege! Or at least that is what you can tell your kids to get them motivated on the trail.

Start the trail off the side of the road along the Carriage Trail. The first part of the path is paved, then it switches to a hard-packed dirt/gravel path. Around 0.3 mile, turn right at the fork to follow the Carriage Road Trail—do not stay straight to continue on the Carriage Trail. This can be confusing, so make sure to pay attention to the signs. This is when the trail narrows and becomes steeper than the previous section. There are lots of roots and rocks that line the trail, so keep an eye on the surface of the path to ensure nobody trips.

Top: The WWI Memorial Tower under crisp, blue skies
Bottom: A view of downtown Camden and Penobscot Bay from the summit tower

At the 1.0-mile mark you reach the auto road heading up to Mount Battie's summit. Keep your kids close so they don't accidentally run out onto the road. The speed limit is only 10 mph, but that doesn't necessarily mean people are driving that slowly or even paying attention to hikers on the road. Follow the road up to the summit and the photogenic WWI Memorial Tower.

Hopefully you have kept some walking sticks that you might have picked up on the trail. They might come in handy in case a duel is requested of you or your kids—just pretend though! When the duels have been won, head up the stairs of the WWI Memorial Tower to take in the 360-degree views. On clear days you can see all the way up to Mount Desert Island and Cadillac Mountain in Acadia National Park.

When you have finished your time on the summit, head back the way you came and enjoy some time down in the town of Camden. There are several great spots, including River Ducks Ice Cream, Camden Deli (get the lobster roll), and Zoot Coffee in case you need a little caffeine to get your energy back up after the hike.

Top: A trail marker leading back down to an
alternate parking lot on Megunticook Street
Bottom left: A steep spiral staircase leads you
to the roof of the tower to take in 360-degree
views.
Bottom right: Looking northeast on top of the
tower toward Isleboro

MILES AND DIRECTIONS

0.00 Start at the Carriage trailhead.

0.30 Turn right onto the Carriage Road Trail.

1.00 Meet up with the Mount Battie auto road. Walk along the road to the summit.

1.20 Reach the Stone Tower and overlook. Head back the way you came.

1.40 Take a left to veer off the road and head back on the Carriage Road Trail.

2.10 Veer left to head back down the Carriage Trail.

2.40 Arrive back at the trailhead.

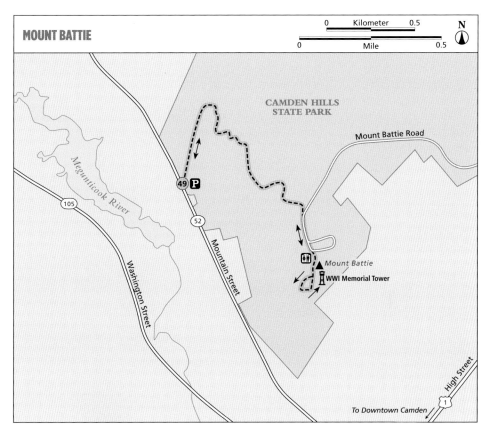

MOUNT BATTIE

0 Kilometer 0.5

0 Mile 0.5

N

CAMDEN HILLS
STATE PARK

Mount Battie Road

Megunticook River

105

49 P

52

Mountain Street

Washington Street

Mount Battie

WWI Memorial Tower

High Street

1

To Downtown Camden

WHAT'S THE DEAL WITH THE BROWNTAIL MOTH?

You might see a lot of signs across several of Maine's state parks discussing the browntail moth. This invasive species is found only on the coast of Maine as well as on Cape Cod. When it is in its larval stage (i.e., the caterpillar version), its hairs are extremely poisonous, which can cause dermatitis if it brushes up against you. Even if the hairs have brushed against a leaf and then your skin brushes against that leaf, it can cause serious skin irritation.

This is why it is super important to wear long pants and sleeves when hiking on any of the trails along the coast of Maine. Even on the hottest of days, make sure you wear long pants and sleeves. It helps to have quick-drying, wicking material to keep your body cool even when it is covered up. I know that getting your kids to wear certain clothing can be as pleasant as pulling teeth, but you will thank yourself later (and so will they) when they aren't incessantly itching for weeks on end due to this pesky critter.

50 LILY BAY STATE PARK

Rounding out this list are the Rowell Cove and Dunn Point Trails in Lily Bay State Park. Choose from hiking, fishing, boating, relaxing on the beach, or simply playing on the playground. If you and your family enjoy kayaking, canoeing, or stand-up paddleboarding, make sure to bring your equipment, because you can take off right from the gravel beach.

Start: At the Dunn Point trailhead
Elevation gain: 180 feet
Distance: 4.5 miles
Difficulty: Moderate
Hiking time: 4 hours
Seasons/Schedule: Year-round, 9:00 a.m. to sunset
Fees and permits: Fee required
Trail contact: Lily Bay State Park, 13 Myrle's Way, Greenville, ME; (207) 695-2700; https://apps.web.maine .gov/lilybay
Dog-friendly: Allowed on leash
Trail surface: Gravel, dirt, and pavement
Land status: Maine Bureau of Parks and Lands

Nearest town: Greenville, ME
Other trail users: Snowmobilers and cross-country skiers
Water availability: None
Maps: Lily Bay State Park trail map
Age range: All ages
Toilets: Yes, at the trailhead
Stroller/Wheelchair compatibility: Yes, but only to the beach area at the trailhead
Resting benches: Yes, at the trailhead
Potential child hazards: Crossing some roads
Gear suggestions: Water equipment, insect repellent, and a picnic lunch

FINDING THE TRAILHEAD

From Bangor, take Route 15 North for approximately 33 miles. When you reach Dover Foxcroft, turn left onto Route 6 West for 8 miles and then turn right to continue on Route 6 West for another 25.6 miles. The road will turn into Lily Bay Road. Follow that road for approximately 9 miles and then turn left onto State Park Road. Follow the road until you reach the end of State Park Road. Park next to the playground and beach area. **GPS:** 45.569774 / -69.566374

THE HIKE

I stumbled upon this small state park when I was on my way back from hiking Mount Kineo for this book. I did not initially intend for this to be in the book, but once I saw it, I had to include it. I hadn't seen it on any list before, and it turns out that it's a great place for families. Just like Mount Kineo, Lily Bay State Park lies on the shores of Moosehead Lake. Due to its proximity to Mount Kineo, this is a great option to do either before or after your hike up there. It's hard to drive all this way and not have more than one hike planned for the area.

Start the hike along Dunn Point. The parking lot at the gravel beach and playground is the better spot to start and end your hike rather than in Rowell Cove. The trail begins on the north side of the parking lot in the opposite direction of the playground. Start walking along Dunn Point Trail until you hit the road that loops around the campground. You will continue straight through until you hit the road again and hang a right.

Top: A sign marks the Lily Bay Trail toward Rowell Campground.
Bottom: Looking south along the beach on the shores of Moosehead Lake

A shaded playground greets day users at Lily Bay State Park.

HOW MOOSE ACT IF THEY'RE MAD

Despite how calm they might look, moose are not as friendly as you might think. In fact, I would rather encounter a black bear on the trail than a moose. In the years I have been an ecologist and outdoor enthusiast, I have always equated moose with erratic behavior. But there are a few ways to know if you are making moose mad or if they might charge you. Here are the signs:

- Laying their ears back.
- The hair on the back of their neck or hips is standing up.
- Smacking their lips.
- Showing the whites of their eyes.
- Tossing their heads erratically.
- Urinating on their back legs (eww).

They also may simply charge at you. If that's the case, I hope you brought diapers for more than just your children.

LILY BAY STATE PARK

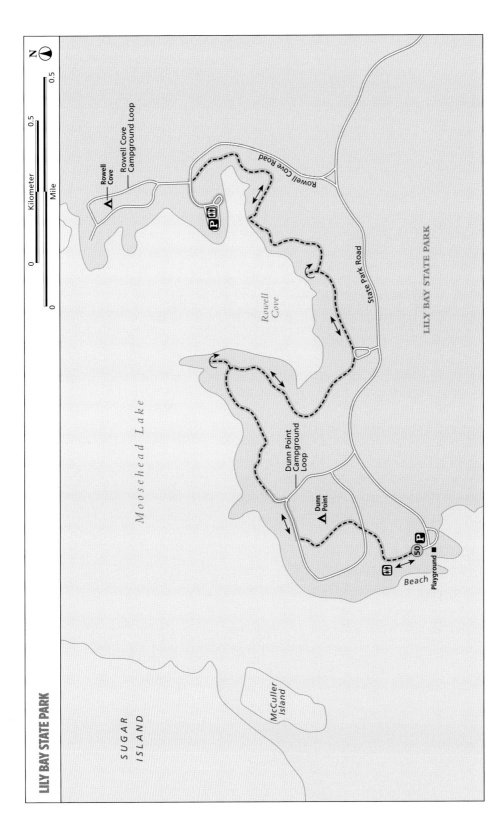

Heading through the campground at Dunn Point will be the only time you aren't close to the shores of Moosehead Lake. Most of the trail skirts along the edges of the water where you can be in constant view of the enormity of the lake. Take a left to stay on the trail after you have walked along the campground road for 0.1 mile. In just under another 0.5 mile, there is a beautiful overlook to your left. Continue on the trail after you've taken in the views.

Once you've been on the trail for about 1.5 miles, the trail will turn into Rowell Cove Trail. Another mile will bring you to the end of Rowell Cove, where you will likely see folks launching their boats or fishing on the shores. Go back the way you came to head to Dunn Point when you are ready.

When you arrive back at Dunn Point, grab beach accessories from your car and set up camp along the gravel beach just west of where you parked. Despite the gravel, the ground is soft and comfortable. What is truly great about a gravel beach is the lack of sand that always seems to get in your food when you are at a regular beach.

If you have brought any water equipment, like kayaks or canoes, you can launch them here. You can also swim in the lake, but I will warn you that it is cold! If none of those things sounds enticing, feel free to sit and watch for boats on the lake or any wildlife that might be flying overhead. Although this state park is a little "out there," that also means more wildlife inhabit the area. You have a much higher likelihood of seeing moose here than you would in Acadia National Park.

If the beach gets boring, there is also a large playground for kids to play on right at the parking lot. There are multiple slides and swings for everyone to play at once. It is a great way to get kids' energy out before snoozing in the car on the way home.

MILES AND DIRECTIONS

0.00 Start on the Dunn Point Trail to the north of the parking lot.

0.05 Stay right to continue on Dunn Point Trail.

0.10 Cross Dunn Point Campground Loop. You are walking through the campground.

0.30 Cross Dunn Point Campground Loop again (it's a loop) and take a right.

0.40 Take a left to stay on the trail.

0.80 Reach an overlook of Moosehead Lake.

1.30 Stay straight to continue on Rowell Cove Trail.

2.25 Reach the northern end of Rowell Cove. Return the way you came.

3.20 Stay straight to get back on Dunn Point Trail.

4.10 Turn right to stay on the trail.

4.20 Take a left to head back through the campground.

4.40 Cross Dunn Point Road again.

4.50 Arrive back at the trailhead.

THE TEN ESSENTIALS OF HIKING

American Hiking Society

American Hiking Society recommends you pack the "Ten Essentials" every time you head out for a hike. Whether you plan to be gone for a couple of hours or several months, make sure to pack these items. Become familiar with these items and know how to use them. Learn more at **AmericanHiking.org/hiking-resources**

1. Appropriate Footwear

6. Safety Items (light, fire, and a whistle)

2. Navigation

7. First Aid Kit

3. Water (and a way to purify it)

8. Knife or Multi-Tool

4. Food

9. Sun Protection

5. Rain Gear & Dry-Fast Layers

10. Shelter

HIKE INDEX